ESSAYS

IN

MILITARY BIOGRAPHY

BY

CHARLES CORNWALLIS CHESNEY

COLONEL IN THE BRITISH ARMY AND
LIEUTENANT COLONEL IN THE
ROYAL ENGINEERS

NEW YORK
HENRY HOLT AND COMPANY
1874

PREFACE.

OF THE ESSAYS here republished, the first four relate to the great war in America, the military excellence displayed in which has been unduly depreciated by comparison with late events on the Continent. There is a disposition to regard the American generals, and the troops they led, as altogether inferior to regular soldiers. This prejudice was born out of the blunders and want of coherence exhibited by undisciplined volunteers at the outset,—faults amply atoned for by the stubborn courage displayed on both sides throughout the rest of the struggle: while, if a man's claims to be regarded as a veteran are to be measured by the amount of actual fighting he has gone through, the most seasoned soldiers of Europe are but as conscripts compared with the survivors of that conflict. The conditions of war on a grand scale were illustrated to the full as much in the contest in America, as in those more recently waged on the Continent. In all that relates to the art of feeding and supplying an army in the field, the Americans displayed quite as much ability as any continental power; while if the organization and discipline of their improvised troops were inferior, the actual fighting was in fact more stubborn, for no European forces have experienced the amount of resistance in combat which North and South opposed to each other. Neither was the frequently indecisive result of the great battles fought in America any proof that they formed exceptions to the ordinary rules of military science. These actions were so inconclusive, first, from deficiency in cavalry, and next because the beaten side would not break up. The American soldiery, in thus refusing to yield to panic when losing the day, retiring in good order, and keeping a good front to the victorious enemy, displayed, let us venture to believe, an inherited quality. In order to pursue, there must be some one to run away, and, to the credit of the Americans, the ordinary conditions of European warfare in this respect were usually absent from the great battles fought across the Atlantic. Hence partly the frequent repetition of the struggle, almost on the same ground, of which the last campaign of Grant and Lee is the crowning example. Nor have those who study the deeds wrought by Farragut and Porter, with improvised means, any reason to hold American sailors cheaper than our own, or to think lightly of the energy that raised the fleets they led.

The essays on DE FEZENSAC and VON BRANDT bring to notice memoirs which not only deal with a most interesting period of history, but may be studied with special advantage at this time. They will prove that the present fashion of depreciating the French military character and ascribing German successes to an innate superiority, though carried to extravagance, is more reasonable than the belief in French invincibility which was as commonly entertained in the earlier days of the first Empire. These memoirs show clearly that the French victories of that era were not due to any intrinsic superiority of a military organization in which might be discerned broad-sown the germs of the faults that have lately been manifested but to the extraordinary imbecility of the powers that controlled the opposing forces. The military qualities of the two races appear to have been then very much what they are now.

The essay on Lord CORNWALLIS is an attempt to illustrate the life of a man who, without conspicuous ability, effected by common-sense, high-mindedness, and force of character a complete revolution in the Indian Public Service, overcoming in doing this the dearest prejudices of his employers, as well as the self-interest of his subordinates. In his early days Lord Cornwallis had taken an honorable, if not glorious part in the war of American independence, perhaps the most ill-conducted of the many ill-conducted wars in which England has ever been engaged ; and the memoir which follows that on his Indian career gives a curious picture, by one of the loyalist militia he raised, of that almost forgotten struggle, when the Southern states especially were divided almost man against man, as personal feeling declared itself on the side of Congress or King.

The remaining essays in this volume are designed to record high work done by two brother officers, name-sakes, though not related to each other: one, a man who lately ended a life of which heart-whole devotion to duty had been throughout to a degree hard to parallel, the unswerving guide; the other, a soldier still young, whose brilliant military genius has already saved an empire from ruin, and is still happily available for the service of his country.

CONTENTS.

ESSAYS

IN

MILITARY BIOGRAPHY.

THE MILITARY LIFE OF GENERAL GRANT.

IT is not very many years since, that a needy man was lounging in the streets of St. Louis, with scarce a friend or a hope in the world. He had left an honorable service under a cloud ; and after trying his hand at the national pursuit of farming, which had brought him much toil and little gain, had turned in vain to other pursuits. As a dealer in wool, as agent for collecting debts, as auctioneer, as house-agent, he had failed to compete successfully with the sharper or better trained minds around him ; and now what he had regarded as his last chance, his application for a petty local appointment, had been rejected curtly, with the intimation that fit testimonials were lacking in his case. To this ex-captain, bankrupt in fortune, name, and hope, some demon may be imagined whispering, " Why struggle any more against your fate ? The world has no place for you and such as you. Your chances have slipped from you. Your day of hope is past. Your friends are growing tired of your existence. Your ac-

quaintances slink away, lest they should hear of your
need. Give up the useless effort to recover yourself,
and cast yourself away." On the other hand, his better angel intervening, may have urged him to good
courage, reminding him that he had been known on
the distant plains of Mexico for distinguished gallantry
and conduct ; that the name then gained was not yet
wholly lost ; and that in the seemingly peaceful money-
seeking country in which his fortune lay, there were
hid the elements of a deadly strife, soon possibly to
break out, when the soldierly qualities within him
would shine forth, and place him as high above more
common-place men in fame and fortune, as now he
seemed hopelessly beneath them.

Whether thoughts corresponding to these crossed
his mind, and the better in the end predominated,
who can truly tell? Certain it is that the ex-captain
Hiram Ulysses Grant,* leaving St. Louis and its
temptations behind him, turned towards Galena in
Illinois, where his father lived, and was received into
his employment. Thus it came about that the future
General-in-Chief and President passed the next two
years of his life in the humble capacity of assistant to
a leather-dealer, taking his turn of rougher and harder
occupations in the winter. So passed his time peace-
fully, but with no recovery of his lost position, until
the great events of April, 1861, brought Southern policy to a decisive issue at Fort Sumter, and electrified
the North with Lincoln's sudden call, the first hint

---

* Such is the President's Christian name. He was entered however as a cadet (by some unexplained mistake) as Ulysses Sidney, and
has retained the initials thus received ever since, calling himself
Ulysses Simpson. Simpson was his mother's maiden name.

the outer world gained of the dimensions of the contest, for 75,000 volunteers.

In common with all educated men in the United States, Grant had watched the approach of the rupture with intense interest. A Western man by birth, and now a denizen of the great free state which boasted the new President among her sons, instinct and patriotism made him eager to strike for the Union : nor self-interest less, since here appeared the long-desired opening by which to raise himself at once to the level from which he had fallen. Like many another ex-officer of the army who held to the North, he wrote at once to Washington to beg for a commission. The War Office was not, however, to be his door to fame. General Scott, the aged soldier who commanded for the first few months of the war, was stern against the offence of which Grant had been once accused. With Hooker, and some other less known officers who had left the service under similar circumstances, the ex-captain found his application totally neglected. He had not, however, happily, trusted to it alone. Before making it, he had begun to form and drill a company at the town of Galena, and in eight days after Lincoln's first proclamation had his little charge in sufficient order to present it to Governor Yates at Springfield, the state capital. Military men of any real training were exceedingly scarce in the West, while military and patriotic enthusiasm abounded. The governor, less prejudiced than General Scott, after some conversation with Grant, gladly took him into his own office to assist in organizing the volunteers of the state. His professional knowledge (for he had served as a quartermaster), his energy, his

strict attention to details, here made him a most serviceable assistant; and when, five weeks later, the Twenty-
first Illinois Regiment begged the governor to give
them a colonel (since no one in the battalion could profess the least military knowledge), Mr. Yates pointed
to the humbly dressed individual who sat writing in a
corner of his room, and said to the deputation, "Gen-
tlemen, I cannot do better than give you Captain
Grant." The appointment was soon made out. Not
instantly, however: for Grant, before accepting it,
twice visited Cincinnati, where M'Clellan was then
collecting the troops which soon after raised him to
distinction in Western Virginia. Grant had known
M'Clellan well in former days, and hoped to find a
place upon his staff; but missing the general on each
occasion, returned finally to Illinois to receive charge
of his regiment of volunteers. This was, of course,
like all such commands, only mustered for three
months; and hence, no doubt, Grant's anxiety to find
some more permanent, though nominally lower appointment. It is a curious study for the military
biographer, to conjecture what would have been the
fortunes of Grant had he become attached to those of
M'Clellan. It is not to be doubted that his opportunities of separate personal distinction would have been
greatly missed, at least for a time, and that his disappointment in not meeting his old comrade was in
truth a remarkable piece of good fortune.

Taking command of the Twenty-first Illinois Volunteers early in June, 1861, Grant was ordered forthwith across the border to Missouri, each district of
which was at that time rent by contests for the possession of the state, waged by the slaveholding inter-

est on the one hand, and the Free-soilers, aided by a powerful contingent of German immigrants, on the other. The first regular officer he served under was General Pope, who ordered him to the town of Mexico. Here, meeting some other volunteer regiments, the colonels begged him, as the only trained officer present, to act as brigadier until some general arrived; but a week later the "Gazette" contained his commission, with those of thirty-three other officers, as brigadier-general of volunteers. Mr. Washburne, a well-known member of the House of Representatives, and a resident of Galena, though he had never noticed his humble neighbor during the peaceful days before Fort Sumter fell, had marked the strenuous exertions which Grant had made to give military cohesion to the volunteers of first the town and then the state. Supported by the other representatives of Illinois, he had pressed the new colonel's name on Lincoln as one likely to do well in a higher command; and Grant thus came to form one of the first large creation of generals which the growing dimensions of the war made needful. The promotion was altogether unexpected, and reached the acting-brigadier at Mexico, at first solely through the papers, without his even knowing who had thus befriended him.

Major-General Fremont at this time commanded the so-called Western Department, lately formed of Illinois and the states west of the Mississippi. His headquarters were naturally at St. Louis (saved to the Union by the happy vigor of the deceased General Lyon), where he had already assumed those extravagant airs of dictatorship which very soon after caused his removal. He had serious fears for the southern portion of Missouri, which, though now freed from the imminent danger of secession, was still penetrated by partisans from Arkansas, and threatened by the large forces known to be assembling for the Confederates in Tennessee. The key to its defence was naturally the town of Cairo, the junction point of the Ohio with the Mississippi; and hither General Grant (selected by Fremont for his name for care and order rather than for supposed higher qualities) was sent at the opening of September with two brigades, to command "the district of South-east Missouri," which included large portions of the adjacent states. Fremont's intention at this time appears to have been chiefly to remain on the defensive; but his lieutenant was otherwise minded, and at once looked around for the opportunity of action.

This was afforded ready to his hand by the acts of the Confederates in the vicinity. They had hitherto been separated on the east side of the Mississippi from the Federal forces near Cairo by a strip of Kentucky, which state had declared its neutrality in the contest, Disregarding this, Polk, the well-known Southern bishop-general, had just entered the state to seize and fortify Columbus, an important point on the great river. An officer of his staff had reached Paducah, a small town standing at the point where the river Tennessee, ending with a northward course, drains the state of that name and the western end of Kentucky into the Ohio. It was probable that the Confederates would, once lodged there, close the Ohio as effectually as they had already closed the Mississippi, while their batteries would also guard the approach up the Tennessee into the heart of the central members of the new

Confederation. Grant resolved at once to prevent this. The pretended neutrality of Kentucky he had now no reason to respect, and could therefore strike boldly foɪ the threatened point. Arriving on September second, at Cairo, he heard on the fifth, of Polk's advance, and telegraphing forthwith to Fremont that he should proceed on his design, "if not forbidden," he started up the Ohio, and was before Paducah soon after daylight the next morning. The Confederate recruits who were being raised fled hastily from the place, which Grant occupied with a strong garrison; and he had got back to Cairo before he received Fremont's permission to move "if he felt strong enough." He incurred his chief's rebuke soon after for having entered directly into correspondence with the Legislature of Kentucky; but the latter, hitherto led away from the Northern cause by their governor, now passed resolutions on the Union side, and the state neutrality which they at first had affected to maintain, was heard of no more. Small as are the details of these events, the energy which they display in Grant; the readiness with which he used the raw land and water forces newly entrusted to him; the decision with which he moved into ground hitherto neutral, forestalling a too tardy permission; finally, the clear strategical view which led him to Paducah, a place which was to prove presently of the highest importance: all testify to his possession at that time of the very qualities of generalship for which all the world has later given him credit. The moderation, tact, and good sense of the politician appeared as plainly in the address he issued on entering the town; and as this was the first important public document of his life, it is well to read it in the original words:

"Paducah, Kentucky, Sept 6, 1861.

"To the Citizens of Paducah,—I am coming among you not as an enemy, but as your fellow-citizen ; not to maltreat you nor annoy you, but to respect and enforce the rights of all loyal citizens. An enemy, in rebellion against our common government, has taken possession of, and planted his guns on the soil of Kentucky, and fired upon you. Columbus and Hickman are in his hands. He is moving upon your city. I am here to defend you against this enemy, to assist the authority and sovereignty of your government. I have nothing to do with opinions, and shall deal only with armed rebellion and its aiders and abettors. You can pursue your usual avocations without fear. The strong arm of the government is here to protect its friends and punish its enemies. Whenever it is manifest that you are able to defend yourselves and maintain the authority of the government, and protect the rights of loyal citizens, I shall withdraw the forces under my command.

"U. S. Grant,
"*Brigadier-General Commanding.*"

Having thus secured the Ohio to its mouth, with Paducah as the key to future operations up the Tennessee, Grant next turned his attention down the Mississippi, where Polk was converting Columbus into an important post commanding the stream. "If it was discretionary with me," he wrote Fremont, on September tenth, "with a little addition to my present force, I would take Columbus." But his chief, who looked on the garrison at Cairo as entirely subsidiary to his own action in the interior of Missouri, made no reply. Not until November was Grant permitted to do more than organize his volunteer battalions and strengthen his position : but on the third of that month came orders to detach a force westward to .co-operate with Fremont's movements on the frontier of Arkansas. This was sent under Colonel Oglesby; and on the fifth, Fremont telegraphed to Cairo that Grant should " make a demonstration " towards Columbus to prevent Polk from sending detachments over the Mississippi to aid the Arkansas Confederates. Next day, therefore, he moved down the stream with the transports previously provided for his command, taking all his available troops, 3,000 men, of whom a large part had only received their arms five days before. So rough was the material in the action which followed.

At two A. M. on November seventh, Grant learned from friends on the Kentucky side that Polk had crossed a large detachment the day before to Belmont, a low point lying opposite to and under the guns of Columbus, with the design of cutting off Oglesby from Cairo. He at once resolved to turn the "demonstration" ordered into a real attack, and by the sudden capture of the Confederate camp to check the proposed operation. His purpose was at first fairly carried out. Landing his men on the western bank just out of sight of Columbus, he left one battalion in reserve to cover his boats, and with the rest moved on the camp, three miles off, spreading out his men in skirmishing order as he approached. The Confederates were soon met, and there was much noise and little advance for a long time, as might be expected with such untrained soldiers: but the gallantry of Grant and General M'Clernand, a brigadier of volunteers commanding under him (both of whom had their horses shot in the attack), carried their raw-troops on until the camp was taken, and the enemy, 2,500 men under General Pillow, pushed to the river bank.   Here pursuit and success ended ; for, to use the words of one northern account, the men losing all attempt at order " behaved like so many school-boys, while their colonels took to making stump speeches for the Union."   Nor was it until Grant's own staff had set the camp in flames, and brought on it the fire of the guns at Columbus, that any order was restored.   There was no possibility of holding what was gained, since the site of the camp was completely commanded by the enemy's works.   An orderly retreat to the trans-ports was all that the best troops could now have ac-complished, and to this task under the circumstances, the Federals were not equal.   Polk had not been idle in the interval, and had dispatched five regiments across the stream in boats to take the assailants in flank.   Three of these had already landed, and their skirmishers were spreading in the woods between the Federals and their transports.   "We are surrounded," said one of the staff riding up to Grant, with the warmth of a man in action for the first time.   "Well," was the calm reply, "if that is so, we must cut our way out as we cut it in."   Some of the troops, at the first thought of their being entrapped, had been for laying down their arms at once : but taking heart at their leader's coolness, they pushed on and cleared their way without difficulty.   Grant had in truth already discovered the secret which he so often after-wards used with success ; that when both sides are equally undisciplined and confused, success belongs to that which makes the boldest front and moves the most promptly to attack.   The re-embarkation was no easy matter : for he was anxious to carry off as many of his wounded as possible; his men were too confused to attend to orders; not one of his staff had the smallest experience: and the reserve battalion which was to have covered the rear, had gone off to the transports on its own account. Grant was the last man on the bank when the boats were moving away; and the Confederate skirmishers got so close to him that he would certainly have fallen, but that they were bent on trying to disable the crews, and not distinguishing his rank under his private's overcoat, suffered him to slip almost from under their hands.

The Battle of Belmont, as this combat, the first of any serious nature in the valley of the Mississippi, was magniloquently termed, has formed a subject of controversy beyond its natural importance. Polk, who had driven off the assailants finally, having seen them embark in much disorder, and captured many of their wounded, claimed it loudly as a victory. Grant, who had attained his immediate object, gained the confidence of his men, and inflicted on the enemy a loss (including nearly 200 prisoners whom he brought off) greater than his own, regarded it as a valuable success for his side; and the improved tone of his troops fully justified the boast. But the North was looking already for advance at all cost into the enemy's country; and seeing only the fact of the troops retiring from the point which they had occupied, long spoke of it as a disaster which was atoned for by the leader's later successes. No doubt it was for this reason that Grant, years afterwards, when he had climbed to the highest military honors, withdrew the summary report of the affair which he had originally sent in, to substitute for it an elaborate narrative showing fully what were the objects of the expedition, and how far they had been accomplished. It is worth while to note that this later report coincides fully, except as to the exact numbers lost, with a graphic account written the very morning after the battle to his father, by the general, a dutiful son as well as a good correspondent throughout the war. This account concludes with the following sketch of the retreat:

"We found the Confederates well armed and brave. On our return, stragglers, that had been left in our rear (now front), fired into us, and some recrossed the river and gave us battle for a full mile, and afterwards at the boats when we were embarking.

"There was no hasty retreating or running away. Taking into account the object of the expedition, the victory was complete. It has given us confidence in the officers and men of this command, that will enable us to lead them in any future engagement without fear of the result. General M'Clernand (who, by the way, acted with great coolness and courage throughout and proved that he is a soldier as well as a statesman) and myself, each had our horses shot under us. Most of the field officers met with the same loss, besides nearly one third of them being themselves killed or wounded. As near as I can ascertain, our loss was about two hundred and fifty killed, wounded, and missing."

The mistaken view of the Belmont affair taken by an excited press was not that of the trained soldiers now rising to control of the war. One of these, General Halleck, a man deserving more credit for his organizing faculties than he ever obtained in Europe, arrived at St. Louis to supersede Fremont not many days later. He not only retained Grant in his command, but in December largely augmented it, allotting nearly the whole of Kentucky to his district, and thus making him the chief instrument in the strategy of the coming campaign. For it was of this Kentucky, the state most central to the operations of the war viewed as a whole, that Sherman, to the great indignation of sanguine politicians, and to his own temporary damage, had already prophesied that "it would need 200,000 men to keep her to the Union."

The year 1862 opened on a new phase of the war. It had now passed entirely beyond the stage of local divisions, constitutional measures, and separate action of states, and had become a grave struggle of the vastest dimensions between two great sections of a divided nation ; a civil war, in fact, such as the world had never witnessed before, on the issues of which depended not merely the unity of a country, but the shaping the whole destinies of a continent. The sword of the North, slow to move but terrible in its force, was now fully drawn ; though the time had not yet come for Lincoln, by his proclamation against slavery, to fling away the scabbard, and pledge the Union of the future to enforce emancipation, so winning the world's opinion to his side.

To understand the strategy of the spring campaign which followed, it is necessary to take a general survey of the Confederate line to be attacked. This began far to the east in Kentucky, where Sydney Johnston, at that time the best known of the Southern officers, lay with 25,000 men, by rumor magnified to 100,000, and it ran across Kentucky to the Mississippi at Columbus, and thence into Arkansas, where forces of vague but very considerable strength were collecting, to repel any advance from Missouri. The centre of the line may be regarded as the strip of Kentucky stretching from the Mississippi for sixty miles eastward across the Tennessee to the Cumberland, a large stream running near the latter river and parallel to it in the northern portion of its course, into the Ohio. The weakness of this part of their line was not unknown to the Confederates; since the Tennessee and Cumberland are open to steamers high up during the spring, and the Federals, holding the mouths of both ever since Grant's seizure of Paducah, were known to be augmenting their transports constantly at that place and at Cairo, with a view either to forcing the Mississippi, or penetrating through Kentucky into the state of Tennessee by the two minor streams. It was supposed, however, these might be easily closed by works, as the former was already; and at one of the narrowest points between the two, where they are but fifteen miles from each other, Fort Henry on the right or eastern bank of the Tennessee, and Fort Donelson on the left or west of the Cumberland, were thrown up for that purpose. The operations that followed have been often described, and their credit, as a whole, assigned to Halleck: but it is but fair to state that both Grant, and the naval commander with him, the gallant Foote, had early in the year sought permission to capture Fort Henry, as their letters of January prove; so as at least to keep the Tennessee open and paralyze the Confederates on the Cumberland, as well as those on the Mississippi at Columbus, by breaking the line between them and threatening each in reverse. On the other hand, Halleck's instructions, which were issued in detail on January thirtieth, and the care with which he had accumulated his means under Grant's hand, prove sufficiently that he had resolved, before hearing from them, on the very course his lieutenant had agreed to adopt; and as he alone could control the operations on the whole western theatre, it is just that the praise of the original conception should remain his. Grant and Foote started, accordingly, with 17,000 men and seven gun-boats, on February second, and the spring campaign of 1862 was opened, a campaign which Grant's energy was destined to carry to infinitely greater results than the designer dreamed of.

The plan of the joint commanders was to first attack Fort Henry by water and land simultaneously, so as to invest the garrison and take it with the works. The combination party failed however, for Tilghman, who commanded, sent his infantry off to avoid such a contingency; but finding his gunners unable to maintain their posts in face of the fire of the gun-boats, surrendered presently to Foote at discretion. Halleck's next instructions pointed rather to a strong occupation of the point in the enemy's line thus taken than to any similar operations on the Cumberland; but his bolder lieutenant, rising with success to the height of his position, at once telegraphed his intention to march across the neck of land between the streams against Fort Donelson, and issued orders to his troops accordingly. His design was stayed for the time by the sudden rising of the Tennessee, which flooded the roads eastward, and, as he reported at the moment, "perfectly blocked in" the army. Hearing of this, Halleck still spoke in his orders solely of defensive measures. Grant's resolution, however, had been taken, and with that determination of character which marks his whole military career, he wrote to Cairo during the delay for all possible reinforcements, and to Foote (whose gun-boats were exploring the Tennessee), to move round to the Cumberland and help him. " I feel that there should be no delay in this matter," were his words on the tenth ; and finding himself able to move on the twelfth, he marched across at once on Fort Donelson. The distance was about twelve miles ; and as the enemy remained entirely on the defensive, though at this time not inferior in numbers (as careful inquiry has since proved) to their bold assailants, Grant got in sight of the works in the afternoon, drove in the pickets, and prepared to invest the place as coolly as though he outnumbered the defenders threefold. The few days that followed were probably the most anxious in his life. His gun ammunition fell short. His men, having marched without tents, were benumbed by the cold showers of sleet. The iron-clad gun-boats were fairly beaten off in their attempt to subdue the river defences on the fourteenth, and Foote himself hurt. It was not until the same night that Grant's numbers were raised by reinforcements to a strength superior to that of the force he held enclosed ; and when the enemy issued forth next day in an attempt to force his lines, he was absent on a visit to the wounded commodore, and returned in haste to find his troops demoralized and shaken by their losses, although they saw the foe retiring. His own tenacity and military quickness of perception here changed a doubtful struggle into a brilliant success. " Are their haversacks filled ? " he asked, as he saw some prisoners led in, carrying each a heavy load. Three days' rations were reported to be found in each. "Then they meant to cut their way out, and not to fight," he said; and, looking at his own disordered men, added, "whichever party first attacks now, will whip;" then riding sharply to his left, which had not been attacked in the sally, he ordered an immediate assault upon the works. General C. Smith commanded this wing, an excellent officer of regulars, though now somewhat advanced in years. When last they were thrown together, he had been the College Commandant of West Point, and his present chief one of the cadets who held him in awe. "I am now a subordinate, and know a soldier's duty," he had said shortly before to Grant, observing the natural hesitation with which the latter issued him some orders. "I hope you will feel no awkwardness about our new relations;" and as he had already shown his thorough subordination in the preceding movements, so now he led on his men with all the ardor of a youthful soldier. For once, an event seldom repeated during the war, the intrenchments were fairly assaulted and carried with the bayonet. False attacks, directed by Grant with his right and centre at other parts of the work, distracted the attention of the Confederates, and prevented their concentrating to drive Smith out; and at dark his division still held the key of Fort Donelson. The rest of the story is too well known for us to do more than refer to its strange details; the disgraceful personal fears which caused Floyd and Pillow successively to abandon the troops under their command; the fine escape of Colonel Forrest (afterwards a Confederate general of mark) with the cavalry; the vain attempt of Buckner, the third commander of

2

the garrison, to procure terms; the decisive demand
of Grant (who saw into the condition of affairs) for
unconditional surrender, with the famous threat, " I
propose to move immediately upon your works ; " and
the triumph that followed ; all these are fully set forth
in the official narratives of either side.   While disgrace justly overtook the two fugitive leaders of the
South, a cry of exultation went through the North at
this unhoped-for success.   The 14,000 prisoners borne
off to Cairo formed a solid presage of future successes
in the West, which was sufficient to balance the dis-
credit of Bull's Run, and to leave the advantage
already on the stronger side. Grant was at once
recommended by Stanton for a major-generalcy of
volunteers, and his name passed from the Secretary to
the President, and the President to the Senate the
same day.   Halleck alone appears to have dissented
from this arrangement.   Old prejudices probably more
than mere jealousy of his lieutenant's vast success,
caused him to recommend Smith to be promoted over
Grant's head, as the true author of the victory.   But
this recommendation, which came late, received no
attention at Washington, where it was plainly seen
that it was Grant who had achieved success by taking
large responsibility upon himself. Stanton declared
that his historic message to General Buckner should
be the true motto for the conduct of the war, and gave
the victor an unfailing support from that time until it
came to an end. As to the good old man himself
whom Halleck would have elevated over his commander, when speaking of the assault to Buckner (an old
West Point acquaintance) on the day of the surrender,
Smith said, " It was well done, considering our force ;

but no congratulations are due to me; I simply obeyed orders."

The gratitude and reward which Grant at once met with were fairly his due for the tactical success of his exploits. He had marched boldly up to a fortified camp held by numbers equal to his own; enclosed them in their works until he received reinforcements; defeated them on open ground when, too late, they moved out to battle; finally, assaulted and carried the most commanding point of their intrenchments, and forced them to lay down their arms on the spot. All this was done with a loss of 2,500 Federals killed and wounded—a number not quite equal to one-tenth of those engaged! It is hardly surprising that the effect of this victory told much upon the character of Grant. We shall see it avowedly influencing his tactics in the battles that soon followed, and that to the advantage of his army and his fame: but, on the other hand, it is no less plain to the discerning student of the war that it taught the chief Federal general to overrate the effect of dogged resolution and brute strength, and caused him to suffer some fearful lessons in consequence, when he carried out his favorite idea beyond the bounds of prudence against a veteran and determined enemy.

Great as was the immediate effect of the victory on the confidence of his soldiers and of the North, the results were in truth much larger than the most sanguine of those unobservant of its strategic bearing could possibly have expected. The Confederate line of defence thus pierced at its centre, the ends were cut off, fell back, and the whole gave way to a general advance of the Federals. Bowling Green on the east,

and Columbus on the west, were hurriedly abandoned.
Kentucky and the greater part of Tennessee passed at
a blow into the hands of the North.   Halleck's designs rose with these successes far beyond the original views of that general; and though he had written on the morning of the surrender to Grant " not to
be too rash," and two days later to " limit the operations of the gun-boats " on the rivers thus opened,
he had in two days more attained a clearer perception
of the state of affairs, and telegraphed to M'Clellan
to ask for himself the command of the whole armies
of the West, for " hesitation and delay," he added,
" are losing us the golden opportunity." - It would
have been better for his fame had the credit gained
by his lieutenant served to rouse no other feeling than
emulation of his energy.

One of these armies of the West was that of General Buell in Kentucky, which had been opposed to
that under Sydney Johnston, and was now following
the Confederates on their retreat from Bowling Green.
The line lay through Nashville, the capital of Tennessee : but as this city lies upon the Cumberland, it was
as directly open to Grant to enter it as to Buell.
Grant, however, knew that any further decisive operations must be dependent on the line of strategy chosen
by Halleck.   He therefore sent only his advanced
guard fifty miles towards Nashville, and wrote to sug-
gest a movement onwards to the city.   This, however,
the leading division from Kentucky had reached and
occupied unopposed before Halleck's answer came ;
and Grant having heard of the event, went on to
meet Buell and arrange as to the disposition of the
troops, the two armies being wholly independent of

each other. It is painful to record what followed, for it would seem that Grant's chief had either conceived a genuine distrust of his lieutenant, or had some meaner motive for seeking a quarrel with him. On February twenty-eighth, Grant had returned to his army, and received instructions to make more regular returns of the forces under his orders. Next day, March first, Halleck wrote him to move back from the Cumberland to the Tennessee, with a view of using the line of that river for operations towards Corinth, a great railroad junction in the state of Mississippi. On the third, with no previous intimation to Grant, Halleck telegraphed to Washington two complaints against him, in a severe dispatch:—"... He left his command without my authority, and went to Nashville. ... I can get no returns, no reports, no information of any kind from him. Satisfied with his victory, he sits down and enjoys it. ... C. Smith is almost the only officer equal to the emergency." Next day, after receiving a reply which has not been recorded, he directed Grant to place Smith in command of the troops about to go forward, and to remain himself at Fort Henry, adding, " Why do you not obey my orders to report strength and position ? " On Grant's replying next day, " I have reported almost daily the condition of my command, and reported every position occupied," he received a stern reply, beginning, " General M'Clellan directs that you report to me *daily*," and ending with the complaint now first mentioned to himself, of his going " to Nashville without authority "—Grant was naturally much hurt :—

" I have averaged writing (was his reply on the sixth) more than once a day, to keep you informed of my position, and it is no fault of mine if you have not received my letters. My going to Nashville was strictly intended for the good of the service and not to gratify any desire of my own. Believing sincerely that I must have enemies between you and myself, who are trying to impair my usefulness, I respectfully ask to be relieved from further duty in the department."

And after another rebuke of precisely the same tenor, Grant renewed his request on the ninth and eleventh in stronger terms. Halleck probably had changed his mind as to the wisdom of the course he was pursuing, or was satisfied to have shown his own authority supreme; for on the thirteenth he replied in a friendly and almost apologetic strain, concluding,— " Instead of relieving you, I wish you, as soon as your new wing is in the field, to assume the immediate command, and lead it on to new victories;" a wish which Grant at once received with good will, and forthwith withdrew his resignation. Halleck now wrote to Washington (in reply to inquiries his own complaints had produced), that Grant had " made the proper explanations, and been directed to resume his command in the field." Thus ended this strange episode of the first Federal victory, the most pleasant comment on which is, that it in no wise interfered with the cordial working of Grant with Halleck, when their positions were reversed two years later by the rise of the former to the chief command of the whole armies of the Union.

Joining the forces which had gone in advance up the Tennessee under Smith, who died soon after from the effects of his exposure before Fort Donelson,

Grant, by Halleck's orders, collected his divisions, amounting to 38,000 men, and remained on the defensive, awaiting the arrival of Buell from Nashville with as many more ; for that general was now also put under Halleck. General Smith had already placed the army on the west, or hostile bank of the Tennessee, regarding his position as a base for future operations into Mississippi ; and Grant made no change in the disposition but by drawing his troops more together. Yet there was some obvious danger in this arrangement, because the enemy was known to be rapidly concentrating a large force at Corinth, twenty miles off, by means of his railroads ; and Grant's camp lay open to their attack, inasmuch as the Federal soldiers had not yet begun to educe, from sharp experience, the knowledge (which afterwards proved of such countless value to them) of the use of rough intrenchments. The Confederates were estimated, vaguely enough, at 100,000 men, their real number being just equal to that under Grant ; and the Federal general (as letters since published show plainly) grew more and more anxious as time ·went on, and his colleague, a deliberate man much given to cautious movement and elaborate bridge-building, failed to arrive. From Columbia, ninety miles off, which Buell reached on March nineteenth, it took him seventeen days to attain the Tennessee at Savanna, a point on the other side of the river, and seven miles lower down than Grant's camp at Pittsburg Landing. This was April fifth. Grant directed the leading division (Nelson's), which only reported itself that day, to move up the river and hold itself ready to reinforce his army, for there was skirmishing along the front of the camp in the woods, and the enemy's cavalry had been seen in force. Next morning Johnston's forces issued from the cover they had secretly occupied close to the camp, and fell upon the Federals, resolved to overwhelm them and drive them into the stream.

It is a great mistake to say, with the vulgar version, that Grant was completely surprised at Pittsburg. At the first firing he sent to Buell, words which prove the contrary. "I have been looking for this, but did not believe the attack would be made before Monday or Tuesday." Moreover, General Prentiss, who held the part of the camp towards Corinth, had been warned of the danger, and had doubled his guards and pushed his pickets some way in advance the day before, though not far enough for security. Ere he could collect his startled men from their untasted breakfasts and form them, they were driven in upon the other divisions, and the battle became general and severe. Grant received no aid until late in the day from Nelson, nor from L. Wallace, who, with one of his own divisions, lay farthest down the river. Indeed, the latter officer, one of the Federal commanders who was unfortunate throughout the war, did not move until he had had his orders five hours, and then took the wrong route, arriving at seven P.M.; whereas, according to Grant's report to the War Department, the division might, but for its commander's personal conduct, have been on the ground at one o'clock. The Federals in his absence were outnumbered; and though little of tactical skill was displayed on either side, they gave ground gradually, leaving General Prentiss, with part of his division, who had stood their ground too long, in the enemy's hands. The fight was carried on in the simple form of two long parallel lines firing hotly at one another at no great distance, until at four P.M. the Federals were driven close to the landing-place, where those that were steady held their ground till dark.

" All around the landing" (says a Federal historian, writing of the moment when Buell came up) " lay the cravens who had swarmed in from the front, as many do in nearly every battle ; these, however, were not stragglers nor laggards, but the panic-stricken mob, who had fled from that danger which so many of their fellows seemed to court. As the two generals were conversing at the landing, Grant explained the situation of affairs, then apparently at the worst; and Bueil inquired : 'What preparations have you made for retreating, General ?' His remark was hardly concluded, when Grant interrupted him at once, exclaiming : ' I haven't despaired of whipping them yet.' "

He had seen that the efforts of the assailants were slackening. Exhausted with their long day's work, thousands of Johnston's men had left the ranks to plunder the abandoned camp of the Federals. Their chief himself had fallen in pressing them on to the victory he saw so near, and their loss had not been much less than that of Grant's forces, which amounted to full 10,000 put *hors de combat*, including Generals W. Wallace killed, Prentiss taken, and Sherman wounded. The Confederates were unable to push forward for the final effort, which would have driven the Federals on their boats ; and seeing this, Grant resolved to resume the offensive next day, unsupported or not, it being on his side impossible to urge his jaded men into an offensive that evening. As the turn in the battle has been naturally enough, both in America and elsewhere, ascribed to the arrival of Buell, it is as well to make the matter clear by the narrative of General Sherman, written in 1865. This exactly confirms the assertion made by those who knew him best that Grant from the time of Fort Donelson, believed in there being always a time in every hard-fought battle when both armies being nearly exhausted, and it seeming impossible for either to do more, the one that first renews the fight will win it. Sherman writes in so admirable a spirit of candor and fairness, that his words should be read in full :—

"I never was disposed, nor am I now, to question any thing done by General Buell and his army, and know that approaching our field of battle from the rear, he encountered that sickening crowd of laggards and fugitives that excited his contempt, and that of his army, who never gave full credit to those in the front line who did fight hard, and who had, at four P.M. checked the enemy, and were preparing the next day to assume the offensive. I remember the fact the better from General Grant's anecdote of his Donelson battle, which he told me then for the first time—that at a certain period of the battle he saw that either side was ready to give way, if the other showed a bold front, and he determined to do that very thing, to advance on the enemy, when, as he prognosticated, the enemy surrendered. At four P.M. of April sixth, he thought the appearances the same, and he judged, with Lewis Wallace's fresh division and such of our startled troops as had recovered their equilibrium, he would be justified in dropping the defensive and assuming the offensive in the morning. And, I repeat, I received such orders before I knew General Buell's troops were at the river. I admit that I was glad Buell was there, because I knew his troops were older than ours, and better systematized and drilled, and his arrival made that certain which before was uncertain."

Grant's army passed the night under arms amid storms of rain; but the transports were busy through the darkness, and in the morning 20,000 of Buell's force were ready for the action, with the remains of the divisions which had fought the day before. This great accession of strength told at once, when, in accordance with Grant's resolve, the Federals advanced to make their counter-attack at early morning. The ground was very heavy from the rain, and the movements in consequence even more slow than the ordinarily heavy maucœuvres of the early days of the war. Beauregard, who had succeeded Johnston, found himself from the first obliged to give ground, and falling back slowly, left the scene of contest altogether about noon, retreating upon Corinth unpursued; for Buell's men were declared by their officers exhausted by their efforts to get up, as Grant's own were by the long battle just ended.

This had been not merely the severest contest of the war thus far, but its fierceness was hardly afterwards repeated. General Sherman has expressly said that he never saw fighting so terrible; possibly because the panic among some of the raw troops of his division, rendered necessary the exposure of his own person in a wholly exceptional manner, and made the conduct of the rest seem heroic. Grant has compared the battle to that of the Wilderness; but with little justice, as it seems to us, inasmuch as at Pittsburg the losses on either side (excluding those of Buell, all suffered on the second day) were as nearly equal as

possible,* like the strength of the original armies;
whereas at the Wilderness, as will be seen hereafter,
the disproportion was extraordinary. The victory
was claimed by either side; by the Confederates,
because they had captured their enemy's camp with
many prisoners, and had at one time all but destroyed
his army; by the Federals, because they had at last
successfully repulsed the assault. In all such cases
the only safe method is to consider what was the real
object of a battle, and how far it was attained: and as
that of Johnston and Beauregard was undoubtedly to
crush Grant before succour arrived, and of Grant to
hold his own until Buell joined him, the true success
should belong beyond dispute to the Federal general.
Its moral effect was, however, impaired by the over-
cautious conduct of Halleck, who coming up at this
time to assume charge of the united armies, kept
them from directly following up the enemy, and approached Corinth by the slower process of advancing
solely under breastworks, thus giving to his soldiers
as well as to their country the impression that he was
afraid, after late events, to trust them in the open
ground.

In another respect the battle greatly disappointed
Grant. He had supposed, with most other Northerners, and in opposition to the views which made
Sherman unpopular, that one or two sharp blows, like
that of Fort Donelson, would end the war. The vigor
and determination with which General Johnston had
taken the offensive so soon after that great loss,
showed plainly that any such expectation was a fal-

* Grant's loss was, excluding Buell's, 10,040; Beauregard's 10,699,
by their own official reports.

lacy. Then Grant arrived at the conviction, on which
as a whole he thereafter ever acted, that the war
would never end until the Southern armies were
crushed and worn down, and that they, not forts or
cities or territory, should be the chief objects of the
strategy which controlled the greater resources of the
North. From this time also he, and those that followed him, gave up the notion of sparing the property
of the South. The Confederacy had succeeded, they
admitted, in making this a war of the people. The
people, therefore, must suffer, until the people yielded.
Hitherto he, with most of the Federal generals, would
have protected slavery as an institution. Henceforward that too must perish, with state rights, independent Constitutions, and whatever else stood in the
way of one grand object, the unity of the nation.
These sentiments of her chief generals, conservative
men by nature, but clear-eyed as to the nature and
issue of the struggle, were soon to become the policy
of the North. The peninsular campaign of M'Clellan
had now begun, with its tedious advance, weary stoppages, and final discomfiture. Then followed the triumphant counterblow struck on his army by Lee, the
new Confederate chief in Virginia, Jackson's magnifi-
cent flank marches, the second battle of Bull's Run,
the confused retreat of Pope on Washington, the
summons of M'Clellan to his old command by the
terrified Cabinet, the first invasion of Maryland (that
of September 1862,) and its sudden check at Antietam. Lincoln saw clearly that a drawn battle under
such circumstances was the defender's victory, and
launched the Emancipation Proclamation until now
kept back, making reconciliation no longer possible

but by the submission of the South to a social revolution. Pledged to set free the slaves of the revolted states, the North could no longer grant them acceptable terms.   Henceforth it became clear that the contest must go on to the bitter end, the ruin of the weaker section of the Union.

This seems to be a fit opportunity for noticing a subject which, though not as yet surveyed by any historian, is intimately connected with the history of the war.   It is usually thought because Jefferson Davis pressed, and General Lee consented to the design of carrying the war into the Northern states, that its wisdom was unquestioned.   It is time that this delusion—for it is no less—should be removed.   There were opinions expressed which should have been of the highest value, opinions of soldiers which might have weighed in council even against that of Lee, which opposed most strongly these attempted invasions.   In their view, it was throwing away a great political advantage to reduce a defensive struggle for rights to the mere level of a civil war for mastery. Hundreds of thousands in the North, who had looked coldly on a war of conquest against the alleged rights of the sister states, would be ready to rush to arms the moment that their own soil was violated by rebels in arms.   The military advantage was most doubtful, seeing that neither men nor warlike material (in both of which the South was inferior) could be recruited to any great extent by conquest ; whilst the political evil was so great as in all probability to be ruinous. To the naturally weaker party, the defensive was, according to all rule, the appropriate course.   In this case it was the only safe one as regarded the ultimate issue, the assertion or surrender of independence. Such were the arguments urged against the invasion : but bolder or rasher counsels prevailed at Richmond, and Lee was urged on into Maryland, and Bragg thrown into Kentucky, to be arrested each in turn by the gathering of superior forces, and to retire from the invaded territory, leaving those Northerners who had hitherto been neutral or friendly, banded, by this threatening of their own hearths, with the bitterest enemies of the Confederacy.

To return to the fortunes of Grant. We left him in April 1862, before Corinth, superseded by the arrival of Halleck, who carried on the campaign until Beauregard retreated from the contested point at the end of May. Then followed a complete breaking up of the great army gathered on the Tennessee. Buell's force was once more separated from that of Grant, and sent eastward. Four divisions were soon after stripped from the latter, and Grant was reduced to a defensive in the heart of the hostile state of Mississippi, having under him at one time less than 20,000 men, while an army about equal in numbers covered the country to the south, including Vicksburg, the key of the great river, and Price and Van Dorn hung with light forces on his eastern flank, and threatened his communica tions. Thinking him to be perilously advanced, they twice came down upon his rear ; but being seriously checked at Iuka (September nineteenth), and utterly defeated (October second), in an attack on Corinth which place Grant had well intrenched, they fell back once more into Alabama. Rosecrans, who had been left by Grant at Corinth, received the chief credit of the action, which gained him the command of

Buell's army, on the supersession of that general, and
Grant was relieved of a lieutenant who had more than
once thwarted his superior, and plainly thought less
of his judgment than those who had shared his victories in the spring. The general course of the whole
summer operations of 1862, in the Western states, is
well described in the words of General Badeau, the
best of Grant's biographers, whose account throws
special light on this portion of the war :

" The truth is, that Grant's extreme simplicity of behav-
iour and directness of expression imposed on various officers,
both above and below him. They thought him a good plain
man, who had blundered into one or two successes, and who,
therefore, could not be immediately removed ; but they
deemed it unnecessary to regard his judgment, or to count
upon his ability. His superiors made their plans invariably
without consulting him, and his subordinates chose sometimes to carry out their own campaigns in opposition or
indifference to his orders, not doubting, that, with their superior intelligence, they could conceive and execute triumphs
which would excuse or even vindicate their course. It is
impossible to understand the early history of the war, without taking it into account, that neither the government nor
its important commanders gave Grant credit for intellectual
ability or military genius."

The time was now about to come when this estimate was to be greatly changed ; when those who
would give him credit for naught else, would learn to
admire his undaunted tenacity and hopeful perseverance in the face of discouragement ; and when, pursuing one great object steadfastly, he was to win it at last
by a display of resource such as the most brilliant or

scientific of modern generals could not surpass. The town of Vicksburg, little known before the war, had taken the place on the Mississippi first held by Columbus, before that port was turned by the fall of Fort Donelson, and then by Memphis, which the retreat of the Confederates from Corinth rendered similarly untenable. It barred the passage of the stream to Federal use ; its batteries, high-raised in air, defied the skill and valor of Farragut's and Porter's fleets ; it separated Banks' force at New Orleans from the rest of those of the North ; it formed a *point d' appui,* whereby the Confederates on the west side of the Mississippi could connect their operations freely with the main armies on its east. They might still indeed by bringing in the great left wing, which they had kept uselessly scattered through Arkansas into Texas, have added over 50,000 men to the centre of their line of defence, and possibly turned the scale of the war. As there has been indicated one grand error in their conduct of the war, the making invasions beyond their means on the eastern side, so it was possibly no less fatal to them that they wasted a large part of their fighting strength in a defensive occupation of their semi-barbarous western states. At the time of Beauregard's retreat from Corinth there were, according to the official report of Cooper, the Adjutant-General, 55,000 fighting men enrolled under General Holmes and ready for service in the trans-Mississippi part of the Confederacy. It was proposed to Mr. Davis to bring these across as secretly as might be, and so overwhelm Grant's army near Corinth, and that in Tennessee, in turn, if possible ; but the advice was rejected. And finally a great part of Holmes's army, tired of

3

inaction, dispersed gradually, and were never employed at all. Never was the necessity of the concentration of force on the decisive point more forcibly illustrated than in this false strategy.

To return to the operations about Vicksburg, which were to make of Grant the acknowledged hero of the war on the side of the Union. We left him more than 100 miles to the north of the city, with a country intervening which was but little known, and crossed by three great streams, each ending near the Mississippi in a labyrinth of swamps and creeks. Yet he had his eye already steadily on the important point; for when his command, after his unsuccessful defence of Corinth, was suddenly enlarged in October, and a further increase of force promised, he wrote at once to propose to Halleck a new and bold plan of operations, ending: " I think I would be able to move down the Mississippi central railroad, and cause the evacuation of Vicksburg." This was his first official mention of the historic name. From that time forward, until he entered the works as victor on the fourth of July following, his life, and that of his friend Sherman, were bound up with the operations against the great stronghold of the West.

It is not within our scope to recount these in detail, interesting as they are as a military study. Their general features are so well known that we need only remind the reader of them. The first attempt was by direct march overland, which failed, owing to the brilliant surprise by Van Dorn of Holly Springs, the most important post in the long line of communication Grant had formed with his base near Corinth. The Federal General had not yet discovered the secret, afterwards so freely used by Sherman, of working an army in these rich but depopulated states of the South, without a base at all, by living on the enemy. He fell back, therefore, checked for the time. Then, while he still acted inland, threatening another advance, Sherman, with a separate force, descended the river, and strove (about the Christmas of 1862) to carry the works by a *coup de main*, a plan which failed with heavy loss. But the North had now tasted enough of success elsewhere to nerve her to put forth her strength. 130,000 soldiers obeyed Grant's orders in January, 1863, and of these fully 50,000 were employed in the swamps opposite Vicksburg, in his next scheme of endeavoring to divert the course of the Mississippi. English writers have been accused of exaggerating the sufferings that ensued ; let an American one, therefore, who served with distinction in the Western campaign, give his own account :

"The troops were put in camps along the west bank of the river, on the low swamp land, overflowed this year to an unusual extent. This protracted freshet, together with the extraordinary fall of rain, greatly increased Grant's difficulties, as well as the hardships of his army.

"The camps were frequently submerged, and the diseases consequent to this exposure prevailed among the troops ; dysenteries and fevers made sad havoc, and the small-pox even was introduced, but speedily controlled. The levees furnished the only dry land deep enough for graves, and for miles along the river bank this narrow strip was all that appeared above the water, furrowed in its whole length with graves. The troops were thus hemmed in by the burial-places of their comrades."

No wonder that, as is added by the writer :

"Exaggerated rumors of disease and even pestilence were circulated by the enemy, and at the North; these added to the anxieties of the country, as well as to the difficulties of the commander."

This bold effort to deprive the place of its command of the stream having failed, in March 1863 a new attempt was made. It was now sought to turn the works of Vicksburg on the north side by carrying some of the gun-boats and troops into the Yazoo (which flows into the Mississippi above the place) through the net-work of swamps which lies between it and the course of the great river; but this also miscarried from the inherent difficulties. Grant had now tried three sides of the place in vain, and had brought so much odium on himself as to make his removal on the next failure certain; yet in May he was found landing on the west bank, thirty miles south of the city, on a new enterprise against it, which involved his throwing himself into a hostile country, between forces of unknown strength, arriving in the rear of the place, and dropping the base he had marched from and held at first with his left, to seize a new one with his extended right; that new one being itself dependent on the success of his march turning the hitherto impregnable works on the Yazoo, and so admitting Porter's fleet to form for him a new line of supply to it from the great depôts further north. The boldness of the design, and the unity and vigor with which it was carried out to a perfect result, show a strategy as remarkable, if it was somewhat slowly conceived, as that tactical use of pressure in the crisis of battle which seemed instinctive in the Federal general, and had given him his previous successes. The mistakes of Pemberton, the too late arrival of General Joseph Johnston (only now recovered from Virginian wounds) did the rest; and July fourth, 1863, saw Grant, in spite of Meade's hard-won victory of Gettysburg the day before, the foremost man in the armies of the Union. No longer a mere volunteer-general, commissioned but for three years, he received his well-earned brevet into the regular army, and was numbered with the most honored members of the profession from which he had not many years before parted in despair.

The fame of this happy general, whose merits were made more conspicuous by the faults of others, was not to rest long upon the conquest of Vicksburg and the triumphant opening of the Mississippi. The shattering defeat of Rosecrans at Chickamauga by Bragg and Longstreet, as he sought to force his way from the Tennessee into Georgia, brought Grant upon the scene in the autumn, summoned by telegraph to retrieve his former subaltern's disaster. Thomas, who had succeeded the disgraced general at Chattanooga, was apparently shut in by the victorious army; but his line of supply was never wholly broken. Grant (now commanding all the armies west of the Alleghanies) hurried up a powerful reinforcement under Sherman; Halleck dispatched Hooker round with two corps from Virginia; and every day lost by Bragg after his victory diminished the Confederate chances. There was no greater mistake (it has been said by very high authority) in the history of the war, than this so-called investment of Chattanooga, in truth no investment at all, by a numerically weak army distributed over a position

which necessarily cut it in two. Too confident to retire and too weak to attack, Bragg lay idle on his hills
before the camp, until the enemy within it had gathered in irresistible strength. Then Grant, attacking
him at last in his own lines, drove him back with
heavy loss on Georgia, and opened the centre of the
Confederacy to be pierced next spring, as its western
portion had already been severed from it by his success on the Mississippi. The month of March 1864
saw him, with the new rank of Lieutenant-General
created expressly to do him honor, assuming, by a
sort of national appointment, the chief command of
the Union armies, with unlimited control over a million of men ; whilst Halleck, superseded by his former
lieutenant, was henceforth confined to those administrative functions at Washington, which it is but bare
justice to say that he performed with constant energy
and success. The good discipline of the Federal armies in the coming campaign owed much to the strong
measures he used during this spring, and especially
towards the lower ranks of regimental officers. On
the other hand, that of the Confederates, always lax
and neglected, fell off under the influence of discouragement, until it resembled rather that of a band of
undisciplined volunteers than such as becomes the
tried soldiers of a national army. So loose, indeed
was their order that, however great the courage of the
men, no officer could count upon the number of men
he should bring in at the end of the day.

His new rank attained, Grant parted from the
comrades by whose help it had been won, prepared to
try his fortune elsewhere. Before the spring campaign
of 1864 was to open, it was necessary that he should

choose his own field of action, and assign those of his
subordinates. The Mississippi being now unquestion-
ably secured to the North, there were but two great
lines on which the General-in-Chief could fitly conduct
the operations of 1864; that which his late success
against Bragg had laid open, or that which led direct
to the Confederate capital. Many reasons might have
tempted him towards the former. Here he would
command tried troops, who had in him the implicit
confidence gained by great achievements already done
under his leadership. Here he would be seconded by
lieutenants of the rarest powers; for it was hard to say
whether he leant most on the calm courage and unfailing resource of Sherman (long recognized by him
before the world perceived them), or the subtle genius
and daring spirit of the lamented M'Pherson, a soldier
of the very highest promise who fell before Atlanta,
having attained, at the early age of thirty-three, the
honor of commanding an independent army. Here
too, Grant had thoroughly examined the scene of operations, and understood that a moderate series of successes would plant his army across the main lines of
communication yet left to the enemy, dividing absolutely the Atlantic states of the South from those near
the Mississippi, and restricting the government of the
Confederacy within such limits as must necessarily
cause its extinction. Against these and all such considerations was set that weightier than any, the will
of his country; for the North expected the general of
her choice to show his powers on the field where her
military honor had been so sadly tarnished. While
victory after victory and progress after progress had
accompanied her arms in the West, in Virginia the

Army of the Potomac was now nearly as far from Richmond as when it was first raised ; and though holding its own when on the defensive, and with especial success since Meade had the command, it had never advanced without recoiling shattered, or at the least wholly checked, before the unconquerable strategist who held it at bay with his inferior force. Honor, therefore, called Grant to Virginia, and policy also plainly pointed out that to defeat Lee and to occupy Richmond would, if not destroying the inner resources of the Confederacy, at least damage her external prospects beyond all hope. In April, therefore, it was announced that Grant was to command in person in the next Virginian campaign.

He had left Chattanooga suddenly on March third, on a private intimation of his coming promotion : but his own wish had been, as was natural, to return and conduct the Georgian campaign in person, a wish which he cheerfully relinquished when understanding fully what the nation expected at his hands. There is nothing a military biographer could offer more honorable to the character of Grant than the terms in which he now took leave of his great lieutenants. Flaws may be found in his tactics, or deficiencies in his strategical power ; yet, if not absolutely perfect as general or soldier, as a commander full of generous sentiment to the deserving, who could desire to serve under a better chief? Not that Grant's praise was of that cheap sort which is easily earned and little valued. On the contrary, few commanders have spoken more severely of their subordinates' errors when censure was called for ; and Hooker, Burnside, and Butler are notable examples that the scathing rebukes which he administered in his reports spared neither rank nor standing. Unqualified praise from such a chief is doubtless the more valued; but it is rather in justice to himself than his lieutenants that we insert the letter he wrote, on the decision already mentioned, to the general who, next to himself, had earned most largely the gratitude of the Union their swords aided to preserve:

"DEAR SHERMAN,

"The bill reviving the grade of lieutenant-general in the army has become law, and my name has been sent to the Senate for the place. I now receive orders to report to Washington immediately, *in person,* which indicates a confirmation, or a likelihood of confirmation. I start in the morning to comply with the order.

"While I have been eminently successful in this war in at least gaining the confidence of the public, no one feels more than I, how much of this success is due to the energy, skill, and the harmonious putting forth of that energy and skill, of those whom it has been my good fortune to have occupying subordinate positions under me.

"There are many officers to whom these remarks are applicable to a greater or less degree, porportionate to their ability as soldiers; but what I want is, to express my thanks to you and M'Pherson, as the men to whom, above all others, I feel indebted for whatever I have had of success.

"How far your advice and assistance have been of help to me you know. How far your execution of whatever has been given to you to do, entitles you to the reward I am receiving, you cannot know as well as I.

"I feel all the gratitude this letter would express, giving it the most flattering construction.

" The word *you* I use in the plural, intending it for
M'Pherson also.   I should write to him, and will some day,
but starting in the morning, I do not know that I will find
time just now.   Your friend,

"U. S. GRANT, *Major-General.*"

Less than a fortnight after this letter reached him
Sherman found himself promoted to the chief command of the Southwestern states, which Grant had
left on his advancement to that of the whole land
forces of the Union; and a few days earlier (March
ninth) the latter had publicly received at Washington
his commission of Lieutenant-General, bestowed by
Lincoln under the authority of the special Act of
Congress.   The new Commander-in-Chief had already
decided to take the personal direction of the Virginian operations, and the protracted campaign was to
begin which never actually can be said to have ceased
until Richmond fell, and with it the Confederacy that
Lee defended.

The main purpose of the new campaign was a concentration of the scattered Federal invasion on two
points of the long line hitherto assailed.   The front
of the Union armies had thus far practically extended
along a vast irregular curve from New Orleans to the
Lower Potomac.   Three years of bitter welfare had
not sufficed to make any change in the strategic situation at the eastern end of this line; although the superior Federal resources, wielded with ability and tenacity by Grant and his lieutenants, had greatly contracted the limits of the Confederacy along its southwestern border, forcing it back from the Ohio to the
Tennessee, and wresting point after point on the Mis-

sissippi from its grasp. It was now resolved at Washington to give up the system of embracing with separate attacks, the whole front of the enemy, who had by it been permitted to avail himself of his shorter lines of communication, and to bring unexpected numbers to bear on the points most threatened. The whole weight of the Northern pressure was now to be thrown by the Commander-in-Chief upon the enemy's capital; by Sherman upon that vital point of the Confederacy which the endurance of Rosecrans' army and the brilliant victory of Grant had laid bare to the next advance from Chattanooga. The first-named object of this double invasion was of course political. Notwithstanding the boast of the Confederate President that the war did not in any manner depend upon Richmond, it was manifest that the fall of that city would be felt as a terrible blow to the Southern Government both at home and abroad, and would greatly justify the expectation of the mass of the Northern people that the Union was to be reconquered by the sword. Against the devoted capital Grant was to bring forces more vast and powers more uncontrolled than any general since the days of Napoleon. And should these, aided by his prestige and his proved vigor and activity, cause Lee in the defence to exhaust the resources of the South, Sherman, furnished with a mighty army, would be able to penetrate into and hold the whole centre of Georgia, threaten or seize such warlike magazines as the forethought of Davis's administration might have placed in that remote and hitherto untouched state, and sever the Carolinas and Virginia from the rest of the Confederacy. That the complete success of either invasion would give the

latter its death-blow was the not unnatural expectation of even those more far-seeing Federals who
were not blinded to the difficulties each must encounter.

The key to the whole campaign of 1864 in Virginia
is to be found in Grant's design (formed long before
on the spur of his success at Vicksburg) of assailing
Richmond by a double method, combining direct attack and wide-spread investment. He was himself to
move straight on that capital, or rather on the army
that defended it, with a host as large as it was possible
to manœuvre in the country through which he must
pass ; while two minor but considerable armies, advancing to the right and the left of the main one, were to
sweep through the territory beyond the city and aim
at the railroads which supplied it from the west and
south. His calculation, made on very reasonable
grounds, was that in opposing his own march Lee
would require to bring into line every available man
in the Virginian armies, and would thus be compelled
to strip the districts entered by his subordinate forces.
It was perfectly ascertained at Washington that the
very considerable population of the rival capital, as
well as the large army under Lee that covered it, were
maintained chiefly by food brought from great distances. Indeed, the district to the north of the James
had been so harried by the Federal expeditions, and
so stripped of its negro laborers, as barely to produce
enough food for its own scattered rural population.
To sever completely the railroads which led to the city
would therefore quickly bring both its inhabitants and
Lee's army to a state of starvation, and inevitably
force the latter to retreat, not less than a series of

defeats in the open field. Grant believed himself thus to have two distinct chances in his favor, and diligently applied himself to work out the details of his scheme.

The first part of this which naturally came under consideration was the line of operations to be chosen for his own advance. The Army of the Potomac, with which he had fixed his own headquarters on assuming his new office, at this time lay around Culpepper, north of the Rapidan, and its supplies came straight from Washington by the Alexandria railroad. The problem to be solved as to the best means of approaching Richmond was precisely that which had first produced open difference between M'Clellan and the President two years before. The preference of the latter for a direct movement across Eastern Virginia, which should at the same time keep his own capital covered, is well known. The objections to it we prefer to give in M'Clellan's own words, which are here quoted from his letter of February third, 1862, addressed to the President in reply to that of the latter, challenging him to show the superiority of his design :

" Bearing in mind what has been said, and the present unprecedented and impassable condition of the roads, it will be evident that no precise period can be fixed upon for the movement on this line. Nor can its duration be closely calculated ; it seems certain that many weeks may elapse before it is possible to commence the march. Assuming the success of this operation, and the defeat of the enemy as certain, the question at once arises as to the importance of the results gained. I think these results would be confined to the possession of the field of battle, the evacuation of the line of the Upper Potomac by the enemy, and the moral effect of the victory ; *important results it is true, but not decisive of the war, nor securing the destruction of the enemy's main army, for he could fall back upon other positions, and fight us again and again, should the condition of his troops permit.*"

With the exception of the Confederate army of Virginia being intrenched behind the Rapidan instead of near the Potomac, there was but little change in the main conditions of the question which M'Clellan had treated. But Grant did not rely like his predecessor on the single hope of success from his own direct attack. On the contrary, he intended (as we have already pointed out) to use the latter partly to cover a separate system of acting on his enemy by destroying the latter's communications. Further it would have appeared a servile copying of a plan which had already failed in the execution, and a reflection on the President's judgment, if he had proposed to move his main army by water to the peninsula, or to the mouth of the Rappahannock (according to M'Clellan's original idea), and worked his detached left, as it was open for him to do, from Norfolk far beyond the south of the James. He had already decided, therefore to move across the difficult country which his predecessor had dreaded to attempt. His force for this purpose would be, as we shall presently see, fully as numerous as that which M'Clellan had commanded before his rupture with Lincoln. Although the staff, the organization, and the spirit of the soldiery had most wonderfully improved under the stern discipline of actual service, he yet felt the

necessity of keeping near to some better line of supply for his numerous wants than cartage, however
liberally added, could furnish. The railroad he now
had at his back continued onward to Richmond; but
even if he could drive Lee from the part his army
now covered, the line thence runs due east for forty
miles, and could only be followed by exposing a flank.
For this cause he resolved, if failing to surprise Lee's
position, to move the army of the Potomac round it
to his own left, so as to seize that short railroad from
Acquia Creek to Richmond, attempts to master the
Rappahannock passage of which near Fredericksburg
had successively proved so ruinous to Burnside and
Hooker. From the fords of the Rapidan, which his
left nearly touched, to Bowling Green, a station on that
line, is but twenty-seven miles. A rapid march south-
eastward on the latter place, through Spottsylvania
Court-house, would plant him with his back to Fredericksburg and his face to Richmond; and if Lee were
not crushed in the coming collision, nor even forced
back into a strictly defensive attitude, the Federal
army could (as Grant believed) so use the difficult and
wooded country as to cover the movement effectually
by the peculiar tactics now become familiar to all its
branches.

For this part of his campaign Grant made earnest
personal preparations during the six weeks that followed his appointment. The five whole corps of the
Army of the Potomac were not only recruited, but
also broken up and redistributed into three, under
Sedgwick, Hancock, and Warren, all men of proved
ability and courage. The chief cavalry generals were
superseded; the most active of them, Kilpatrick,

being sent to act in the army of Sherman, from which
Grant drew a still younger officer, General Sheridan,
whom he had previously marked out as the most
fitting leader for his 12,000 horse. The whole of
these arrangements were made under the supervision
of Meade, who retained the nominal command of the
Army of the Potomac, and carried out his new
superior's instructions with a whole-hearted earnestness worthy of Wellesley himself under the like
trial.

The three infantry corps numbered about 30,000
each, distributed in four divisions. They were to be
joined, at the last moment, by another, that of Burnside, which, on Longstreet's retreat from East Tennessee, had been brought round from Knoxville to a
depôt in Maryland. Its regiments being filled up
with conscripts, and a large division of colored troops
just raised being added, it mustered 35,000 strong at
the end of April. This corps was purposely held back
in order to cause the Confederates to believe it to be
intended for some separate expedition, and so to keep
their government from reinforcing the Army of Virginia. When the roads at length were reported fit
for use, and all Grant's preparations on the Rapidan
complete (and these had included separate reviews
and movements of each corps to test the efficiency of
the staff), Burnside's divisions advanced through
Washington, and having defiled before the President,
joined their new chief at his headquarters in the last
days of April. With Sheridan's cavalry, the Lieutenant-General had now assembled, for his immediate
command, a fully equipped force of 135,000 men,
being in number only slightly larger than that which

M'Clellan had prepared for his first campaign, but for the major part composed of veteran troops.

Beyond the Blue Ridge, on his right, a separate army of 25,000 fighting men had been assembled under Sigel, to act in the Shenandoah. The supersession of that general (who had been in retirement since the days of Fredericksburg) had given much umbrage to the German Republicans. This, Lincoln had lately striven to disarm by offering him a new and detached command in the great valley. Augmented now into a formidable army, his force was to be led, in co-operation with Grant, straight upon Lynchburg, the important point which commands both the railroad and canal leading from the Upper James to Richmond. Grant believed there would be but little opposition on this side; and as the advance would necessarily cut the line from the Shenandoah into Richmond, the Confederate capital would be by it thrown entirely for supplies on the railroads passing to the South.

These are in number two only, regarded as main lines. The one runs from Richmond due south through Petersburg to Weldon, and so along the Atlantic side of North Carolina. The other nearly southwest through a richer country to the border of that state at Danville. To completely sever these we have shown to be a vital part in Grant's original design; and the operations for the purpose were to be conducted by an army assembling at M'Clellan's old base between the York and James Rivers. A mere threatening of Richmond, to be followed by a hasty change of manœuvre to the south side of the James, from whence the expedition should rapidly penetrate far

4

into the interior and destroy, or if possible, hold the railways, was the general plan. Thirty-five thousand men were allotted to it.

Next to the fitness of Grant's main army for its own share of the drama was evidently needful to him the proper conduct of these subordinates; and here we come to the weak part of his strategy. Sigel's appointment had taken place before his own, and could not well be revoked (no present fault being alleged against him) without great odium to the government on the part of the German soldiers and voters. Grant therefore did not attempt to change the staff in the valley. But for the still more important change on the James he had designed his protégé, W. F. Smith, whose promotion to Major-General he had just with difficulty succeeded in forcing from the Senate, inclined at first to reject it from jealousy of his dictation. Here, however, he found an absolutely insurmountable obstacle in the obstinacy of Lincoln, who had resolved not to allow the supersession of Butler, already selected for this service: so that after some discussion, Grant was forced to content himself with a half measure of putting Smith at the head of one of Butler's two corps (the other being formed of troops from Charleston under Gilmore), in the vain hope that the civilian would be guided by the soldier in the actual operations; a hope which Butler's character for self-assertion rendered vain from the first.

The forces available for the defence of Richmond against this triple invasion, though far inferior in numbers, were yet of formidable strength. Longstreet had lately returned from East Tennessee with his corps, which, with those of Ewell and Hill, mustered 70,000

infantry nominally, and could put 52,000 bayonets into
the line of battle. Lee had but few cavalry near the
Rapidan, great part of Steuart's command lying nearer
to Richmond to watch against such raids as that of
Dahlgren, which had alarmed that city not long before.
There had been but little change in the staff of Lee's
force since the days of Gettysburg.

In addition to this, the so-called Army of Virginia,
Richmond was defended to the south by Beauregard
and his troops, released from their duties at Charleston. These were disposed along the Weldon railroad,
ready for concentration on any point threatened between Richmond and Wilmington, at the further
extremity of North Carolina. They numbered about
20,000, exclusive of a well-trained militia which guarded
the capital itself. Twelve thousand troops, in great
part newly raised, were all that could be allotted to
the defence of the valley against Sigel, where Early
was now succeeded by Breckinridge. With this
marked inferiority in every quarter, the Confederate
strategy was necessarily of the defensive order, and
made dependent upon that of their opponents. Nor
was this hardly less the case in Georgia. There
Sherman had collected an army of 98,000 men at
Chattanooga, exclusive of the vast trains for rail and
common roads which were to force and maintain an
unequalled system of transport; while Johnston con-
fronted him with but 76,000, and this disproportion
of numbers was enhanced by doubts whether his contingent from Tennessee would hold to the Confederacy
from which their state was now wrested.

All things being now prepared for his great adventure, and orders given for a simultaneous advance to

Sherman as well as to Sigel and Butler, Grant
launched his army by its left across the Rapidan.
The well-known passages at Ely and Germaniatown
Fords, used by Hooker in his disastrous attempt of
the year before, which led to his defeat at Chancellorsville, were unguarded by the Confederates, and
crossed without difficulty on the night of May third.
The cavalry divisions of Gregg and Wilson moved
first before dark to lay the pontoon bridges at these
two points, three and seven miles respectively west·
of the fork of the Rappahannock. Hancock's (second)
corps followed Gregg at the former place, and Warren's (fifth) and Sedgwick's (sixth,) forming a right column, passed after Wilson at the latter. A train of
8,000 wagons, carrying supplies for the whole army,
passed in rear of Hancock, thus interposing the bulk
of the force between itself and the enemy. From the
moment of beginning the march all connection with
the Alexandria railroad was thrown aside, and the
troops made dependent for all supplies on their moving commissariat until a new base should be gained.
Burnside's (ninth) corps alone remained on the ground
where the army had lately stood, to deceive the
enemy as long as possible. But this for twenty-four
hours only; after which he too moved across the
river, following the right column by Germania, and
rejoining the other corps on the fifth. That day saw
the first fighting of a long and bloody series of engagements.

It was far from being Grant's desire to force his
foe to an immediate action. His wish was to pass
beyond the Confederates to Spottsylvania Court-
house, the central point of all the tangled mass of

woods which covers the country to the south of
Chancellorsville, before Lee could discover his real
object. He had, indeed, fair ground to hope that the
latter would form his army behind the strong line of
Mine Run, a brook running north into the Rapidan
between Grant's new position and the Confederate
right, under the idea that the Federal army had
crossed the river (as under Meade it had attempted
in the November preceding) to threaten that flank
and turn his entrenchments. If Lee had been thus
deceived, the hostile army would soon have gained
ground sufficiently in its intended line to threaten his
direct communication with Richmond, and force him
to seek to dislodge it at any cost. But this was not
to be; and Hancock was recalled from his advance
on the coveted point; and wheeled rapidly into position, to meet the attack which Lee (much stronger
now than when opposed to Meade on the same ground
in the autumn) moved instantly to make. Of this
attack Grant received warning from his cavalry in
good time to form his line facing to the west, and
covering the road along which he would have pressed.
Hancock naturally formed his left. Sedgwick protected the road near the ford, with Warren more to
the centre. Burnside arrived in time to fill the interval between the latter and Hancock; and as soon as
this disposition was complete, the shock fell on the
Federals. The column reported on the turnpike
road from Orange proved to be Ewell's; that more to
the south on the new or plank road was Hill's. So
desirous was Lee (who evidently hoped to take his
adversary by surprise) to commence the battle that
day, that he entered on it without the aid of Long-

street, whose cantonments were so distant that he could not reach the scene of action before the sixth. Night closed upon it without decisive advantage to either party.

At dawn on the sixth the battle was renewed; but by this time the Federals had intrenched the more prominent parts of their position, and the contest assumed the normal character of the great majority of the battles of this war. The beginning of this system is to be found in M'Clellan's operations before Richmond; but it had now been fully developed. We purpose to explain its details, which done, there will be but little need to follow particular incidents; for all such contests bear of necessity a striking family resemblance.

The tactics used in Europe, where the commander of an army can sweep the battle-field with his glass, and direct the march and instantly know the actual danger or success of each division, are evidently not to be applied to warfare conducted in the midst of forests, broken only by clearings too small in many cases for the free movement of a brigade. Combined movements can here be done by guesswork only; and the front of the army, instead of being at least at double its artillery range from the enemy at the close of the day, is often within earshot. Hence sprang the practice early in the war, of each corps entrenching slightly the ground on which it was to sleep. The facility with which that could be done (in a manner presently to be described) caused the same system of breastworks to be applied extensively in the midst of battle, so as to avoid the constant danger of being taken in flank by sudden movements of the enemy through the wood.

Flank attacks are alarming to the best of troops, and are especially applicable to the case of a forest engagement, where the enemy's line, broken into skirmishers, each covered by a tree, could be forced back from the front only by slow degrees, and with considerable sacrifice of men; and yet may be approached without observation at either extremity. At the period of the war of which we are writing, it had become a fixed habit of the armies to cover every hundred yards gained by a breastwork wherever the materials could be found. It followed that the so-called battles degenerated into a series of long and bloody skirmishes, carried on chiefly from under rude shelter, and occupying sometimes many days without any decisive result. The fighting, in fact, had grown to resemble rather the last part of a siege on a great scale, with its constant intrenching, sorties, counter-attacks, and vast expenditure of powder, than such conflicts as Europe has seen on her great fields. Indeed the latter have often been fought (as Leipsic, Waterloo, Wagram, Borodino testify) upon ground of remarkably open character, naturally fitted for the parade movements of mighty hosts. Yet the length of the American conflicts, the often-repeated attempts of their generals to search the enemy's lines, and the deadly fire of the arms employed, have made their character scarcely less bloody than that of the actions with which we contrast them.

We must now describe more particularly the breastworks which are so identified with our subject, and in the forming of which the Federals especially were so skilful and laborious as greatly to counteract the individual inferiority of their soldiery; for many of these, town-bred or recent immigrants, were no match in

regular skirmishing for the active Southerners, trained
from their youth to free use of the rifle, who formed the
mass of the hostile army.

Given a piece of ground to be occupied, and thickly
covered with trees, there would be found in every
brigade some hundreds of stout arms ready to wield
the formidable bushman's axe, used throughout the
North American continent, and carried in profusion
with the regiments. A line being roughly marked, a
few minutes sufficed to fell the trees along its length,
letting each fall towards the front; and some further
chopping completed a rough " abattis," (or " entangle-
ment" as it is technically called) forming a very awkward obstacle to an advancing enemy. Behind this,
and against its rear, two or three hours of spade labor
were enough to throw up a line of parapet with ditch,
or row of rifle-pits, sufficient to shelter the defenders
of this woodland barricade. But to enclose the
whole of the army's front in this fashion would be to
renounce all attempt to advance. Openings had
therefore to be left at frequent intervals, and these
again were covered by separate intrenchments, with
guns disposed to flank each other, and the approach
to the general line. If a retreat were thought of, other
lines formed to the rear might be so arranged as to
make it secure. If the enemy were forced from his
opposing works, a little ingenuity converted them to
the captor's use. Allow but a little time in advance,
and it is hard to say how resolute men could be forced
from a succession of such works as these. They were
indeed but the revival on a larger scale of those
against which British valor and discipline were shattered at Saratoga, to the ruin of our war against the

revolted colonies. But it is time to return to our narrative.

The battle of the Wilderness, begun late on the fifth, was renewed next day, and continued even after darkness closed over the scene. Longstreet had come upon the ground at dawn, to the great relief of Hill, whose corps showed symptoms of giving ground before the pressure of Hancock. The newly-arrived general restored the day, and sought soon after to decide it by turning the extreme left of the Federals with one of those wide sweeping movements so successful under Jackson. To do this it was needful to march his troops to their right; and in guiding his advanced brigades that way, he was shot at through the cover by some of his own men while passing along the front of his second line, and desperately wounded, General Jenkins being killed by the same volley. Less happy in this respect than his great comrade had been at Chancellorsville, the fall of Longstreet ruined the success of the manœuvre he had undertaken, and the Confederates made no real progress during the rest of the day. As it closed, however, General Gordon, whose troops formed their extreme left, stole up to the breastworks which covered Sedgwick's right near the Rapidan, and carried them by a swift surprise made before the pickets were posted for the night. Great part of two Federal brigades were captured, and the rest of the division fled. But the pursuers were checked by another line of intrenchments raised by some reserve artillery close at hand; and Sedgwick, by gallant exertions, rallied his men behind this, which, though somewhat at an angle with the general

front, served to protect the right of the army sufficiently for Grant's purpose.

Lee in these encounters had already incurred a loss
of 7,000 men, including two of his best generals; and
although the Federals estimated theirs at double that
number, yet the spirit of their soldiery was good, and
their position unshaken. Another day would see it
so strengthened that the Southern marksmen would
lose the advantage of that greater activity and quickness of aim which had told hitherto in their favor, and
Grant would be enabled to guard his front sufficiently
and yet to continue his original movement by a gradual extension of his left. Lee's offensive battle, in
short, had failed in its object; and, with the versatility
of true genius, he shifted it at once for the opposite
course. For the rest of the campaign we shall find
him steadily pursuing that defensive warfare which
the great German writer, Clausewitz, points out for the
natural course of the weaker party, and which here became especially necessary to him, as he discovered
that his new antagonist was unsparing to a marked
degree of the lives of his men. Grant has in fact
much to answer for in this year's history as regards
the charge of wasting his army by pressing it on
against unfair odds of position. To justify him in any
measure, it must be borne in mind that he came to his
new work in Virginia after a train of striking successes
won greatly by the judicious employment of superior
numbers; that he had sound reason to believe that
the enemy had no such supplies of recruits to draw
from as were available to himself; and that the government he served was of necessity compelled to insist on constant advance, and on seeming advantage

at any present sacrifice. Add to these conditions that the general was of disposition as obstinate as brave; and his troops resolute and patient rather than daring in their character; and we may account for much of the waste of life now so notorious. A little more of success in the results, and we should have heard noth-ing but praise. Doubtless Grant is deficient in that sublime quality of genius which instinctively knows the impossible, and recoils from it alone. His war-fare shows marvellous resemblance to that of Masséna, whose obstinate clinging to his purpose and patient waiting for opportunity saved France and covered himself with glory in 1799, as they proved the ruin of his fame and of Napoleon's Peninsular designs when met by Wellington and Torres Vedras.

The morning of the seventh saw Lee resting on the defensive, and expecting Grant to advance. But the latter, finding himself no longer pressed, began in the afternoon to detach to his left in the direction of Spottsylvania, the coveted point where, as before no-ticed, the chief roads of the district intersect. His movement was complicated by the attempt to conceal it, and the march of the Federals filled so much time that daybreak arrived on the ninth, and found the cross-roads occupied by a mere advanced guard; while Lee, being warned of the operation by his cav-alry, and at once divining the full purpose of the Fed-erals, had resolved to throw himself across their path, and compel them to become the assailants. His right (now under Anderson, who had taken Longstreet's place) marched rapidly for this purpose; and arriving at the double-quick, drove the Federals sharply from the neighborhood of the Court-house. This corps was speedily supported by Hill and Ewell; and the Confederates intrenched themselves at once in their new position, which covered the cross-roads, and ran in semicircular form through a piece of ground peculiarly adapted for their purpose of defence.

The tremendous losses which Grant endured on the fifth and sixth of May (amounting to no less than 20,000 men, not including those of Burnside's corps) must have shown him plainly that troops so hastily made up as his own (the brigades in some cases being composed four-fifths of recruits lately armed) were helpless as skirmishers among these dense woods before the veterans of Lee, each man of whom was hardened to the work. In the words of Swinton, at once the ablest and the fullest of American writers on this campaign:

" The result was a grievous disappointment to General Grant, for he shared an opinion commonly entertained in the West—the opinion that the Army of the Potomac had never been properly fought. This belief was perhaps natural under the circumstances ; nevertheless it was fallacious. Sharing it, he had hoped at one blow to finish the troublesome, and seemingly invulnerable adversary. And to achieve this end, he made little account of those arts that accomplish results by the direction and combination of forces : for at this period he avowedly despised manœuvring. His reliance was exclusively on the application of brute masses, in rapid and remorseless blows, or as he himself phrased it, in ' hammering continually.' "

This statement is not made at random. It is founded on the highest testimony; for as the same work states:

"Shortly before the opening of the Rapidan campaign, General Meade, in conversation with the lieutenant-general, was telling him that he proposed to manœuvre, thus and thus; whereupon General Grant stopped him at the word 'manœuvre,' and said, 'Oh! I never manœuvre.' This characteristic utterance, which the suavity of biographers might readily pass over in silence, cannot be omitted here; for it is the proof of a frame of mind that essentially influenced the complexion of the campaign. The battle of the Wilderness can hardly be understood, save as the act of a commander who 'never manœuvred.'"

In quoting this, it is but justice to General Grant to add that if he used such expressions and acted here with such apparent rashness, it was plainly owing to a mistaken view of the particular army he had under him; for in the previous campaigns of Vicksburg and Chattanooga he had shown the very highest powers of manœuvring, those larger qualities of strategy in fact, which will more and more be demanded in modern war, as the means for great combinations multiply.

Then followed for twelve long days the bloody contest around Spottsylvania. Once only (May twelfth) did Grant's troops break fairly in upon the breastworks, on which they were moved again and again, searching out the weak points in Lee's long enciente; and then, although the capture of a single projecting angle with many guns and prisoners rewarded Hancock's bold assault, the enemy's position was but slightly contracted, not really changed. This day, too, the Army of the Potomac lost 8,000 men in retaining the ground thus won, for the scene of the contest (says Swinton, speaking here as an eye-witness) was literally, and by

no figure of speech, "covered with piles of dead." Bu
two days before, in a less fortunate attack, "the los
was between five and six thousand, while it is doubtfu
whether the enemy lost as many hundreds;" anc
finally, "after General Grant had carried out witl
much fidelity, but very indifferent success, his owr
principle of hammering continuously, ... the carry
ing of the position was seen to be hopeless, and he
abandoning the effort after twelve days, resolved by a
turning operation to disengage Lee from it." Grant
had paid the penalty of his want of discernment with
another 20,000 men put *hors de combat*, whilst the Confederates, even including nearly a whole division captured by Hancock's surprise, were again diminished
by only one-third of the number. "Grant's exhausted
army," says the same writer before quoted, "began to
lose its spirit. It was with joy that it turned its back
upon the lines of Spottsylvania."

Largely reinforced from the reserves about Washington, Grant moved on May twentieth to the west,
passing beyond the right of the enemy, and then
making southward; but only to find the Confederates
again established across his front on the North Anna
river, in a position so admirably chosen that even his
audacity admitted it unassailable. Another flank
march, the fourth within the month, carried him over
the Pamunkey, and finally brought his army, at the
end of May, in sight of the very ground occupied by
M'Clellan two years before. Close to the army's front
was the Chickahominy, with the very passages which
had connected the wings of that general's forces when
pushing along that stream in 1862; but between it
and these passages, in a line of hasty intrenchments

covered by swamps and thickets, lay the ever-watchful Lee, in that strictly defensive attitude which he held throughout this campaign after the failure of his first attack in the Wilderness.

Leaving the two great hosts once more facing each other after a month of constant fighting, marching, and intrenching, we turn to follow the courses of those minor operations on which Grant had counted for the success of his double scheme. In addition to the movements of Sigel and Butler on their respective lines, he had detached Sheridan with the cavalry of the Potomac army as soon as the course of the first two days' battle had shown this arm to be unavailable about Spottsylvania, with orders to pass through the country to the north of Richmond, and operate between it and Lee. In this there was nothing original; for Stoneman had received the same charge from Hooker the year before. Nor did Sheridan perform any more striking feat upon his raid, which would be little noteworthy, but for its having led to the death of General Steuart, who was shot down in a charge upon a party of the Federal horse which had appeared close to Richmond on May eleventh. Though this once famous leader had never, though for two years in constant command, made any reform in the wasteful over-work which wore Lee's cavalry away; yet was he unrivalled in the outpost duties of that difficult country, and doubtless was sorely missed by his old commander, and the army for which he had so long kept watch.

Sigel's expedition up the Shenandoah was chiefly remarkable for its fully revealing to the Federals the intense hostility to their cause which the severities of former generals in that district had created. This, and a natural hesitancy, caused him to strip his column so much in order to guard his communications, that when met suddenly by Breckinridge far up the valley, he was very decisively beaten on May fifteenth, with heavy loss in guns and men, and driven again far north. Lincoln instantly superseded, this time without a murmur against the act, the unsuccessful commander, and sent General Hunter in his stead. The latter, in the absence of Breckinridge (called at this time to the aid of Lee on the Chickahominy), began another of those advances up the great valley which the high land on either side throughout the war kept so distinct from other operations.

Butler at this time aided his chief but little more than did Sigel. His first movement was a feint upon York River to draw the attention of the enemy from the south of Richmond, and it so far succeeded, that when he debarked his force high up the James, he struck without difficulty the railroad mentioned as running through Petersburg, and sent his cavalry far across country to that of Danville, promising in his first dispatches to wrest them from the enemy. But neither of these important lines was retained by the Federals. Alarmed by a report that Lee was falling back on Richmond, Butler drew in his posts, and confined his operations to a feeble demonstration against Fort Darling, the chief work upon the river; and being sharply attacked in flank by Beauregard on May sixteenth (when the Federals lost, by surprise a whole brigade captured), he abandoned the offensive entirely, and intrenched himself upon a deep loop of the James. His campaign had failed decisively as a separate operation, and half his force was now called suddenly from him to join the main army on the Chickahominy.

Then came the darkest spot in the career of Grant as a commander. It had seemed as though, when he recoiled a few days before from Lee's position on the North Anna, without attempting it, he had learnt by bitter experience that the "continuous hammering" in which he not long since had trusted might break the instrument while its work was yet unfinished. Not even the vast resources on which he had power to draw could long spare 20,000 men a week for the continuance of the experiment. It requires, therefore, more excuse than has any where been offered for the sacrifice which followed. It may be that Grant's usually imperturbable temper was ruffled by the continued readiness with which his adversary met him ; or that he believed the Confederates already so worn down by their unsupplied losses as to be unable to man their works ; or that he judged that his new command had not yet been sufficiently put to the proof by the stern doings of the month just past ; or that all these causes acted together. Possibly he was influenced more than all by the uneasy consciousness that he had brought the criticism of the whole world upon his strategy by his famous dispatch, " I propose to fight it out on this line, if it takes all the summer : " for had not this chosen line been already abandoned and no result won ? At any rate his conclusion was to try once more to force Lee out of his path by direct attack So having called up 16,000 of Butler's forces from the James to aid him, he ordered a general assault of the kind so often made in the course of this campaign

5

along the whole front, to be made at half-past four on the morning of June third.

The most eulogistic biographer of the great Federal general, speaks, as it were, under his breath when he tells the story of the battle of Cold Harbor. "There was a rush" (says such an one), "a bitter struggle, a rapid interchange of deadly fire, and the army became conscious that the task was more than it could do." The testimony of Swinton, himself an eyewitness is more emphatic and complete: "It took hardly more than ten minutes to decide the battle. There was along the whole line a rush—the spectacle of impregnable works—a bloody loss—a sullen falling back, and the action was decided." Then after some details, he concludes:

"The action was decided, as I have said, in an incredibly brief time in the morning's assault. Rapidly as the result was reached, it was *decisive;* for the consciousness of every man pronounced further assault hopeless. The troops went forward as far as the example of their officers could carry them : nor was it possible to urge them beyond ; for there they knew lay only death, without even the chance of victory. The completeness with which this judgment had been reached by the whole army was strikingly illustrated by an incident that occurred during the forenoon. Some hours after the failure of the first assault, General Meade sent instructions to each corps-commander to renew the attack without reference to the troops on his right or left. The order was issued through these officers to their subordinate commanders, and from them descended through the wonted channels ; but no one stirred, and the immobile lines pronounced a verdict, silent yet emphatic, against further slaughter. The loss on the Union side in this sanguinary action was over thirteen thousand, while on the part of the Confederates, it is doubtful whether it reached that many hundreds."

It was in fact not half as many, if the most authentic Confederate reports may be believed.

It is vain to enter into elaborate criticisms of such an action. Grant's mode of assault, made " along the whole line," and without any reserve, was contrary to all the tactical rules of theory or practice. There is, indeed, an exception in one important case, where the enemy is decidedly worn out and shaken by previous events. So Wellington ordered his general charge at Waterloo when the Prussian shock had shattered and laid bare the French right flank, and made Napoleon's battle a hopeless struggle. So Radetsky, acting on the same instinct of genius, threw all his front line suddenly on the exhausted Italians at Novara, ere Hess, his more methodical chief of staff, could array the reserves for a final assault. Grant had no such motive for his battle. The troops that he attacked were not the ill-led swaggerers whose indecision at Fort Donelson had been patent to his observant glance, nor the wearied stragglers whose officers stayed to plunder with them at Pittsburg. They were veterans, war-hardened to suffering and danger, confident in their general, feeling themselves invincible on the defensive, and making up by their priceless value as individual soldiers for their want of discipline and numbers. It is better for those who would think well of Grant, to pass onward from the subject, with a word of pity for Burnside, so often condemned for the like fault committed earlier in the war at Fredericks-

burg ; and to add only that the error of the Federal
generals was older than their day : since Napoleon
(whose mode of fighting battles it is the fashion to imagine faultless) threw away nearly the same number
of men in 1807, in a vain assault on the Russian intrenched camp upon the Aller ; an assault ordered apparently without reason, for the works were afterwards
turned strategically without difficulty by a simple flank
movement.   The holocaust thus offered by impatience
at Heilsberg was even more inexcusable than those of
Fredericksburg and Cold Harbor ; for no excited nation
was crying out to the French Emperor for action at all
cost.

Unconscious, it may be, of his imitation of Napoleon, whose tactics in his later period were not unlike
those of the great Federal general, Grant now once
turned aside from the works he could not carry, and
with a wide sweep to his left, the fifth and last of the
year, passed away from the blood-stained meadows of
the Chickahominy, crossed the James thirty miles
below Richmond, and establishing himself south of
Petersburg (which place should have been captured
but for a miscarriage in the movement), spent the rest
of the year intrenched before that place.

To do this was no strange conception, forced upon
him by his previous failures.   On the contrary, in letters to Washington written before his late promotion,
he had strongly urged that the future campaign
against Richmond should be conducted not by any
direct advance, but rather by just such an operation
conducted south of the James and based upon the
coast ; the tendency of which would be ultimately to
sever Richmond (viewed thus as a sort of advanced

fortress thrust northward) from the rest of the Confed
eracy, and by straightening its defenders, to enclose them
as Pemberton was shut in Vicksburg, or at the least com
pel its evacuation. Strong indeed must have been the
political and personal motives which had induced him
when nominally uncontrolled, to lay aside this plan
and adopt, in deference to the well-known anxiety of
Lincoln for the national capital, the line of advance
on which M'Dowell and Pope, Burnside and Hooker,
had met their successive disasters, and had led him
when forced to abandon this, to try that on which
M'Clellan had failed. The result had proved the
sagacity of his original choice; for now he found himself at last in the position which he might have assumed
at the first, and he had only reached it after suffering
a loss of nearly 70,000 men, while Lee's rolls were
diminished by about 25,000. The moral energy of
the North sustained its commander-in-chief still; but
Sherman's successful advance into Georgia had, it may
well be believed, much effect at this time. Had that
general been as rash as his chief, and his campaign as
unfruitful in aught but losses, " it would," in the opinion of the Federal historian already cited, " have been
difficult to have raised new forces to recruit the Army
of the Potomac, which, shaken in its structure, its
valor quenched in blood, and thousands of its ablest
officers killed and wounded, was the Army of the
Potomac no more."

From that time forward, Grant, not too proud to
learn by adversity, abandoned the costly tactics which
had served him so ill. His campaign took the shape
of a siege, or rather a blockade, and the cumbrous
form of warfare which the world had not witnessed

since Turenne and Montecuculi checked one another
in the Palatinate, was revived on a grander scale.
Lines of circumvallation round the enemy in front
arose, and lines of contravallation against the enemy
in rear. Works mounted with the heaviest guns
guarded the camp of the Federals, and a railroad
brought the rations along its lines. Bit by bit Grant
strove to extend his left inland to seize the three lines
of railroad which connected Richmond with the Confederacy. Bombardment and mining of unknown
dimensions failed to shake Lee's defences in front,
and the struggle gradually narrowed to the continuous
effort to reach beyond him by successive operations
on the western flank. August saw Grant in possession
of the coast railroad that led to Weldon; but the
year waned, and the spring of 1865, found the
"Southside" branch line leading from Danville
through Petersburg to Richmond still intact, while
the more important one direct to the city was yet far
from the Federal grasp. Grant not the less for many
failures held tenaciously his threatening position,
being well supplied from those vast and ever-develop-
ing resources of the Union cause which Sherman's
brilliant successes had quickened into vigorous action;
and being warned minutely by deserters and spies of
the waning strength of that heroic army which had so
long bidden defiance to the efforts of the North.

We have not space here to point out fully how
fatal was that political determination which caused
General Lee, against his own opinion and all true military rule, to maintain himself in Richmond at the cost
of ruin to its defenders. Two causes operated with
terrible effect upon his army; the want of men, and

the want of supplies. The Confederacy was not as completely stripped of its manhood as Grant believed when he publicly declared that winter of his enemies, " they have robbed the cradle and the grave : " but the conscription, badly managed at the first, failed altogether in its object as the powers of the Confederate government were lessened ; and this failure, coupled with the proposed refusal of the exchange of prisoners, prevented all recruiting for the forces at the capital. As remarkable, and probably even more decisive of the result, was the utter break-down of the commissariat system in force. This department, it is now well known, was confided to a man as incompetent by nature as ignorant of his duties; and the mode he adopted of pressing supplies at a nominal price caused evasion wherever force was actually wanting. So much is now generally admitted, and has been written plainly in American works ; but, in addition to these errors of the government, it is plain that there was a certain weakness on the part of Lee himself, which contributed largely to the result. If kept at Richmond against his will, there was all the more need of his being fully rationed ; and, strong as he was by his position and prestige, had he insisted on taking the commissariat of his force into his own hands, and seen to its working, the failure of the supplies need not have occurred. We have been informed by irrefragable authority that, when Richmond was abandoned, there were stored up not far off, on the North Carolina railways, four months' provisions for such an army as his, which had only required exertion to have been forwarded long before. The food was there, and the railroads still serviceable ; but there was a lack of that personal energetic supervision which in such cases smooths difficulties away, and brings provisions and army together.   In excuse it may be said that a retreat into North Carolina was constantly kept in view ; but this should not have prevented the measures necessary to meet immediate wants.   For lack of such the strength and spirits and number of those glorious soldiers fell ruinously away.

Lee discovered this too late.   Desertion had thinned his ranks in the winter, and increased so rapidly in the spring of 1865, that the month of March found him guarding forty miles of intrenchments with but forty thousand men.   The strength of the enemy was meanwhile constantly increasing, and it became absolutely necessary to make an effort to extricate the army from a situation no longer tenable.   To retreat from Richmond was, however, no longer easy nor safe.   The necessary movement would involve the march of long columns past the left flank of Grant, who was constantly on the watch ; and Lee resolved therefore to force his enemy to draw this in by threatening the eastern or right end of his lines before Petersburg by a sudden assault.   The sortie took place accordingly on the morning of the twenty-fifth of March.   It was confided to Gordon, the youngest and most daring of Lee's corps commanders, whose courage and conduct had raised him from the rank of simple brigadier to his present charge during the autumn campaign.   His attack at first promised to be successful, one of the strong redoubts which guarded the Federal camp being carried at a rush, and three of the neighboring batteries abandoned by their guards.   But the advantage could not be followed up ; for the supports which were to have aided Gordon to establish himself beyond the works by a further advance, failed to answer the call upon them : and then the Federals, recovering from their surprise, drove back the assailants by a counter-charge, taking many of them prisoners, and inflicting further heavy loss in killed and wounded, the retreat taking place under a severe artillery fire. The task had not seemed impossible, nor the odds hopeless ; but the Army of Virginia had failed because the energy and spirit which had made it the world's wonder for the past three years, were decaying for lack of nour-ishment and hope.

Grant detected his enemy's increasing weakness under this show of offence, and made haste to give the counterblow that was to conclude the long cam-paign. With his wish arrived the ready instrument in the person of Sheridan, the most impetuous and active of that new class of generals, young in years, but veterans in war, whom the long series of contin-uous campaigns had raised to high charge upon the Federal side. Grant had marked him out first in 1863, at Chattanooga, where he led on his division of infantry to break the lines of Bragg, with all the fire of youth and the skill of a practiced soldier. Struck by his spirit and tactical ability, he restored him to the cav-alry service (in which Sheridan had first distinguished himself in the West), choosing him out, first to com-mand the whole horse of his army, and then to take charge of the independent operations in the Shenan-doah valley, where he had been opposed during the autumn to General Early. Having first checked, he finally routed and ruined that general's army ; and then, his separate task accomplished, returned to his

chief to take part in the final struggle, arriving at
the Federal headquarters on March twenty-seventh,
two days after Gordon's repulse. His arrival was
the signal of the opening of the spring campaign of
1865.

Grant's first plan as laid down in his own orders,
was simple enough, and indeed may·be regarded as a
continuation of the efforts made on his left in the
previous autumn. Sheridan, with the cavalry, was to
strike boldly inland, and destroy the Southside and
direct Danville Railroads. The other corps, taking
for lightness' sake part only of their guns, were to
move by their left, for the double purpose of "turning
the enemy's positions, and insuring Sheridan's success." The Ninth Corps alone was to remain and
guard the lines before Petersburg. These, therefore, would be watched by 20,000 men, while 10,000
horse and 80,000 foot moved beyond them, and cut
Richmond off from the rest of the South. The troops,
well fed, well armed, and confident of success, took
every man his four days' rations; and light wagon-
trains bore supplies for eight days more. This was
enough, it was thought (nor was the reckoning false)
to finish well the work in hand. The greatest Civil
War, as some prefer to call it, the greatest Rebellion
ever known, had drawn to its close. The energy and
resolution with which General Grant had carried out
his purpose, unwearied by delay, undaunted by failure,
were at last to bring their full reward.

The movement began early on the twenty-ninth
of March. That evening the fifth and second Infantry
Corps, under Warren and Humphreys, got well outside the lines, and found slight intrenchments ex-

tended by the Confederates into the woods beyond. Along the front of these they skirmished, feeling their way cautiously. Sheridan lay that night at Dinwiddie, six miles further to the west (or left), preparing to start on his distant expedition next day. Suddenly there fell upon Grant that sort of inspiration which, in such great events, precedes and presages success; and changing his first plan, he resolved to turn his left inwards, and crush the enemy where they stood. "*I now feel*," he wrote that evening to Sheridan, "*like ending the matter*, if it is possible to do so, before going back. I do not want you, therefore, to cut loose and go after the enemy's roads at present. In the morning, push round the enemy, and get on to his right rear. We will act altogether as one army here until it is seen what can be done with the enemy."

Lee was neither surprised nor idle. With his usual insight, he had discovered the Federal manœuvre, and drawing 15,000 men from the weak garrison of Petersburg, he moved to his right, to try his old method of war once more and strike at the exposed flank of the enemy while they were yet extending it. The thirtieth of March found his troops gathering, despite storms of rain which that day stayed the Federal march at Five Forks, important cross-roads close to the Southside Railroad and ten miles beyond the Petersburg lines. Intrenching themselves here, they stood almost between Sheridan and the nearest corps of Federal Infantry, that of Warren: the next morning the blow fell on each. Warren was at first surprised; but, improving on the ordinary Federal practice, he had disposed his forces deeply in echelon, so as to meet a flank attack by mutual support ; and being reinforced by part of the corps of Humphreys, he finally regained his ground. The Confederates, retiring before him, now turned against Sheridan (who had reached Five Forks with his advance), and drove him roughly back upon Dinwiddie. On the whole, therefore, this battle of the thirty-first of March was indecisive; though Grant's orders that night, show that he was inspired with grave anxiety about Sheridan, and Warren was ordered to march directly to his quarters, and support him.

The morning of the first of April decided the campaign. It showed Sheridan that the enemy had retired on Five Forks; and he followed them with his horse, keeping Warren's corps back, concealed from observation. When arrived before the enemy's intrenchments, a simple line of breastwork, without flank protection, held by Pickett's and Bushrod Johnson's divisions, he engaged their attention with some of his dismounted troopers, and made as though about to turn the right of their works with another division, while Warren's whole corps was secretly formed to march in upon their left. These tactics (for no general had mastered, like this young American commander, the new art of using, amid infantry manœuvres, his mounted riflemen), succeeded perfectly. Warren swept on in irresistible strength upon the astonished Confederates, when occupied with the attacks of Sheridan on their front and right. A panic seized them; they broke; and 5,000 of the defenders of Five Forks fell captives into the victors' hands.

Next day, Grant followed up vigorously the success which his lieutenant's energy had won, and attacked the whole front of the Petersburg lines. The outer defences, too weakly manned for serious resistance, fell at the first assault; and although Longstreet (delayed until now at his posts on the other side of the River James by a feint) arrived in time to restore the fight, and save the inner line of works, it became necessary for Lee to order the retreat at all risks that night. But the Federals were as near as their enemies to the Danville Railroad, by which alone could Lee hope to feed his army in that wasted region while on his way to North Carolina: and Grant's forethought had already furnished the provisions necessary for a lengthened pursuit, while the Confederate general had no nearer supplies than at Danville, and was uncertain if these would reach him in time to meet his wants on the retreat. His uncertainty began to change into despair when, early on the fourth, after a severe march, he reached the railroad at the designated point, Amelia Court-house, to find his trains missent to Richmond! Meanwhile his adversary, the general who had long since " felt like ending the matter," had now taken up the pursuit with relentless vigor, and was not slow to profit by the disparity of supplies. While the starving Confederate columns were waiting for the foragers sent out to gather up a meal, Grant himself directed his infantry on a line parallel to that of Lee ; and Sheridan, pushing impetuously past them, struck the railroad just south of Amelia, where he was soon joined by the Fifth Corps, the same which had turned the scale at Five Forks, and disposed his force so as effectually to block the way.

Not even then did the great Confederate commander yield to his fate. Twice he struck westward

with a wide sweep; attempting to first pass around the
enemy and gain the Danville line beyond; and when
that hope failed, to win the branch railroad which ran
to Lynchburg and the mountains. All was in vain
against the prescience of Grant, the fire of Sheridan,
the fatal odds they wielded. His famished troops
could bear the pressure of their misery no more.
" Hundreds," says an eye-witness, " dropped from
exhaustion, and thousands let fall their muskets from
inability to carry them any farther." On the ninth,
the gaunt relics of the Army of Virginia were finally
brought to bay near Appomattox Court-house, and
were surrendered shortly afterwards by their beloved
chief on terms so liberal, and enforced in so delicate a
manner, that one knows not whether the transaction
reflects most credit on the victor or the vanquished.
When President Johnson, not long after, in the first
vindictive impulse of triumph, would have singled out
the Confederate hero and his favored officers for trial
and vengeance, General Grant showed no less resolution in maintaining the capitulation inviolate than he
had displayed in the campaign by which he won the
right to offer it. All honor to the noble instinct which
saved the restored Union from the crime her Chief
Magistrate meditated in the newness of his power!

It is not within our present purpose to show how
far Sherman's masterly strategy had contributed to
the successful issue of the struggle. The war was recognized as practically finished from the day when Lee
laid down his sword, and the cause of the Union
needed that of Grant no more. And soon the nation,
grateful for his services and expectant of more, resolved
to raise her favorite general to a yet greater charge

than that of army or bureau. As in the crisis of the war the voice of the North called Grant to supreme command, so after peace was won, it named him as the man who best could solve the difficulties the war had bequeathed. It is not for us to prophesy the final result. Great, though not faultless, as a general, active and successful in administrative office, the character of Grant as a statesman and the effect of his personal character as President are enigmas which time must solve. We know that he has steered so clear of shoals of party that the Republicans have charged him with being at heart a Democrat, and the Democrats abused him for his gross Republicanism. We have seen that fulsome and inappropriate praise, virulent and personal abuse, have failed to shake his reticence, or cause him to commit himself unreservedly to the arms of faction. Yet the task before him needs more than mere prudence and reserve. It demands high wisdom as well as enduring resolution, and statesmanship no less than self-restraint. To bind up the wounds left by the war, to restore concord between the victorious and vanquished sections of the Union, to insure real freedom to the Southern negro, and full justice to the Southern white; these are indeed tasks which might tax the powers of Washington himself, or a greater than Washington, if such an one could be found. It would seem as though his friend and adviser, Sherman, had foreseen coming events to the letter when he wrote, five years ago, on Grant's elevation to be Lieutenant-General, the warning prophecy which we may quote as peculiarly appropriate now:—" You are now Washington's legitimate successor, and occupy a position of almost dangerous elevation; but, if you can continue

as heretofore, to be yourself, simple, honest, and unpretending, you will enjoy through life the respect
and love of friends and the homage of millions of
human beings, that will award you a large share in securing to them and their descendants a government of
law and stability."

We would hope that this worthy counsel of his
friend to the commander may find its full fruition in
the actions of the President. We trust that there was
a deep inner meaning, as well as fine political tact and
generous sentiment in the words with which General
Grant closed his brief acceptance of his first nomination for the Presidency, and that generations of American citizens yet unborn may identify his name with
the most noble aspiration a successful soldier could
utter, " LET US HAVE PEACE."

A MEMOIR OF GENERAL LEE.*

YEAR after year had passed by since General Grant first publicly sought the presidency of the great republic which owed so much to his services in war; but the peace which he then made his motto has not yet smiled on the reconquered South. The world from outside the narrow sphere of American politics has looked on with surprise at the petty warfare against individuals which succeeded the gigantic contest between Union and Secession. Amnesty upon amnesty, ever repeated, never complete, tells the tale of mistrust still nourished on the victor's side, or of party intrigue defeating national generosity in its purposes. Traveller after traveller through the limits of the overthrown Confederacy brings back the sad story of ceaseless dissension and widespread ruin. Rival legislatures, born of mean fraud or open violence, contest the political supremacy here. There negro revolt, unchecked by law, threatens summary vengeance for the long-endured wrongs of the slave. In other districts secret and bloody societies strive by illegal combination to prolong the rule which has passed away from the white. Everywhere rises the same story of corrupt administration and finances involved to enrich the mean adventurers who have swarmed in upon the prostrate states for booty, as foul birds seek their prey

* *A Life of General Robert E. Lee.* By John Esten Cooke.

6

when the carnage is over. The successful general, raised to rule the Union saved by the sword, who had called upon the nation that elected him to join in the noble wish, "Let us have peace," found his task of political pacification more arduous, more thankless, and withal far more prolonged, than the command of the Union armies for the overthrow of Secession.

If to us afar off this defeat of the first hopes that came with the victory of the Union seems sad and surprising, how must those feel it who dwell near the contending parties that prolong the strife, without sharing their political passions? Even among those that lend themselves to prolong the intolerable state of things in the reconquered states, must be many who regret the results bitterly, while they excuse the means used by the false reasoning of expediency. And doubtless in the Northern States there are thousands of good men to whom each phase of the political conflict that makes its market in the strife of the South seems an unmixed evil, which mars, in their view, the full freedom and growing greatness of the Union. But all these can look on with comparative serenity. For how much happier are such than those whose lot has been cast among the storms that sweep over the face of what they once dreamed of as an independent, well-governed republic: who have watched sorrowfully the growth of the evils they could not ward off from the states which gave them birth: who had offered their lives freely in battle to save these from what they deemed oppression, and yet, when the cause for which they had fought fell, bowed their heads meekly before the victors' yoke, in hopes that their submission, possibly their sacrifice, might save

their humbler fellow-citizens from ruin: who, when
called upon to set the example of prudence, thought
it no shame to ask pardon at the hands of that government which once their victories had shaken: who
urged the writers that would extol the brief-lived
glories of the Confederacy to "avoid all topics that
would excite angry discussion or hostile feeling:"*
who turned their faces steadfastly away from the
ambitions and hopes of the dead past to seek com-
pensation for defeat and loss in the steady performance of humble daily duties: whose blameless lives
and peaceful bearing in adversity have testified to
their love of country more gloriously than deaths upon
the battle-field: whose conduct, in short, when conquered, has won involuntary admiration from the
adversaries who once heaped curses upon their rebellious names. Many such there must have been, vic-
tims of fate, sacrifices to political necessity, innocent
expiators, if the truth be told, of wrongs done in ages
past to helpless Africans, among the leaders of the
late Secession. One such, at least, all recognize in
Robert Edward Lee, General-in-Chief of the ex-Con-
federate forces, better known as the Commander of
the Army of Virginia, who passed away, after five
years' endurance of his altered position, without the
sign of ailment outwardly, without a word of pain,
that great heart which repined not for his own loss of
dignity or of ancestral fortune, giving way at last
under the continued pressure of the ruin and degradation of the beloved state to the freedom of which
the prospects of his whole life had been sacrificed.

* General Lee's words to an author undertaking to write the life of
" Stonewall " Jackson.

While he lived, General Lee never ceased to contemplate (as we know from his private correspondence with ourselves) giving a record of his own career to the world. But the time never came when in his judgment this could be honestly and fully done without stirring up the bitter feelings he would have sacrificed all he could give to allay. Now that he has passed away, others cannot be so reticent. And Mr. Cooke has produced a life of the dead hero, which, if wanting in many particulars, is more so perhaps from the greatness of the subject than from the imperfections and partiality of the writer. A large part of his volume is, of course, directed to those campaigns which have placed the name of Lee in the very foremost rank of the world's great commanders. These, however, have long been treated of and studied in England in their general outlines. They were known and admired here before the American public could bear a critical recital of the defeats of the Union generals. Be it our present task rather to speak of those portions of Lee's eventful life which are less known on this side of the Atlantic: what sacrifices he made when he cast in his lot with the South: how, brought into command by an accident, his first stroke raised him to the eminence he never lost: how he fell, carrying in his fall the tottering Confederacy which had ceased to hope in any other name: how he bore himself in his retirement, when vanquished by fate, yet crowned with undying fame, he rivalled in patience the patriarch of Uz, and waited in sad watch over surrounding ruin through his appointed time for the change which he longed for but would not anticipate. Some eulogist, worthy of the grandeur of the theme, will, we hope, arise hereafter. But it is time that at least an attempt should be made to do justice to the virtue and patriotism of the man, known hitherto to Englishmen chiefly as one of the greatest of modern generals.

When the American colonies, finding remonstrance vain, rose in arms against the overbearing policy of the mother country, the descendants of the Cavalier families which had transplanted to Virginia the loyal traditions and sentiments of the King's party in the Civil War, were to a man found foremost among the defenders of local independence. How this apparent contradiction came about it is not here pretended to explain. But it is certain that the so-called Royalists of 1776 were for the most part very recent immigrants. Those of their fellow-citizens whose interests were fairly bound up by long association and descent with the fortunes of the rising colonies, espoused almost without exception the cause of the latter, no matter how earnest their loyalty had been in theory before. And it is of itself enough to condemn the measures of King George and his Ministers that they should have alienated from the very outset of the struggle the class whose natural sentiments would have been on the side of loyalty, had there been fair room left for them to doubt. One member of this aristocracy of Virginia, then a youth of twenty, was Henry Lee, a direct descendant of Richard Lee of Stratford Laughton in Essex, who had been an ardent Cavalier in the Revolution, and one of many supporters of the falling cause of the Monarchy whom fear of political persecution after the overthrow of the Royalists, or disgust at the then triumphant Puritan Government, had driven to hasty emigration. Settling in Virginia with considerable means, Richard Lee had built what was an exact reproduction of the old manor-house of a country gentleman in the east of England, acquired gradually a large estate, and maintained, so far as possible, the dignity of a rich esquire of the old country. For those were days when the abolition of primogeniture had not been introduced into America ; and settlers of Richard Lee's rank and fortune seem to have looked confidently forward to a continuance in the new country of all the privileges and enjoyments possessed by their class in Great Britain. A great English writer, who has made the " Virginians " of the last century the subject of one of his most skilful and touching fictions, had in view precisely such a family, by race and tradition, as that from which General Lee was descended : and if his hero had left descendants to our own times, they would have played the same part as the illustrious representative of this other Virginian race.

In the manor-house of the Lees once burnt, but soon rebuilt on the same spacious lines, the family were still living more than a century later, when young Henry Lee, just graduated at Princeton College, came forward to offer his services in the Revolutionary army, and received a commission from the Congress as captain of horse. From the very first he displayed military talent of a high order, and became before long the most noted leader of his army for dashing enterprise in separate command. A special gold medal was awarded him by Congress for his capture of the fort at Paulus's Hook, and in 1781 he was sent to command

the cavalry of the Republican forces in the Carolinas
under General Greene, there matched against Cornwallis. That Greene failed on the whole in his encounter is well known. He was in fact in a position
of inferiority, until Cornwallis left the South for Petersburg and the Richmond peninsula, in the vain
hope of effecting the decisive junction with the forces
of Clinton, which the timidity or insufficient resources
of his Commander-in-Chief never allowed to be accomplished. Greene, however, though defeated,
never ceased to hold his own stoutly against Cornwallis for the time, and afterwards recovered the Carolinas fully for Congress: and his successes were due
in great part to the talents and energy of his young
cavalry commander. General Henry Lee had a
worthy opponent in Colonel Tarleton, a cavalry officer of no mean merit in light warfare. But the republican cavalier established his superiority very fully in
the series of skirmishes that ensued. And although,
in his own Memoir of the War, he has the modesty to
attribute his own successes over Tarleton to his superiority in horse-flesh, readers of his interesting
work may discern for themselves that his own skill
and judgment were the prime causes of the advantage,
and will be disposed to agree to the full with General
Greene, who wrote in his personal thanks, " No man,
in the progress of the campaign, had equal merit with
yourself;" an expression of strong meaning coming
from a plain, blunt soldier of honest character. And
this praise was fully confirmed by Washington's own
words of " love and thanks," in a letter of later date,
written long enough after to show how strong in that
great man's mind was the memory of the services of

" Light-horse Harry," as his contemporaries familiarly called General Henry Lee.

Retiring from command, when the close of the war turned the swords of revolutionary generals into ploughshares, Henry Lee married his second cousin, Matilda Lee, heiress of the old family estate of Stratford, and thus coming, as it were, into the place of the head of the family, gave himself up to local political life. Alternately governor of his native state of Virginia, and her representative in Congress, he yet found leisure to write the really thoughtful and accurate account of his Southern campaigns already referred to, as well as to indulge largely in the open-handed hospitality which was the tradition of the family, and which in his case was carried so far as to impoverish his estate. His cousin did not long survive their union; but a subsequent marriage gave him three sons, the second of whom, Robert Edward, became the renowned general, whose fame has almost caused that of his father's reputation for warlike prowess to be forgotten. He was born on January nineteenth, 1807, in the same room where Richard Henry Lee, his father's cousin, first saw the light, the orator to whose charge was intrusted the moving of the Declaration of Independence, and one of the leading members of the original Congress which voted it.

" Robert was always good," wrote his father some ten years later to a relative, in a description of his young family. The boy was then growing up in a healthy out-of-door life, taught to ride almost from his infancy, and enjoying the constant good health which a serene conscience and temperate habits preserved to him until the close of a long life. For several years

of his later boyhood the family lived in the town of
Alexandria, where there were facilities for education
not attainable in the country, and here, after General
Henry Lee's death, his widow remained for the same
reason. Before arriving at manhood, Robert Lee had
avowed his earnest desire to follow the military profession in which his father had been so distinguished.
The services of the latter were too conspicuous to
make it difficult to procure an appointment to West
Point for his son; and in 1825 he entered the Military
Academy for that long and complete course of study
by which it is aimed in the United States to fit the
future officer, not as with us for one, but for every
branch of the service. Young Lee was as remarkable
here as through the rest of his career for the blameless
simplicity of his life and his devotion to the duties of
the hour. No entry was recorded against him in the
defaulters' book during his four years' residence, and
when his class graduated in 1829, he took the second
place, and was appointed to the Engineers, a small
corps regarded as the *élite* of a highly trained service.
His manly form, great personal beauty, and sweetness
of manner were noted then; and in the young lieutenant's carriage and appearance were the pledge of the
noble presence and calm bearing which won the instant
confidence of the high-spirited but wilful troops of the
Confederacy, almost from the first sight of their new
commander thirty years later. Three years after being
commissioned, he became the fortunate suitor of Mary
Custis, the daughter and heiress of George Custis,
Washington's adopted son. By his marriage with her
he came into possession of the hereditary estates of
the founder of American liberty, and was the nearest

representative before the world of that great man's family. This fact, as well as the traditions of his own family, should be distinctly borne in mind by those who would understand fully his painful position at the outbreak of the Civil War.

Seventeen years of peace service passed by, and Captain Lee had hitherto found no special opportunity of distinction. In 1846, however, the Mexican War began, and his character and attainments were so well known as to cause him to be selected as Chief Engineer to the army under General Scott, in which capacity he served through the first campaign that any American officer of his standing shared in. It is not our purpose here to enter into the details of General Scott's difficulties and successes. Suffice it to say that from first to last Lee fully justified the choice which had been made of him for his post, and was mentioned in almost every important report. "Indefatigable in the siege operations, in reconnoissances as daring as laborious, and of the utmost value everywhere," was the character he earned in his commander's dispatches. Three times specially breveted for his services, he returned to his own country after the close of hostilities, acknowledged as one of the most promising of her officers, and possessing the confidence of his chief beyond any other of the many distinguished men who had served with him. From duty on the defences, or as Superintendent of West Point, Lee soon passed again to a service which had more promise of adventure. In a fit of sudden liberality the Congress in 1855 voted two regiments of cavalry to be added to the permanent establishment of the army. Energetic officers of all branches naturally sought commissions in the new corps, which were specially designed for active frontier duty; and Lee, being among the number applying for transfer, became Lieutenant-Colonel of the Second Cavalry, in which he found among his comrades Albert Johnston, whose death lost the Confederates their advantage at Shiloh, and, it has been declared, saved Grant's army from ruin; Thomas and Stoneman, in after days leading generals on the Northern side; with Hardee, Van Dorn, and Hood, who were equally well known on that of the South. The regiment was ordered to Texas, where Lee spent the four years following in guarding the new frontier of the Republic.

The next event of Lee's life brought him prominently into collision with the stormy elements already brewing to burst later in civil war. He chanced to be on leave at Washington in the autumn of 1859, being then on a visit to his family at Arlington, his seat close by, when he was sent for very suddenly by President Buchanan. A gang of desperadoes, he learnt, under one John Brown, had attacked and taken the military depôt at Harper's Ferry, and declared their intention of raising a servile war against the slaveowners of Virginia. To proceed there with the party of marines placed at his disposal, attack the rioters in the building they had fortified, and give them over, when presently captured, to the civil authorities of Virginia, was a duty executed with such completeness and promptitude as the service called for. But far-seeing and sagacious as Lee was, he probably, as little as any man in the states, could foretell that the small cloud thus easily dispersed was but the forerunner of a tempest of civil war of more terrible extent and fury than the world had ever witnessed. He was again in Texas, commanding his department, when the storm was gathering rapidly after the election of Lincoln in 1860; and early in the following spring he was recalled to headquarters by General Scott, under whose command were the modest forces which formed the whole army of the now threatened Union.

Men's minds were on all sides growing fevered as the coming struggle revealed its inevitable shape more certainly. To none was it more vital and terrible than to the sons of Virginia, a state in which the sentiment of pride in the growing greatness of the Union balanced her natural inclination to side with her more forward and passionate sisters of the South. Bordering too on the capital of the country and the Northern states behind it, interest, as well as a loyal repugnance to break up the republic, united to arrest her tendency to follow the example of South Carolina, which had seceded in December. But when Lincoln issued his decisive proclamation, pronouncing secession to be open rebellion, and calling on each state which had not departed from the Union to send its contingent to repress the contemplated crime, an absolute choice could no longer be deferred. Virginia must fight either with or against the South. She chose the former alternative, as that which, if the more immediately dangerous, was the more certain to carry the sympathies of her people. On the seventeenth of April her Ordinance of Secession was passed, and her lot for the future cast by this measure with the new Confederacy.

To none of her children was the crisis a severer trial than it was to Colonel Lee. On the one hand were the traditions of his family, whose whole career from the time of its establishment in Virginia had been identified with the honor and progress of the state. She was his country proper in his eyes, having been originally an independent colony, and only by her own act long afterwards leagued with other independent colonies into a Federation for the maintenance of common rights and liberties. Brought up in this faith, he could not view any other claim as more than subordinate to that of his native state.

On the other hand, his professional interests—we lay stress on this fact, because it has been hitherto unrecognized in England—were absolutely on the Union, since termed the Northern side. Distinguished by position and pedigree above all those of his standing in the service he had chosen, beloved and blameless in his private life, he had been recognized by all as one of the ablest of the country's officers during the Mexican War; and what was more important than all, he had impressed his genius for war so strongly on General Scott, that the Commander-in-Chief, conscious of his own growing infirmities, did not hesitate to announce his intention to propose Lee as his successor in his now weighty charge. A warm personal regard for his junior made the aged general all the more anxious not to lose his services. He recommended him, therefore, on his arrival at Washington for the first vacancy as brigadier-general in the regular army. And although there is no record of the personal conversation which ensued when the conqueror of Mexico and his trusted staff-officer were closeted together in that eventful April, we may be sure that no argument or appeal was left unused which could avail to save the Union the loss of Lee's servi-

ces. Up to the last hour before the die was cast by
the state Legislature at Richmond, Lee probably
hoped that its decision might be stayed, and his own
rendered unnecessary. But when certain news came
that Secession was accomplished, and he must choose
between the flag he honored and the state he loved,
he decided that the latter claimed his first allegiance,
and he could no longer delay what he believed to be
his painful duty. His last sad interview with his old
chief took place the following day, and found his resolution fixed unalterably. On the twentieth he sent
in his official resignation of his commission, and apolo-
gised for the two days' delay by saying:

"It would have been presented at once but for the struggle it has cost me to separate myself from a service to which
I have devoted all the best years of my life and all the
ability I possessed. During the whole of that time—more
than a quarter of a century—I have experienced nothing
but kindness from my superiors and the most cordial friendship from my comrades. To no one, General, have I been
as much indebted as yourself. . . . Save in defence of my
native state, I never again desire to draw my sword."

Writing to his sister the same day, he lays bare
his feelings with a candor which even those who least
approve his decision must honor. No doubt his words
express generally the feelings of many others less
gifted with the power of expression; and in these
days, when State independence has been swept away
by the keen arbitrament of the sword, it is well to
recall what was thought on the subject at that time
by one of the most pure-minded and unselfish of those
who were forced to choose:

" The whole South" [he writes] " is in a state of revolution, into which Virginia, after a long struggle, has been drawn; and though I recognize no necessity for this state of things, and would have forborne and pleaded to the end for the redress of grievances, real or supposed, yet in my own person I had to meet the question whether I should take part against my native state. With all my devotion to the Union, and the feeling of loyalty and duty of an American citizen, I have not been able to make up my mind to raise my hand against my relatives, my children, my home. I have therefore resigned my commission in the army."

He adds here the same expression of his hope, before quoted, that he may not be called upon to serve save in defence of his own state : but Virginia's fortunes were now to be bound up for weal or woe with those of the Confederacy that she was about to join.

The very mansion of Arlington from which he wrote these letters was his first sacrifice to his decision. Situated as it was in sight of the capital, it must needs be abandoned, with the fine estate on which it stood. Perhaps in quitting it and leaving its contents intact, he may have vainly hoped that the venerated relics of Washington with which it was crowded might save it from spoliation. But personal losses could weigh nothing with such a soul as his ; and leaving to its fate of almost certain occupation by the first advance guard of the Union army that house in which he had spent the happiest hours of his life, he set out for Richmond. Ere, however, he had reached the capital of this state, soon to become that of the Confederacy, he had been appointed Major-General of all the Virginian forces by the spontaneous choice of the

governor and legislature, and on the twenty-third
he was publicly received in his new capacity at Richmond.   He accepted the trust conferred on him
in a few simple and dignified words, again expressing
it to be his sole desire to defend his native state.
There was general joy, the American biographer
states ; for it had been feared that he would adhere
to the Federal Government, and Virginia would have
looked upon his loss as a public calamity.

He was now, though fifty-three years of age, still
remarkable for the manly beauty of his face and form,
as well as for his singular temperance and the calmness of his manner :

"Grave, silent, with a military composure of bearing that
amounted at times to stiffness," says Mr. Cooke.   And he
adds that although then "looked upon by those who held intercourse with him as a personage of marked reserve, the
truth and frankness of the man, under all circumstances, and
his great, warm heart, full of honesty and unassuming simplicity, became known only in the course of the war."

No doubt General Lee felt at that time the
weight of his responsibilities and the serious character
of his decision, and possibly he discouraged the frivo-
lous conversation in which the excitement of lesser
men would naturally vent itself at such a crisis.   Be
this as it may, it is clear that the innocent gayety of
heart for which in earlier years he had been noted had
disappeared under the weight of official duties, or was
banished by the gravity of his new charge ; for this included the whole supply and training of the state forces,
which were collecting in large numbers, and gave him
incessant employment.   But the defence of Virginia

soon became merged in that of the Confederacy which she joined formally in May. Her capital was declared the capital of the South. The Southern Congress soon met there. New men pressed in to take the lead in the affairs of what claimed to be a nation, and for a time, General Lee was relegated to duties of a secondary order, the late period at which his state had declared for the Confederacy, having put others already into the chief military posts. His immediate charge for the present became that of fortifying Richmond. It is natural enough that the works he raised should have extorted admiration from the Northern generals whom they so long defied ; but their best eulogy is contained in the simple fact that though often threatened they were never seriously attacked. From the time that he thus girdled Richmond with the full resources of the engineer's art, aided by the use of that " eye for positions" for which he had been admired in Mexico, the capital was destined to fall only with the Confederacy itself. To other commanders, however, Davis had been compelled by the political situation to assign the first honors of the defence of the South.

While the fortifying of Richmond went on, the battle of Bull's Run, the first great encounter of the war, was fought and won by Beauregard, aided by Johnston, who had marched to join him from the Shenandoah Valley. Though this event concerns us little here, it is right to say that the surprise of the Confederates on their flank was a real one, and their defeat at one time very near, being only averted by the superiority in steadiness of Jackson's troops to their comrades. And as we laughed so loud and long at the behavior of the raw militia of M'Dowell when once in

7

retreat, it is well to add that there is not the least
reason to believe, judging from the testimony of
Southern officers, that their men would have behaved
one whit better had the reverse been on their side.
More than this. Those among ourselves who know
most of war are agreed that, however highly one may
think of the spirit of the levies we call our Auxiliary
forces, there is no ground whatever, beyond a vulgar
national vanity, for the common belief that a mass of
these, once beaten and panic-stricken, would show
conduct very different from that of M'Dowell's volunteers in 1861, or of the Mobiles of the Army of the
Loire ten years later. "Nations deceive themselves
very much in this matter of their untrained troops,"
was the remark made to the present writer by the
chief of the Swiss army ; one composed wholly of mi-
litiamen. And what is true of Frenchmen, of Swiss,
and of our own kith and kin in America, would hardly
be greatly falsified if misfortune fell upon ourselves.
Whatever may be thought of this deduction, certainly
nothing could be more mistaken than the judgment
hastily passed by our press on the conduct of
M'Dowell's raw troops, sent as they were into the
field untrained, and through the ignorance of Congress
left unfurnished even with the semblance of a staff.
Nor was the general result of the battle at all as favorable to the Confederacy as was then supposed. For,
in fact, the Northern army had been hitherto composed only of three-months' volunteers ; and though
not in proper fighting order, it was absolutely necessary to employ them, before they dispersed to their
homes, in checking the hostile forces which had gathered to threaten Washington. And although com-

pletely defeated in his attack, M'Dowell yet left his enemy so shattered as to be not only quite incapable of an advance upon the capital of the Union, but according to the confession of the best Southern officers, unfit for some time later for any serious operations. Brave as the Confederates individually were, there was not at this time any real power of discipline in their commanders' hands which could enable the latter to reap the fruits of victory. And what is more surprising, the best generals never wholly established this moral force over them. But discipline on the other side, though far from being ever brought up to the stricter European standard, was certainly improved during the war ; and to this difference, hardly less than to the greater resources of the North her final triumph was due.

Poor as the military results of the battle of Bull's Run were, and serious as its political effects proved in rousing the North and her leaders to real earnestness, it naturally caused great rejoicing for the hour at Richmond. Johnston, who from the time of his arrival was the senior officer on the ground, was confirmed in his command of the whole army of Northern Virginia, and Lee still remained at the capital completing its defences. But attention was soon directed to Western Virginia, the part of the state beyond the Alleghanies, which had from the first showed its Union sympathies. Into this M'Clellan, a hitherto unknown Federal officer, had been pushed from Pennsylvania. By July his forces were augmented to 20,000 men, giving him a large numerical superiority over the Confederate troops of Garnett, who attempted to hold it against him. In a series of skirmishes which followed, M'Clellan and his active lieutenant Rosecrans routed the Confederates, killing their general. The officers who succeeded to the latter, meeting with further disasters, began to quarrel among themselves. On this the Southern President dispatched General Lee to the scene of action with reinforcements, and instructions to bring into one common plan the movements along the scattered lines held by the Confederates, but with no orders to take the command,which he never did officially, though for a short time directing the operations. The only active part of these, an attempt to carry a strong position held at Cheat Mountain by General Reynolds, failed entirely, owing, (as we have gathered from direct personal information,) even more to the misconduct of a subordinate commander than to the ill discipline of the disheartened troops. Lee himself left on record a full explanation of the circumstances, but with the express understanding that it should not be made public during the war; and as this confidential report perished in the fire at Richmond, all that can now be known is from the remark he made to a would-be critic soon after. "When you read the story by-and-bye, you will be as much surprised as any one." After this affair, Lee, deciding that he had no forces that would justify offensive operations against a superior enemy to whom the feeling of the country had proved favorable, remained strictly on the defensive, and confined his efforts to restricting, as far as possible, the movements of Rosecrans, who had succeeded M'Clellan. Winter now came on, and in that high region fairly stopped all serious operations. But the failure before Cheat Mountain, where Lee's plans had apparently proved too elaborate for such raw materials, and his subse-

quent apparent inaction, were little calculated to raise
the general's reputation. When he left in the winter,
by Jefferson Davis's orders, to put the defences of
the Carolinas in order, he was spoken of in his new
command as "a Virginia failure," his name being as
unduly depreciated as that of M'Clellan was exalted.
For that officer's early success in Western Virginia
had shed a gleam of light over the North in its humiliation. It caused his instant selection as Commander-
in-Chief when Scott resigned the post he had hitherto
retained. And while Washington politicians spoke
of M'Clellan as the young Napoleon of the Union,
the critics of Richmond and Charleston poured forth
their strictures on General Lee as an over-refining
strategist, too subtle for practical warfare, and declared him the only mistaken choice among their
commanders; judgments which were destined to be
singularly reversed a few months later. And even
while they were being made, the presence of the
latter in Carolina sufficed to bring back confidence to
the forces stationed there, who in the first moment
of panic at the success of Burnside's expedition against
Roanoke were for abandoning the coast defences
altogether. An officer at that time serving on the
North Carolina staff has assured us that Lee's arrival
on the coast worked an effect little less than magical
on the conduct of matters there, and on the temper
of the garrisons along the coast.

During the winter of 1861-2 M'Clellan, wielding
large resources at Washington, showed to the full his
real genius for organization. At length, at the head
of a well-organized army numbering over 100,000 men,
with a large fleet in support, and the strategy—not

without a sharp struggle with the strong will of President Lincoln—left to his own judgment, he disem-
barked in May on that historic peninsula below Richmond which had witnessed in former days the triumph
of Washington over Cornwallis, forced his way along
it despite obstinate resistance near Yorktown, and
crossing his right over the river Chickahominy, which
describes a steady curve at a few miles' distance round
the north and east sides of the city, planted himself
firmly within sight of the spires of the enemy's capital.
The North, under the influence of her first defeat, had
made far more exertions than the Confederacy since
the previous summer. M'Clellan's army was soon
raised to 156,000 men, while Johnston could only collect rather less than half that number to protect the
city, which was really covered mainly by the works
that Lee had thrown up. Co-operating with M'Clellan were further independent armies under separate
leadership. Of these Fremont and Banks, with 30,-
000 men, were opposed by Jackson with half that
number in the Shenandoah Valley; and a more important force of 40,000, under M'Dowell at Fredericksburg, was designed to come in on M'Clellan's right,
and would complete the investment of the city on its
northern side, and bring an immense superiority of
numbers to overbear its defenders.

Such was the programme on the side of the North.
But Jackson's detached command against great odds
proved just such an opportunity as that general needed
to make his rare talent for war conspicuous. Being
ordered by Johnston to take the offensive in the
Valley, and draw some of the pressure off Richmond,
he performed his task so admirably as not only to

neutralize the large forces of Fremont and Banks, but
to cause President Lincoln, in alarm, to direct
M'Dowell to send half the Fredericksburg corps westward to take part in the operations against this redoubtable adversary. This detachment from his
expected support held M'Clellan motionless; for he
had from the first considered his own force insufficient
for direct attack upon the enemy in his works, and,
indeed, overrated the number before him under
Johnston: and while he thus stood indecisive, the
latter suddenly issued from his line of redoubts on the
south side of the Chickahominy, and became the
assailant. The action that ensued on May thirty-first,
known as the Battle of Seven Pines, was the most
obstinate of those fought at this early period of the
war. M'Clellan's front was partly intrenched and well
guarded by artillery, and though the left of his line
was forced, the Confederates gained no decisive advantage over him, while they themselves suffered the loss
of their general, who was severely wounded in the
commencement of the engagement by a shell. It was
of course necessary to give the Southern army a new
chief at once, and the choice fell naturally on Lee.
He had just returned to Richmond from his duty in
the Carolinas. He was more intimately acquainted
with the defences of the capital than any other officer.
And, what was still more to the purpose, his former
rivals in reputation and superiors in the favor of the
South, Albert Johnston and Beauregard, were far away,
the one slain in the hour of his promised victory over
Grant on the Tennessee, the other still in command of
the large forces near that river. President Davis had
therefore full opportunity of exercising his own judg-

ment, and giving effect to the high opinion he had
from the first entertained of the Virginian general.
On June third Lee took charge of the army in which,
save to battalions of his own state, he was unknown or
thought little of, but which was destined under him to
achieve a history, hardly less glorious or less chequered
than that of the African veterans of Hannibal. Accident, rather than the choice of the Confederacy, had
given him his high office. It remained for him to use
his opportunity so as to win at once the confidence of
his soldiers and of the government he served. The
opinion of him at that time was that he was disposed
to be cautious, slow, and somewhat timorous. He was
about to show himself on the instant a master of the
art of strategy, at once as daring as sagacious, and as
brilliant in combination as decided in action.

M'Clellan's force, as we have said, was almost
double of that now placed under his new opponent.
His front was so strong that Johnston's bold assault
had failed to shake it. His left was covered by the
vast morass known as White Oak Swamp, which extended southward from the Chickahominy nearly to the
James. The only part left open to Lee's attack was
the Federal right, which, as before mentioned, was
thrown northward across the Chickahominy, and planted there to await the reinforcements through Petersburg which the Federal general was still demanding
from Washington. Well supplied by the railroad
from the York River behind, he had at first little fear
for his present position; and it was only when he
found as June passed by, that the President was thoroughly alarmed by the ill success of the Northern
troops against Jackson, and had resolved to detain

the promised succor, that M'Clellan determined to withdraw his exposed right, and move through the White Oak Swamp to the James River, where his communications with the fleet would be absolutely secure. In not venturing an attack there can be little doubt that he still overrated the force before Richmond; but while his change of plan had been hardly more than decided on, his enemy was upon him. Lee had assumed the offensive with every man whom he could throw upon his foe.

To explain whence this apparent boldness came is not difficult. From the hour of his first command he resolved on raising the threatened siege by such a decisive stroke as should at once give heart to the army and to the government which watched him anxiously. But to do this with full effect he resolved to bring Jackson secretly to his aid, and hence time for action was practically chosen by that general, whose special task it was to arrive before Richmond without being missed from the Valley: for it was absolutely necessary for the success prepared on the Chickahominy that the alarm of the Federal Government for the safety of Washington should be kept up, and all succor denied M'Clellan. The plan was carried out with a completeness worthy of the conception. The matchless activity with which Jackson marched and countermarched in the Shenandoah Valley up to the very hour of his suddenly quitting it, deceived the Federals effectually there: while M'Clellan was tricked for the time into the same belief that Washington was threatened, by the ruse of sending detachments northward from Richmond—for a few miles of course only—when exchanged prisoners were about to quit the city. So completely was the

5*

Federal commander deceived on this occasion, that he wrote, certainly not with any pleasure, and in contradiction of his former views, to the president on June twentieth, " I have no doubt Jackson has been reinforced from here." The reinforcements imagined had at the time long safely returned into Lee's lines, and Jackson was then making his forced march from the Valley to Richmond with such rapidity and secresy that even the bulk of his own men knew nothing of their destination. To all questions they were directed to reply, " I don't know;" and so when the general himself demanded of a straggler his name and regiment, the soldier, using the license which never left the Confederate army throughout the war, put his interrogator off with the answer the order had enjoined on him, and of course escaped punishment. Jackson's distance from Richmond, being a straight line, was short comparatively to that which any of the forces with which he had hitherto been engaged must have covered in order to move round to M'Clellan, even had they discovered their enemy in the act of vanishing. Never was the advantage of what are technically called " interior lines " more finely used than in this first design of Lee. Never was the execution of such a design more ably accomplished than by Jackson on this memorable occasion. On the night of June twenty-fifth; before one of the Federal officers in the sphere of his late operations had missed him from their outposts; before M'Clellan, now abandoning present hope of support, had issued the orders he was preparing for his change of base from the York River to the James; before Lee himself could hope to greet him; Jackson had left his divisions within a few miles of Richmond, and

entered the city in person after dark to meet his new
chief. The colloquy that followed was but brief.
Both were essentially, in their several ways, men more
of action than words. General Steuart, the henceforward famous cavalry general of Lee, had just distinguished himself for the first time by his raid, or reconnoissance in force, round M'Clellan's position, which
had revealed fully the exposure of the Federal right
and rear. The orders for the attack had been prepared by Lee's own hand the night before. It was only
necessary, therefore, to assign the new comer his part
in the action of the next day, and all would be ready.

Lee's plan in effect was this: Leaving but 25,000
men under Magruder, to guard the front of Richmond
on the south side of the Chickahominy, he resolved to
march the remaining 50,000, under Longstreet and the
two Hills, to the north of that stream, so as to turn
and attack M'Clellan's right, which was under General
Porter. Jackson, keeping still more to the northward,
was to pass behind this mass of Confederate troops,
and carry his divisions beyond it in a decisive turning
movement directed against Porter's extreme right and
rear. Of course this scheme of operation, which threw
some 70,000 men on the 40,000 of M'Clellan's right,
could only be executed at a certain risk to Richmond.
M'Clellan, if fully acquainted with his opponent's
strength and design, would almost certainly have ordered Porter to do no more than defend the Chickahominy bridges, while he himself pressed forward the
bulk of his army to crush the two divisions left alone
under Magruder in his own front ; and if it proved not
possible to attempt the works behind them, he at least
might have got between these and Lee, and so cut the

latter off from the capital he had to defend. But some risk must needs be run by a general, who, with so great an inferiority as Lee's, attempts vast combinations. And he trusted rightly as the event shows, to his adversary's ignorance of his real strength, and to the alarm this pressure on Porter's wing would certainly occasion, as sufficient to keep the Federal attention from discovering the weakness of the force that was left in their front.

The battle of the Chickahominy, which lasted through the twenty-sixth and twenty-seventh of June took exactly that course which Lee had designed beforehand. The brunt of the first attack came from A. Hill's division, which followed nearly the line of the river downwards, and soon got into serious collision with the enemy. Checked until dark that day on the line of Beaver Dam Creek, a small stream running from the north into the Chickahominy, which afforded the Federals a strong line to hold, Hill found them retreating next morning as Jackson with a wide circling movement turned their position. They fell back on Cold Harbor, where they occupied a new line with their backs towards the Chickahominy, holding in part the same ground on which General Grant, two years later, threw away many thousands of lives in a vain attempt the last of many such in his Virginian campaign, to force a roughly intrenched position by direct attack. Reinforced from the south side of the river, Porter held his own stoutly for some hours. In vain did Longstreet, already famous for his fierce courage in action, press his men on to support those of Hill. In vain did General D. Hill bring his division up to his namesake's aid. The Confederates were fairly beaten off: yet their chief did not dare to slacken their attack, for every hour he feared to hear far up the stream the din of battle suddenly rise, which would tell him that M'Clellan had discovered how he was deceived, and was making the counterstroke on Magruder which was the chief danger the Confederate cause had to fear. But at length to his left, as the afternoon advanced, was heard the roar of fresh guns coming into action. Jackson, it was plain, had completed his flank march, and was closing with the Federal right rear. A few minutes more and the gallant soldier himself appeared on the scene, and rode up to greet Lee, cheered loudly by Longstreet's men, already veterans enough in war to understand what his coming meant. Nothing, it has been said, of this first meeting of these great soldiers on the battle-field could be in more striking contrast than the appearance and manner of the two. Handsome in face and figure, finely mounted, a graceful rider, calm-visaged, and carefully dressed, Lee presented the beau ideal of the commander whose outward bearing captivates the soldier's eye. His famous lieutenant rode, apparently by choice, an ill-groomed, raw-boned horse, and sat so short-stirruped as to give his figure the most awkward appearance. An old cadet's cap, evidently a relic of the college professorship he had not long since left, was drawn down over his eyes. His coat was not only threadbare but ill-brushed; and his words were jerked out in short, abrupt sentences, between which he sucked the lemon which was as usual his sole refreshment during his day's work. Yet each already understood the other, and valued him at his true worth. "That is a heavy fire down yonder," said Lee, as the Federal guns opened in reply to Jackson's.

"Can your men stand it?" "They can stand almost any thing. They can stand that," was the emphatic reply ; and after a few words of order and explanation he left his chief to lead on the attack. This was decisive, aided as it was by a fresh advance of the troops before engaged. The Federals were turned, overmatched, and driven from their position, and before dark the shattered remains of Porter's force were crossing the Chickahominy in hasty retreat. Lee's first battle, in fact, was as striking a success, and as well earned, as any of the more famous victories won by him in after days which have been so widely studied and so often extolled. No word henceforward from his government of any want of confidence in his powers, or fear of his over-caution. From that hour he became the most trusted, as well as the most noted, general of the Confederacy. As to his soldiery, his hardy bearing, free self-exposure, and constant presence near their ranks, completed the influence gained by that power of combining their force to advantage which they instinctively felt without fully understanding. From man to man flew the story of the hour. The subtle influence of sympathy, which wins many hearts for one, was never more rapidly exercised. Like Napoleon, his troops soon learnt to believe him equal to every emergency that war could bring. Like Hannibal, he could speak lightly and calmly at the gravest moments, being then himself least grave. Like Raglan, he preserved a sweetness of temper that no person or circumstance could ruffle. Like Cæsar, he mixed with the crowd of soldiery freely, and never feared that his position would be forgotten. Like Blücher, his one recognized fault was that which the soldier readily forgives; a readiness to expose his life beyond the proper limits permitted by modern war to the commander-in-chief. What wonder, then, if he thenceforward commanded an army in which each man would have died for him: an army from which his parting wrung tears more bitter than any the fall of their cause could extort: an army which followed him, after three years of glorious vicissitudes, into private life, without one thought of further resistance against the fate to which their adored chief yielded without a murmur!

Is it therefore asserted that Lee as a commander was faultless? Far from it. We say it with all humility, but without any doubt, that from first to last he committed most grave errors; errors which only his other high qualities prevented from being fatal to his reputation. Chief of these was his permitting the continuance of the laxity of discipline which throughout the war clogged the movements of the Confederates, and robbed their most brilliant victories of their reward. The fatal habit of straggling from the ranks on the least pretext; the hardly less fatal habit of allowing each man to load himself with any superfluous arms or clothes he chose to carry, the general want of subordination to trifling orders, which was the inheritance of their volunteer origin: these evils Lee found in full existence when he took command before Richmond, and he never strove to check them. Nor did he ever use his great authority, as he might have done, to purge his command of the many inefficient officers whose example of itself was ruinous to all discipline. Add to this, that though never careless of the good of his soldiers, he failed altogether to enforce on the Confederate Government the vital necessity of bringing the supply of their wants more directly under the control of those who commanded them; so that at the last they were absolutely starving in Richmond, while the War Department there, uninspired by the proper energy for its task, had left large supplies scattered on the line of railroad leading to the Carolinas. And lastly, there must rest on him the grave responsibility, shared certainly by, but not wholly falling on his favorite cavalry commander, of misusing the limited supplies of horseflesh at his disposal in repeating brilliant but unserviceable marches; so that in their last campaign the Confederates were left almost destitute of that most necessary arm. "Divisions of cavalry," an eminent Southern officer and devoted admirer of Lee has said to us, "were sent in those early days on work which squadrons might have done as well." These are grave charges. But the errors cited all plainly sprang from one flaw in Lee's character; the too yielding generosity of his nature, which made him reluctant to enforce upon others that self-denial he never forgot in his own person. Trifling matters they seemed at the first. The very modesty of temperament which prevented his correcting them, might in another situation have won him fresh admiration. But as the war went on, the rifts caused by indiscipline and carelessness in the Confederate armor widened more and more; and in the end, these faults were hardly less fatal to the fortunes of the South than the greater material resources of her adversary. Her fall was to offer a new proof to the world that neither personal courage nor heroic leadership can any more supply the place of discipline to a national force than can untrained patriotism or vaunts of past glories.

Before leaving the subject of the first relief of Richmond, so brilliantly accomplished by the victory on the Chickahominy, it is necessary to follow M'Clellan's retreat, not only for the story's sake, but in order to do justice to a commander whose ill success before Richmond has diminished in the world's eyes the great services he performed for the cause of the Union, both before and after that fatal check. It has been said that the Federal general had decided before the battle to transfer his operations from the Chickahominy to the James. Of this there can be no manner of doubt. Nor is there any that the deciding causes; the failure of the hope of support to his exposed right wing from M'Dowell at Fredericksburg, and the alarm caused by the havoc which Steuart, in his raid a few days before, produced on the Federal communications with York River; were very sufficient reasons for the proposed change of base. Unhappily for M'Clellan's reputation, he had not, as before noticed, issued his orders for the movement when Lee's stroke fell on his right. It was natural enough that the success of this served to quicken the Federal commander in his intended operation; but it is hardly less natural that when the world learnt from his dispatches that the severe defeat on the Chickahominy was followed at once by the retreat to the James, the one was directly and wholly ascribed to the other: so that M'Clellan's declaration that the movement through White Oak Swamp was but "a strategic change of base," only caused his expression to be caught up and used as a taunt against himself, and became a proverb in all cases where a beaten general

8

excuses the necessity of retreat under a cloud of words.

If M'Clellan deserves sharp criticism for not having sooner made up his mind, and still more for his failure to discover and use the absence of the Confederates in his front, where his advance in mass, according to General Magruder's officially expressed opinion, "would have insured his success, and the occupation of the works about Richmond, and consequently the city;" his character as a commander never shone so brightly as in the hour of disaster and danger, when Porter's wing was driven in upon his centre. The ill-success of his campaign as a whole has caused his conduct at this crisis to be done scant justice to. But there is no military reputation in the world which would not be increased by the manner in which that retreat to the James was conducted from the moment it began. His troops were so demoralized by the shock of the two days' unsuccessful fighting as to begin their retreat, according to the testimony of Hooker, one of the oldest officers present, "like a parcel of sheep; for a few shots from the rebels would have panic-stricken the whole:" expressions strong enough at once to show the importance of this first victory of Lee's which some writers have spoken lightly of, and to give the more credit to M'Clellan for what followed. On the very evening of his defeat he assembled his chiefs of corps, explained his plan for retreating to the shelter of the fleet, and made his arrangements for covering the movement. The roads leading through White Oak Swamp direct to the James were bad, and crossed by many others which the Confederates might advance on. Their outposts on the Chickahominy were close to his own : their confidence as high as that of his own troops was depressed ; and the first movement of retreat discovered, would bring them on in ardent pursuit, Lee's only doubt now being as to which way his adversary would attempt to draw off. Nevertheless M'Clellan succeeded in concealing his design during the whole of the twenty-eighth while his trains were moving off; and when the pursuit was taken up on the morning of the twenty-ninth, his worst danger was already over. Moreover, the coolness and self-possession of the Federal commander not merely stood himself in good stead, but had its natural effect on his subordinates, and through these began to reach his discouraged men. Step by step he fell back, using his heavy artillery with great skill to guard the dangerous approaches to his flanks by the cross-roads through the swamp. On their side the Confederate staff showed a not very creditable ignorance of the scene of contest. No sketch or survey had been made of it, though lying but a few miles from their own lines; and their pursuing columns were greatly delayed for want of this simple precaution. Fighting soon ensued ; but as neither side could form any front, it was never serious, and the advantage naturally on the side of the defenders. So the retreat went on day after day. In vain did Longstreet, relieved in his turn by Jackson, press on the Federal rear. In vain Magruder threw his troops, eager to share in the newly-won glories of their comrades, along each approach towards their western flank by the cross-roads leading from the city. Each attempt was met skilfully and repulsed ; and when, on July seventh, M'Clellan found himself clear of the swamp, and occupied the strong ridge of Malvern Hill beyond it, his men had so far recovered heart as to inflict a very sharp repulse on the advance guard of the pursuers, which Magruder has been charged with engaging with useless rashness. Thus closing his retreat with an unquestioned success, M'Clellan drew off his army, no longer followed, to its proposed encampment by the James, where the support of the gun-boats gave him a position well-nigh impregnable. He had recovered the confidence of his troops. If they shouted for joy when he again accepted their command two months later at Washington ; if they followed him confidently when he moved to check Lee's first invasion of the North, it must be ascribed not to his mere genius for organization, but to the moral effect of his masterly retreat. The battle of Antietam, the first check in Lee's steady career of victory, was in truth saved for the Federal side at Malvern Hill. Lee's dispatch on the subject of the White Oak Swamp affair puts the general facts in a clear light. " Under ordinary circumstances," were his words, " the Federal army should have been destroyed. Prominent among the causes of its escape is the want of timely and correct information. This fact, attributed chiefly to the character of the country, enabled General M'Clellan skilfully to conceal his retreat, and to add much to the obstruction with which Nature had beset the way of our pursuing columns." Nevertheless, though thus saved from ruin, M'Clellan's force was for the time powerless for harm. Richmond was relieved from all pressure, and without strong reinforcements there was no hope of a fresh advance from the James. The political differences between President Lincoln and his unsuccessful general aggravated the former's distrust of M'Clellan's powers. He turned to new projects and new commanders for his hopes of attack on Richmond, and the first phase of the war in Virginia came fairly to an end.

To follow it farther would be to tell a twice-told tale. Lee crowded into the next two years as much personal glory as has ever fallen to the lot of a commander within the same time. Overthrowing one opponent after another by brilliant strategy, wielding an inferior force ; applying with unsurpassed skill to each new purpose the special resources of the country he defended, and the personal weakness of his adversaries ; he failed only when attempting for political reasons an offensive beyond the means of his force. While elsewhere, ill success on the side of the Confederacy became disaster, and disaster grew into ruinous defeat, the defence of Northern Virginia was never shaken. Only when a general advanced upon it whose resources in men and material were practically unlimited, and who used them deliberately in what Union historians, such as Dr. Draper, have exultingly called "the process of attrition," wearing down his adversary's numbers gradually by the free sacrifice of his own, was Richmond once more seriously threatened. But the June of 1864 found Grant almost in sight of the city, upon the very ground which M'Clellan had held on the banks of the Chickahominy two years before. Four times he had changed the line of operations, chosen in obedience to Lincoln's strong desire, on which he had declared his intention to "fight it out all the summer." Four times he had recoiled from the attempt to force his way direct to the rebel capital ; for his indomitable and watchful adversary ever barred the way. Once more, on the morning of June third, he flung his masses fiercely against the line held by Lee, which ran across the very field of battle where that general had won his first triumph over M'Clellan. The result was so fearful and useless a slaughter that, according to the chief Union historian,* when " later in the day orders were issued to renew the assault, the whole army, correctly appreciating what the inevitable result must be, silently disobeyed."

Foiled and exasperated, yet never disheartened, for the fifth time Grant changed his strategy. Following M'Clellan's movement of two years before, he pressed on to the James ; but without halting at that stream in indecision, crossed it at once to invest Petersburg, and gain the approaches to Richmond from the south ; following, in fact, the plan by which he had triumphed at Vicksburg, and which he had himself long before pointed out, when asked to advise freely, as the most decisive mode of attacking the capital of the Confederacy. Gaining the southern part of Petersburg before his advance was fully discovered, he assaulted the works fiercely, and it was not till he had lost 9,000 men more that he desisted, and sat down deliberately to prepare the investing lines which were thenceforward continually to be strengthened and extended until Richmond should be won. But he had still 150,000 men at his command, having been largely reinforced by General Butler's army ; and he had the prospect of continual supplies of men and means. Lee had less than 70,000 men all told. The armies of the South elsewhere were overmatched, and could promise him no help. Want of energy and ability in the adminis-

* Draper, vol. iii. p. 387.

tration of the Confederacy, hardly less than its inferior
resources, left him destitute not only of recruits, but
straitened for the most necessary supplies. And if his
enemy had weakened himself by fully 60,000 men in his
fruitless attempts to gain Richmond, it had cost Lee
more than one-third that number to defend it. He
well knew that this loss could never be replaced.
Firm as his soul was, the sure effect of that " process
of attrition," of which the chroniclers of the triumphant Union now speak with admiration of its success,
was already discovered by the general of the Army of
Virginia, which was melting away under it. The
hopes that had brightened his earlier years of command,
were plainly disappearing as the increasing energy of
the North brought her superior strength into full
play. From the hour that Grant sat down before the
lines of Richmond, already too weakly guarded, and it
became plain that ill success had not shattered the confidence of the Washington Administration in his sagacity, and that his reserves were increasing from week to
week, the result could never be doubtful. Lee, above
all others, could well forecast the event, which might
be delayed but could not be averted. Two years
before, when M'Clellan, after his first retreat, had proposed to cross the James and move on Petersburg, and
the plan which brought Grant triumph in after days
had been summarily rejected by Halleck as "imprac-
ticable," a fact his official memorandum of his visit to
the Army of the Potomac records; Lee had in his
private conversations expressed his own conviction that
Richmond, now freed from immediate pressure, could
be held safely so long as such a movement on its communications with the Carolinas was left untried. Yet

it needed two years of continued victory in the West
to gain for Grant that prestige which could enable him
to patiently carry out, after plain proof of the imprac-
ticability of the President's favorite plan of a direct
advance, the strategy which he, as well as his great
adversary and his predecessor, all saw clearly to be that
to which the defence of Richmond must succumb.

Not in the first flush of triumph when his army
cheered his victory over M'Clellan; not when hurling
back Federal masses three times the weight of his
own on the banks of the Rappahannock: nor even
when advancing, the commander of victorious legions,
to carry the war away from his loved Virginia into the
North; had Lee seemed so great, or won the love of
his soldiers so closely, as through the dark winter that
followed. Overworked his men were sadly, with forty
miles of intrenchments for that weakened army to
guard. Their prospects were increasingly gloomy as
month passed by after month, bringing them no reinforcements, while their enemy became visibly stronger.
Their rations grew scantier and poorer, while the
jocund merriment of the investing lines told of abundance, often raised to luxury, by voluntary tribute
from the wealth of the North. The indiscipline, too,
long allowed, told on them; and, with the pangs of
hunger added, led to desertion, a thing formerly almost
unknown in the Army of Virginia. But the confidence
of the men in their beloved chief never faltered.
Their sufferings were never laid on " Uncle Robert."
The simple piety which all knew to be the rule of his
life, acted upon thousands of those under him with a
power which those can hardly understand who know
not how community of hope, suffering, and danger

fairly shared amid the vicissitudes of war, quickens the sympathies of the roughest and lowest as well as of those above them. He who was known to every soldier under him to have forbidden his staff to disturb the impromptu prayer-meeting that stopped their way when hurrying to the fierce battle in the Wilderness; he whose exposure was seen by all to grow only greater as the hour grew darker; he who was as constant in the lines during the monotonous watch against the foe that never attacked, as he had been when Grant hurled fresh legions on him day after day in the blood-stained thickets of Spottsylvania; he who, in short, had long lived up to the motto he is said to have commended to his own children on entering life, as the only sure guide, "Duty is the sublimest word in our language;" now illustrated in his own person that other motto which he bequeathed to the army when it dissolved, "Human virtue should be equal to human calamity." The vision of becoming the new Washington of a new Republic, had he ever entertained it, had faded away, with all its natural ambition. The very hope of saving from humiliation the state for whose safety and honor he had sacrificed his high prospects in the army of the Union, must now be despaired of. Yet the firmness of his bearing, and his unfaltering attention to the hourly business of his office, never declined for a moment, and impressed alike the falling government of the Confederacy, the dejected citizens of its capital, and the humblest soldiers of its army. Once during the sad spring of 1865 he recommended earnestly the prompt abandonment of the attempt to defend Richmond, and the retreat of his force, while it was still capable of movement, far into the South to concert further resistance with Johnston. This was in February, when he had received the commission of General-in-Chief of all the Confederate Armies; an empty title now, when those armies were melting into nothingness. But though he gave orders to prepare for the march, and looked on it as the only hope of using the few men at his disposal with effect, President Davis, ever buoyed up with false hopes of foreign succour and loth to admit the decadence of his brief rule, forbade the design being carried out. The only effect of this contemplated change of strategy was probably to delay the forwarding of supplies to the troops at Richmond, already too ill-cared for. And when March came, and Sheridan, hot from his successes in the Shenandoah, had joined General Grant with 10,000 mounted infantry, raising the Federals with all deductions to a strength 130,000 men, well fed and efficiently provided for in all respects, Lee's "effectives," a bare 40,000 men according to the best records, were subsisting solely on the daily issue of a quarter of a pound of rancid bacon, with a ration of ill-baked maize bread. Not that they ever murmured at their general. Their cheers for him when he visited their lines were as ready as of old; but their hungry eyes gazed more wistfully and sadly on his retreating form each time that he passed from them. And the supplicating look of the citizens when he entered Richmond, fixed with inquiring entreaty on the man in whom they still believed, there lay the power to save them, must have added a pang hardly less sharp to that felt each time that he saw the increasing gauntness of his unconquerable troops. No wonder that his hair grew gray in these days of darkness. No one so well as he knew the hopelessness of the situation of all. He was fully aware that Johnston, too late restored to the command of which Davis, in alarm at his Fabian strategy, had deprived him in the crisis at Atlanta, was quite unprovided with means to check Sherman's march through the Carolinas; and that that general, moving steadily northwards, was bringing up 100,000 victorious troops to complete the conquest of Richmond and its defenders.

But while Sherman yet approached the ruin fell, under the vehement impulse communicated to Grant's own troops by the ardor of Sheridan. The line of defence, " stretched so long as to break," in Lee's own phrase, and ever more weakly guarded, at last gave way. Sheridan's attack on Pickett's troops, which formed the extreme right or west of Lee's positions, proved completely successful in the decisive action of Five Forks, fought on April second; and Grant followed up the victory by assaults made all along the Confederate lines. The position, so long and so painfully held, was untenable when turned; and was yielded reluctantly, but without hesitation. Those around Lee could judge of the serious nature of his feelings only, by the care with which that day he carried with him the sword he usually dispensed with in action. As darkness closed on that eventful night, he was seen amid the glare of explosions from the abandoned works, standing at the angle of the road chosen for retreat up the north bank of the Appomattox, guiding and cheering his troops in person as they reached the point, and following them only when the last man of his ragged and weary columns had passed by.

Space would fail us did we attempt to follow out

that retreat in its memorable details. Well-rationed, followed by light trains of provisions, and its advanced guard led by one who never faltered nor admitted hesitation in others, the Federal army started in pursuit next morning, following parallel roads. Great praise has been justly bestowed on Sheridan for his nervous and energetic conduct of the pursuit by which Lee was finally completely cut off. Nor less does Grant deserve it, for the free and ungrudging manner in which he supported his ardent lieutenant. But he who, above all, should have earned honor for the conduct of that march now sleeps in the grave; and it is due here to the reputation of General Halleck to say, that the errors which had marked his earlier conduct of the war are amply redeemed in the eyes of those who recognize that to his stern and unflinching insistance on the necessity of bringing proper discipline to bear on the Federal volunteers, was due much of the success with which the arms of the Union were crowned at the close of the war. The disorders which had hindered the efficiency of the Federal levies in earlier years had been purged sharply from their ranks by the stern application of the military code to the embodied volunteers and conscripts on whom the Union relied to save it. While Meade and Grant pressed the enemy home in Virginia, courts-martial at Washington cleared from the service the scum which accident, or bribes, or the favor of state governors, had mixed with the solid materials of the Northern troops. Week after week appeared lists of officers cashiered for crimes, to look back on which is to peruse the strangest records of incompetence and worthlessness that the annals of war ever disclosed. None proved guilty met with mercy.

The general that sold his safe-conduct to the trembling
people of the district plundered by his troops; the
field officer who disappeared from his battalion before
the action; the captain who stole and drank his men's
rations of whisky; these, and others such as these,
typical cases from the official records of the period,
found themselves treated with no more leniency than
the private sentinel who slept before the enemy. And
as gazette upon gazette published the names of culprits
stripped of the epaulettes they had dishonored, insen-
sibly but steadily a higher tone of bearing was instilled
into the officers of the army thus watched over. Soldiers are ever dependent largely for their feeling of
subordination on the conduct of those above them;
and the improvement effected by Halleck's stern measures extended constantly downwards. The Army of
the Potomac, which was at once the nearest and the
most important of those which, as Chief of the Staff, he
supervised, rose that year in its standard of discipline,
if not to the level to which Europe, with the aid of
caste traditions and reverence for rank, brings her
standing forces, at least to a measure of efficiency
which troops recruited as were these, the mixed volunteers and conscripts of a young republic, can seldom
attain. And if Grant and Sheridan were able to press
the success of Five Forks on to a complete triumph
over the retreating Confederates; if the conduct of
their troops after the victory of the second of April
was in marked contrast to the lassitude and indifference which had hitherto followed advantages won on
either side; the difference is to be found not so much
in the circumstances of the time, or the individual character of the generals, as in the moral power of disci-

pline, which had been left unused by both parties alike,
until Halleck brought it into play to add to the advantages of the North.

So the pursuit of the flying Confederates went on
unintermitted from day to day. It is needless here to
follow it in its details. Enough for us to say that the
Federal troops were well supplied by their trains, while
the depôt on which Lee had counted for his men had,
through the blunder of the same official who had reduced them to quarter rations while in their lines,
been removed to the capital, just in time to fall into
the enemy's hands. Starving, except for what could
be collected by their disposal to forage, and moving
round an arc of which their adversaries followed the
chord, the long experience in marching of the Army
of Virginia could no longer avail. By the fifth day
their enemy had passed them, and was across their
path; and on the morning of the ninth of April the
way of escape was completely barred. Up to this time
Lee had resisted the proposals for capitulation which
had reached him from his adversary; but when this
fatal news came from his most trusted officer, the gallant Gordon who led his advance, he resigned himself
to his fate. For a moment those who looked on him
saw him almost overcome; and the first words of complaint ever heard from his lips during the war broke
sharply forth; "I had rather die a thousand deaths!"
Musing sadly for a few seconds, as his men's favorite
cry broke on his ear, "There's Uncle Robert!" in deep,
sad tones he said to those near him, "How soon could
I end all this, and be at rest. 'Tis but to ride down
the line, and give the word, and all would be over."
Then presently, recovering his natural voice, he an-

swered one who urged that the surrender might be misunderstood, " That is not the question. The question is, whether it is right. And if it is right, I take the responsibility." Then, after a brief silence, he added, with a sigh, " It is your duty to live. What will become of the wives and children of the South if we are not here to protect them?" So saying, he sent in his flag of truce without further hesitation to Grant. The coming action was stayed on the instant, and the struggle of the Confederacy was virtually over.

Of the interview between the great commanders which followed, enough has been already written. Those who would understand how highly Lee was held in honor by the very men who fought hardest against him, should study the story of that eventful meeting, not in the loving records of Mr. Cooke, or of other writers whose sympathies were with his efforts, but in the pages of the warmest partisans of the cause of the Union ; in such works, for instance, as the well-known memoir called " With Sheridan in Lee's last Campaign," where the ardent Northern writer, almost against his will, makes the chief of the captive army the hero of the scene. Or they may read it in the cold lines of the anti-slavery historian of the war, where no word of bitterness is ever missing for the politicians whose cause Lee's arm had upheld :

" From the Rapidan to the Appomattox Court-house " [says Dr. Draper, vol. iii. p. 392] " he had indeed made a grand defence. He had shed over Virginia a mournful glory. In the Wilderness, at Spottsylvania, on the Anna, at Cold Harbor, during the siege, and in the final retreat, he had struggled against preponderating power. For a whole year he had tried to stay the hand of Fate. No one can read his gallant acts without lamenting that they had not been in the cause of human freedom and national unity."

His parting words to his troops are historical. "Men, we have fought through the war together. I have done the best I could for you. My heart is too full to say more." But it is not so well known that while he uttered them with voice slightly trembling, tears from the rough soldiers he was parting from, answered those in his eyes, as they pressed around him to wring his hand lovingly, and offer their response in the rude prayer, "May God help you, general!" In his last army-order, issued the next morning, he replied to their sympathy: "You will take with you to your homes the satisfaction that proceeds from the consciousness of duty faithfully performed, and I earnestly pray that a merciful God will extend to you His blessing and protection." His last official act was to intercede with Grant that the mounted soldiers might be granted the use of their horses, so as to set at once to work on their neglected farms; a favor the Federal commander at once accorded with a readiness as courteous in the giver as it was politic in the disturbed state of the country. Indeed, the whole conduct of General Grant on this memorable occasion reflects on him a credit which the severest critic of his chequered life can never lessen. That the two armies so fiercely opposed for four long years, could have parted as they did without one word but those of sympathy and respect, seemed to presage with certainty the day when the last wounds of the recovered Union shall be fully healed, and the great constitutional victory of the rights of the Federation over those of the states shall be spoken of with as little bitterness in South and North as its petty prototype, the War of the Sonderbund, is to-day in all parts of Switzerland.

Leaving his army dispersing on parole, Lee passed into Richmond, declining the public honors which, even in their hour of humiliation, its people sought to offer him. Living here in the strictest retirement, he began his new duty of conciliation, from which he never ceased while life remained. When he received from a Federal general a private and friendly warning that it was resolved to arraign him for treason, despite the military protection of his capitulation, checking his informant's violent indignation, he replied with a smile, " Sir, we must forgive our enemies. Since the war began, not a day has passed that I did not pray for them." But the danger that the Union would be discredited by dishonorable vengeance soon passed away. The firmness of General Grant upon this point impressed itself on the hasty and violent man whom the murder of Lincoln had made President; and when Andrew Johnson ceased to encourage the thought, lesser partisans gave it up, and Lee continued unmolested in his privacy. In vain his fellow-citizens besought his attendance at their public meetings, when these were once more resumed. The one duty he had made his own was to set an example of personal submission to the people who looked on him as the chief representative of the South ; and for this reason he steadfastly discouraged all premature and useless remonstrance at the arbitrary measures by which it was long governed. But despite his reticence and humility, he made no attempt to hide his own personal responsibility for the actions done under the Confederacy ; and when sum-

9

moned before the Reconstruction Committee of Congress he was questioned as to the oath of allegiance to the fallen Government, he answered plainly, " I do not recollect having taken it, or whether it was required. If it was required, I took it : or if it had been required I would have taken it."

Virginia, in her ruin and suffering, could do little for her hero, especially when it became known that under no circumstances, however favorable, would the fallen general meddle with politics. What she could do, however, was soon done, and six months after the surrender at Appomattox Court-house Lee had accepted the presidency of the State College at Lexington, originally designed as a cadet school for the militia officers of Virginia, but now changed into a place of general training for the sons of such Southerners as were still left the means to educate their children. His fortune had perished, like his former professional prospects, with the war. For his wife's sake, therefore, the offer was doubly welcome, when it came to him as the token of the undiminished affection of his beloved state. And employment was not the less grateful to one who had never known idleness during a long lifetime, except in the enjoyment of a hard-earned holiday. He took up his post at Lexington therefore on October first, and devoted himself to his new duties with not the less assiduity that their sedentary nature made them somewhat a physical trial to a man of his active habits. The appointment was a fitting one in all respects, as well as creditable to those who made it. From far over the Southern States parents sent their sons to be trained under the once renowned commander, whose unblemished character was as well known as his military greatness. And the College, which had sunk into nothingness during the war, and reopened in 1865 with but a few of its old inmates, boasted five hundred students before his death five years later. Some of these, too, came from far Northern States, where very early in the days of reconquered peace there were not wanting men desirous to do all that in them lay to bury the remembrance of civil strife in oblivion.

Here then, engrossed chiefly by the steady performance of his daily duties, and in no society but that of his pupils and his neighbors in the country town, the rest of that great life was spent ; varied sometimes by visits to Washington, where he was several times summoned to give evidence on the state and feeling of the South, over the hard fate of which he never outwardly complained, though its sorrows were wearing his heart away. Public cares never prevented his attention to his College labors, nor to the local municipal affairs in which every American citizen of mark is expected to take an interest. He became scarcely less popular henceforward with the students than with his soldiers in his days of fame; while the residents around reverenced his name no less for his patient bearing in his state's adversity than for his heroic defence of her independence. The very children learnt to recognize as a friend the general who had led their fathers to victory, and went out of their way to seek the grave, kindly smile which had won their simple hearts.

Two objects only Lee seemed to have left during these years of retirement : the one, to lead his countrymen back to the Union, against which he had fought with such terrible effect; the other, to make of those

under his charge men who would grow up to do honor
to it. Of the many anecdotes offered us by Mr. Cooke
and other Virginian writers, one or two will suffice to
illustrate the spirit of his life.

"This is one of our old soldiers who is in necessity," were his words to a friend who discovered him in
the act of relieving a broken-down wayfaring man, and
adding kindly words to his gift. "He fought on the
other side," he added in a whisper; "but we must not
think of that." To a lady, one of the many widowed
in the war, who on bringing her sons to the College
burst out into a strain of bitterness against the North,
he said, with a gentleness which gave the more force to
his rebuke: "Madam, do not train up your children in
hostility to the government of the United States. Remember we are one country now. Pray dismiss from
your mind all sectional feeling, and bring them up to
be above all Americans." And all this was while his
feelings as to the original act by which he broke with
the Union remained unaltered. For when asked directly by the Reconstruction Committee, "What are
your own personal views on the question [of the original Act of Secession]?" he replied unhesitatingly: "It
was my view that the act of Virginia in withdrawing
herself from the United States carried me along with
it as a citizen of Virginia, and that her laws and acts
were binding on me." The past tense being plainly
employed to signify, what he constantly expressed in
private, that the arbitrament of the sword to which the
seceding states had appealed had quenched the supposed rights claimed by them before the war, without
affecting their original legitimacy.

Pages of anecdotes might here be gathered to illustrate his care for his other main object, the welfare of his students. That this took a deeply religious form will surprise no one who knows that during the war he had never ceased the regular use of the well-worn pocket Bible which had been his constant companion before it, and which still bore the inscription " R. E. Lee, Lt.-Colonel, U. S. Army." In his comparative retirement, and meditating constantly over the sorrows of his country, which he had little power to heal, it was most natural that this spiritual side of his character should become more plainly developed. He held to the Episcopal Church in which he had been brought up, but never showed any trace of that sectarian feeling which is almost as much a reproach to American Christianity as to that of our own country : and when once pressed by a forward inquirer for his opinion upon Apostolical Succession, he expressed his simple faith in the words : " I have not cared to think deeply of these things ; I have aimed to be a Christian." Of his limited income a large part was regularly devoted privately to charity. And his feelings for his students were expressed to one who congratulated him on the high state the College had attained under him, in words expressed with all the earnestness of the heart's nearest wish : " I shall be disappointed, sir ; I shall fail in the leading object that brought me here, unless the young men I have charge of become real Christians." In saying this, it is recorded, tears sprang to his eyes ; for his feelings were ever warm and sympathetic, and his heart, as his chief biographer has well said, " was so open to every touch of gentle and quick emotion, as to show that beneath his heroic character was a vein of almost feminine softness." " A noble action," are

Mr. Cooke's words, " flushed his cheek with emotion ;
a tale of suffering brought a sudden moisture to his
eyes ; and a loving message from one of his old soldiers
has been seen to melt him to tears."

Thus living and thus minded, he was ready when
the end came suddenly. No failing strength of body
or faculty gave token of the approaching close of that
great life. The unruffled health, which in long years
of war as of peace he had enjoyed unfailingly, never
seemed to leave him till the last. But his heart, long
bowed down by the weight of his country's sorrows, at
last gave way. His death may have been profession-
ally ascribed to cerebral congestion ; but the medical
attendants unanimously declared this to be but the
effect of long-suppressed sorrows : and that this was
the exciting cause no one could doubt who knew how
his hope of complete peace and restored tranquillity
was deferred from year to year, and how the mental
depression he struggled in vain to cast off increased as
post after post brought him piteous appeals for assistance from those who had served under him, many of
whose families were starving.

On September twenty-eighth, 1870, he had spent the
evening at a vestry meeting of the church he attended,
and had headed a liberal subscription for the object
which brought it together. On his return to the sit-
ting-room where the evening meal awaited him, his
wife remarked that he looked very cold. " Thank
you, I am well wrapped up," was his answer ; but the
words were the last he ever spoke articulately. He sat
down and opened his lips to say grace—a habit, it is
remarked, he had never failed to preserve amid all the
haste of war—but no sound came from them, and he

presently sank back in his chair in a half-insensible state, from which he never rallied, expiring tranquilly on October twelfth, with his family around him.

So passed away the greatest victim of the Civil War. Even in the farthest North, where he had once been execrated as the worst enemy of the Union, the tidings caused a thrill of regret. But though America has learnt to pardon, she has yet to attain the full reconciliation for which the dead hero would have sacrificed a hundred lives. Time only can bring this to a land which in her agony bled at every pore. Time, the healer of all wounds, will bring it yet. The day will come when the evil passions of the great civil strife will sleep in oblivion, and North and South do justice to each other's motives, and forget each other's wrongs. Then history will speak with clear voice of the deeds done on either side, and the citizens of the whole Union do justice to the memories of the dead, and place above all others the name of the great chief of whom we have written. In strategy mighty, in battle terrible, in adversity as in prosperity a hero indeed, with the simple devotion to duty and the rare purity of the ideal Christian knight, he joined all the kingly qualities of a leader of men.

It is a wondrous future indeed that lies before America; but in her annals of years to come as in those of the past there will be found few names that can rival in unsullied lustre that of the heroic defender of his native Virginia, Robert Edward Lee.

ADMIRALS FARRAGUT AND PORTER AND
THE NAVY OF THE UNION.*

"To overcome the dangers springing from so formidable an insurrection three results must be obtained. The shores of the Seceding States must be effectively blockaded; the course of the Mississippi and the whole water-system of the West must be mastered; finally, the rebellious government must be driven from Richmond, its chosen capital." Such were the broad outlines (as traced by the Prince de Joinville's clear pen) of the great task which lay before the forces of the Union at the outbreak of the Civil War. The important part borne by the American navy in the contest; its absolute performance of the first portion of the task indicated in our opening lines; the powerful share taken by it in the river campaigns which cut the Seceded States in twain; the vast weight due to its exertions in the final successes of the Federal generals, have been but little noticed as compared to the din and shock of the great battles with which the New World rang. Yet nothing is more surprising in this great contest; no military, political, or financial success more completely defied expectation, prophecy, and precedent; than the work wrought by this arm of

* *Reports of the Secretary for the American Navy for* 1861-65, *with* **Appendices.**

the Union forces, and wrought by it in the very process of creation out of actual nonenity.

European journals have not failed to make occasional comments on the Reports of the Secretary of the American Navy. Yet out of the United States few persons are aware of the extreme penury of resources with which that officer and his chief, the new President, had to contend, when the terrible fact of the unavoidable contest burst upon them. Even in America the full truth of the difficulties which, in this one department alone, beset the Cabinet of Lincoln, has only been made known by the publication of documents which, for personal motives, it had been designed to withhold. An attack upon the political reputation of Mr. Seward, made some months after the actual close of the contest, first brought to light incidentally the full particulars of the failure to relieve Fort Sumter in April, 1861, the papers concerning which had been once laid before the Senate, but suppressed by that body. The report of Captain Fox (afterwards Assistant Secretary of the Navy), the principal actor in the affair, reveals in vivid colors the destitute condition of the department at the breaking out of the war, and the shifting nature of the counsels which prevailed at Washington in the first dread of provoking actual conflict. This officer, who had left the navy for private employment before the era of Secession, was one of many bold and active spirits who flocked back to the public service of the Union when its existence was endangered. Events so vast as to afford a field for the most daring and energetic of the sons of the North were at hand, and were partly foreseen by the more clear-sighted of her politicians, though none fathomed fully their mighty scope and the great results to follow.

On January ninth, 1861, the "Star of the West," a vessel chartered to carry supplies to Fort Sumter, was turned back by shots from Morris Island, the first hostile missiles of the civil war proclaimed by this outrage on the Federal flag. Captain Fox, being then in New York, and well acquainted with the approaches to Charleston, lost no time in laying before certain eminent merchants of strong Union principles his "views as to the possibility of relieving the garrison, and the dishonor which would be justly merited by the government, unless immediate measures were taken to fulfil this sacred duty." Into the details of his proposal it is not necessary to enter here. So much effect did his vehemence and energy exercise on the hearers, that one of them, Mr. Marshall, undertook to furnish and provision the necessary vessels forthwith. While these preparations were made, the authorities at Washington were communicated with; and on February sixth Captain Fox was present at the capital, summoned by a telegram from General Scott. Next day his plan was fully discussed in the presence of Mr. Buchanan; but the simple vacillation of the latter was (as his own confessions indicate) changed into downright weakness when news arrived on the following morning, that the Seceding States had actually proceeded to the election of a President of their own. "I called upon General Scott," says Captain Fox, "and he intimated to me that probably no effort would be made to relieve Fort Sumter. He seemed much disappointed and astonished; I therefore returned to New York on February ninth." Nor can we wonder at the retiring President's hopeless view of the case, when we learn from Mr. Welles's first report that the number of seamen officially under the control of the Navy Department in the first week of March amounted to *less than* 300 *on home service*, with a proportionately low supply of stores! This weakness was, however, in the main ostensible only; for but a brief time was needed to show what a fund of energy private will could supply, and what wealth of means private resources could create when the spirit of the Northern States should be fairly aroused to grapple with the crisis of their fate.

That crisis was rapidly approaching. The day of compromises and expedients ceased with Buchanan; and his successor, Mr. Lincoln, was no sooner installed in the seat of peril, when the naval enterprise which had been at first rejected was again entertained.

Dismissed by the new President with verbal instructions, Captain Fox is again found at New York in consultation with his merchant friends, " and making preliminary arrangements for the voyage." At these interviews, no doubt, was laid the foundation of that new naval system to be created through private agency for the public service, which may be considered one of the most remarkable products of the great Civil War.

Undaunted by the withdrawal from the project of his first ally, Mr. Marshall, who thought " that the people had made up their minds to abandon Sumter," Captain Fox pressed his project forward. " Delays which belong to the secret history of the time;" in plainer words, the irresolution of the majority of Lincoln's advisers and its effect upon their chief,

" prevented a decision until the afternoon of April fourth, when the President sent for me, and said that he had decided to let the expedition go, and that . . . I should best fulfil my duty to my country to make the attempt. The Secretary of the Navy had in commission, in the Atlantic waters of the United States, only the Powhatan, Pocahontas, and Pawnee, all these he placed at my disposal, as well as the revenue steamer Harriet Lane, and directed me to give all the necessary orders."

On April twelfth, Captain Fox in a borrowed steamer made the rendezvous of Charleston, just three hours before the fire on Fort Sumter was opened. The expedition proved unable to succor it. The weather was rough and the means for landing in the night (the pith of the design) totally inadequate. Moreover, the squadron was left unexpectedly incomplete. A heavy gale along the coast fully accounted for the non-appearance of certain hired tug-boats; but the Powhatan was looked for all day, and through the night, signals in vain thrown up. It was not until the next morning, that of the surrender of the fort, that Captain Fox first learnt that the missing frigate had been carried off to another service by still higher orders than those of the Secretary of the Navy. The instructions of the latter to her captain, Mercer (who was to act as senior naval officer), had been issued in elaborate detail on April 5th, the morning after the President's promise to Fox that the expedition should sail. That in this promise the Powhatan was specifically included does not appear; but that both Mr. Welles and Captain Fox so understood it is perfectly clear, although this all-important ship (as they considered it) was in reality already

secretly engaged for another service, destined to be the
first step on his way to honor of the afterwards famous
Admiral, then Lieutenant, Porter, a naval officer whose
talents had already brought him into the private councils of President Lincoln.

For while Fox had been pressing forward his project for the relief of Sumter, Captain Meigs of the
Engineers (distinguished later for his services as Quar-
termaster-General) had been not less urgent with the
President to attempt the reinforcement of the troops
at Fort Pickens, the key of Pensacola Harbor. This
fort was so weakly garrisoned as to be subject to surprise from Bragg's Confederate force on the main land ;
and yet of itself it was known to be far more susceptible
of defence than Fort Sumter; while Porter was confident that its relief by a dash from the sea-side was an
adventure that only needed secresy and speed to insure
perfect success. Whether the merely military view of
the question; or the advice of Mr. Seward, who favored this project ; or the secret belief of the President
that the fall of Fort Sumter was of more political value
than the holding it to the Federal cause, prevailed in
Lincoln's decision over the arguments of Fox, is not
clear. A consolatory letter addressed soon afterwards
to the latter by the President concludes with a remarkable expression, which seems to justify the belief that
the failure to relieve and consequent surrender of Sumter were events foreseen without much reluctance.
The paragraph ran thus :

" For a daring and dangerous enterprise of a similar character, you would to-day be the man, of all my acquaintances,
whom I would select. You and I both anticipated that the

cause of the country would be advanced by making the attempt to provision Fort Sumter, *even if it should fail.*"

Whatever was the motive, the President chose rather to sacrifice his failing hold on Charleston harbor than give up the other fort at Pensacola. And so small was the degree of confidence at that time reposed in his own officials, that Mr. Welles, the Naval Secretary, remained in complete ignorance of the new design, and was actually suffered (as we have seen) to issue instructions which secret and imperious orders from his chief, set aside. For when the Powhatan was ready for sea and about to quit New York for Charleston, Porter and Meigs suddenly stepped on board ; and the former producing the President's sign-manual authorizing the proceeding, assumed command of the frigate and diverted her course from the Carolina coast to the Gulf of Mexico.

" It was not [says General Meigs, in a recently published account] without some hesitation that Captain Mercer gave up the ship. But the positive order of the President, detaching him and placing Lieutenant Porter in command, overruled the order of the Navy Department. The conflict was the result of the secresy with which the whole business was conducted, and to that secresy, in a great measure, was due the relief of Fort Pickens, and the retention of this finest harbor in the South by the United States."

Besides preserving the control of the harbor of Pensacola (which the Union forces never from that time found difficulty in holding), Porter and his coadjutors were enabled on their way to save the islands of Key West and the Tortugas from yielding to the state authorities of Florida. So rapid and complete was their success, that the first news of it was brought back by Captain Meigs himself, up to the time of whose arrival the true destination of the Powhatan, and of the steam transport Atlantic, which had accompanied her, was unknown to any save the President and the officers who executed the design !

It is not surprising that in his first report, that of July 1861, the Secretary of the Navy makes no allusion to an achievement the conception of which had been kept secret from him ; nor that Captain Fox appears to have long harbored a very bitter feeling against Mr. Seward, to whose personal advice he attributed the President's decision. We are not here concerned with the personal or party aspect of the question, but have brought this, the first episode of the naval warfare in America, prominently forward ; partly for the light it throws on the political chaos out of which so much energy, valor, and statesmanship was to be born; partly for the picture it affords of the extraordinary want of any ready means by which the Government of the Union could assert its authority. The Congress adjourning without providing any men or material to meet the threatened danger : the fleet so reduced that but one steam frigate could be found to execute all the designs the President might have for the control of the seceding ports : a Secretary of the Navy so new to his trust that it was thought necessary to keep from him the knowledge of the orders sent to his own department : a lieutenant sent with secret orders to supersede the post-captain on the deck of his own ship, and at the hour of his departure on an important service : expeditions involving civil war urged on the government

by private citizens, who yet made their aid dependent
on the undeclared will of the people; such were some
of the strange circumstances which surrounded the
Executive of the Great Republic in the day when its
power by land and sea seemed rent in twain. Never
if war must come, had a commercial state more need
of a navy. Never were the apparent difficulties of creating one greater; for many of the merchant princes
of the North were inclined to take a more lukewarm
view of the Union cause when its defence seemed to
threaten danger to their foreign trade, than in the first
moments of excitement, before the cost was fully
counted.

Lincoln however was more fortunate in his Cabinet.
Neither he nor any of his advisers shrank from the
mere magnitude of the duties thronging on them, nor
lacked that faith in their cause which should hereafter
carry the whole North with it to a triumphant end.
Mr. Welles swallowed manfully enough the mortification he had felt, and applied himself with diligence to
the vast task before him; while Captain Fox was soon
to find that the President's expressions of satisfaction
with his conduct in the Sumter affair were no mere
perfunctory commendations. An Assistant Secretary
of the Navy was one of the first additional offices rec
ommended for the sanction of the new Congress; and
on the approval of that body being obtained to this addition to the now important bureau, the appointment
was at once conferred on Captain Fox, who held it until the war was brought to a successful end. No better
selection could have been made. The happy combination he possessed of cultivated professional knowledge
with close experience of the details of the Northern

shipping trade, enabled him, in a degree to which perhaps no other man could have attained, to utilize the resources of the latter for the supply of the vast deficiencies existing in the department of which throughout the struggle he held practical charge.

How great these deficiencies were appears sufficiently in the first report of Mr. Welles, made before the appointment of his energetic and able coadjutor. There is a brevity and a frankness about the bare statements in this paper, which contrast not unfavorably with the more labored narratives of the work achieved by the department in those which came later. Forty-two ships in commission, with a complement of 7,600 men, formed the active fleet of the United States at the accession of Lincoln ; and while thirty of these were absent on foreign stations, four only of the remainder, manned by 280 sailors, constituted the exact force left in the harbors of the states adhering to the Union.

But more serious still was the disaffection among the naval officers, a far larger proportion of whom than in the army sympathized to the full with the objects of Secession. It was found possible at a later time to fill the posts of the 260 who resigned their commissions with volunteers, who, like Captain Fox, had been brought up to the service. But before this could be done, one of the principal naval depôts, the yard at Norfolk, had fallen into hostile hands. In it was a large steam frigate, the Merrimack, now nearly complete, which the Confederates, on the hasty evacuation of the place, succeeded in saving from the flames when some lesser vessels perished. Possessing thus at least one formidable vessel of war, they forthwith proceeded,

10

with an ingenuity which made up for the limited means at their command, to convert her into such an invincible iron-clad as might hope to defy all the fleets of the North. To the foresight and activity of Captain Fox it was due that this design was foiled in the end, by the counter-measures adopted at his instance.

Before his official appointment as assistant to Mr. Welles, that statesman had in this report brought the subject of iron-clad vessels before Congress ; and a vote of a million and a half of dollars being granted for the purpose of obtaining experimental models, three of those submitted were speedily selected for practical trial. The first of the ships thus ordered was the " Ironsides ; " a steam sloop armored throughout with 4½-inch plates, and designed to carry eight of the Dahlgren 11-inch hollow-shot guns, up to that time the heaviest piece known in the navy. The next was the famous invention of Captain Ericsson, the " Monitor," the first ship built with a revolving turret, The principles of her construction were (as is univer sally known) altogether new in the history of naval architecture, and on their general scope it is not needful here to dwell. Plated very imperfectly, slow, and dangerously unseaworthy, inferior even in armament to her successors (her two guns being 11-inch, one of theirs always 15-inch), she yet, by her prompt preparation and opportune dispatch to the Chesapeake, arrived to do such service in her single harbor action as few vessels of the longest sea-going history can claim ; for her success secured its naval base to the army of M'Clellan.

Undeterred by the sneers of the numerous critics, who prophesied that the Monitor would never float, or if floating could never venture beyond Sandy Hook,

the inventor and his employer with equal eagerness
pressed her to completion. Such confidence did Fox
and Ericsson inspire in Mr. Welles as the " Floating
Iron Battery " (her first official name) drew near completion, that the Secretary, before the time of actual
test arrived, applied for and obtained, with a little gentle pressure, a special vote from Congress for twenty
more iron-clad gun-boats, the greater part of which
were ordered to be constructed at once on the Monitor principle. The additions already made to the
strength of the navy in the first four months of Mr.
Welles's charge, comprised, besides eight steam-sloops
sanctioned by the previous Congress, twelve large
steamers bought, and nine more hired from the merchant service, to be fitted for war purposes with from
two to nine guns each. Much of the report of July
1861 is devoted to an apology for the responsibility
assumed by the Secretary in making this provision,
and in ordering from private yards twenty-three gun-
boats of about five hundred tons each ; measures which
are especially justified by a reference to the violence
committed at Norfolk on the naval property of the
Union, and to the insurrection against the Washington
authorities of the people of Baltimore. It is evident
that Mr. Welles was yet in some uncertainty as to the
support the Cabinet might receive in their vigorous
action ; an uncertainty at once removed by the prompt
approval of the Congress specially summoned to decide
whether the Union was to be saved by war.

In the next report (that of December 1861) it is
vain to look for any great progress beyond that shown
by returns of expenditure, purchase, and blockade captures. With the exception of the disastrous campaign

ending at Bull's Run, the autumn of this year was
chiefly spent by the North in gathering up her strength
by land and sea for that great war which she now saw
plainly must be passed through if the Union was to be
saved.   Critics there were in abundance, at home and
abroad, ready to denounce the expenditure as profli-
gate, and the hope of reconquest as visionary. Yet
every month added to the majority who supported
Congress in their resolution to place the national forces
on a thoroughly serviceable footing; and Captain Fox
and his superior availed themselves to the full of the
grants made for their department.   Supplemental estimates for five millions of our money had been submitted in the summer session, and sanctioned without
delay; so that now, in addition to the engaging by
special bounties, a respectable number of seamen, one
hundred and twenty-one more vessels had been purchased from merchants and converted into transports
or vessels of war, in addition to fifty-two begun or
actually completed in the yards, or under special contracts—the greater part by the latter means.   Of the
old navy the number of vessels brought into service
was seventy six; but one-half of those were sailing-
vessels, unsuited to the new exigencies of the service.
It had already become evident that the proclamation
of blockade, without an abundant use of steam-power,
would have proved a nullity; while the capture now
reported of one hundred and fifty-three vessels attempting to break it, proved the wisdom of (we quote from
Mr. Welles's fuller description in a later report) " the
steps which were promptly taken to recall the foreign
squadrons, and to augment the navy by repairing and
fitting, as expeditiously as possible, every available ves-

sel, by rapidly constructing as many steamers as could be built at the navy-yards, and by employing, to the extent that we could procure materials, engines and machinery, the resources of the country in adding others from private ship-yards."

On the whole, however, the year 1861 had given but little opportunity to show whether the American navy, under the new conditions would prove equal to its former reputation. The validity of its blockade, the one work really accomplished, was questioned daily in the foreign press. whose critics, swayed often by national or party prejudice, measured it by the notorious number of escapes rather than by its practical effects upon the South. Yet as we now look coolly back, it is evident that the marine department of the Union forces had done more during this period of general girding for the strife than the administration of the sister service. It is true that masses of volunteers were accepted for the army and placed in camp: but until Bull's Run had been lost, not the smallest attempt was made to give them consistency and value by a working staff.

Passing forward another year in our review, we find more conspicuous successes obtained by the energy of Mr. Welles's able assistant than perhaps even he had dreamed of, when the mantle of office fell on him in a fortunate hour for the Union. The general result of his exertions, and of the support and confidence he received from the President and Mr. Welles, is best given in the words of the latter's report of December 1862:

"We have at this time afloat or progressing to rapid completion a naval force consisting of 427 vessels, there having been added to those of the old navy enumerated in my report of July, 1861, exclusive of those that were lost, 363 vessels, armed in the aggregate with 1,577 guns, and of the capacity of 240,028 tons.

"The annals of the world do not show so great an increase in so brief a period to the naval power of any country. It affords me satisfaction to state that the acquisitions made to the navy from the commercial marine have proved to be of an excellent character, and though these vessels were not built for war purposes, and consequently have not the strength of war vessels, they have performed all the service that was expected of them."

Some exceptions may of course be made to this broad statement; but the history of the navy had now become largely the history of the war, and it is necessary to survey its achievements a little more in detail, in order to see how great a share it had already taken in determining the course of events.

The greatest success, as a purely naval operation, of the whole war—the greatest in naval history since Exmouth's victory at Algiers—was that achieved in the course of the spring of 1862, at the mouth of the Mississippi. Captain Farragut, whom Welles had specially selected as fitted by his resolute character to take charge of the active operations in that quarter, arrived at the scene of action in February with the new rank of Flag Officer, soon afterwards raised to that of Rear-Admiral, which a special Act allowed the President to confer on any captain or commander chosen to lead a naval force. The Western Gulf Squadron had been gradually increased from a few blockading vessels to a powerful fleet of 6 steam frigates and 12 large gun-boats. To these a flotilla of 20 bomb-vessels under Porter (raised to commander's rank for his earlier services) was added by the eighteenth of March. But the obstacles to be overcome were of the most formidable character. Two strong forts—Jackson on the west bank, St. Philip on the east—were connected by a huge boom of rafts and hulks, the approach to which, to be made against a powerful current, was swept with their fire of 80 guns, and seemed thus to bar wholly the way up the stream. Above this obstruction a flotilla of gun-boats was ready to support the fire of the works; and iron-clad rams were known to have been some time in preparation in order to employ in the coming warfare that use of the blow of the prow disused for so many centuries, but now revived by the power of steam.

The first attempt of this kind in modern history had been already made off one of the mouths of the river by Commodore Hollins of the Confederate service in the previous October, when he had attacked and all but driven off a blockading squadron with the ram Manasses, a small river-steamer plated rudely with railroad iron. Thus early in the war, however, the means of the Confederates proved unequal to the carrying out their bold designs. The shock of the ram fell partly as it happened, on a coaling schooner alongside the steamer Richmond, the vessel attacked; and although the latter was considerably damaged, she was not reduced to a sinking condition, while the ram suffered so much in her machinery as to be disabled from continuing the contest. A further attempt on the same occasion to destroy the alarmed blockaders with fire-barges failed also, the former succeeding in drifting out of the way of the danger. Hollins then drew off without any practical advantage gained beyond the prestige established in favor of the dashing mode of warfare which he had the credit of being the first to revive, and which the fleet of Farragut had to prepare for, as one of the most dangerous obstacles to their enterprise.

The navy was from the first designed to bear the labor and reap the honor of the capture of New Orleans unsupported; although General Butler, with 18,000 men, was dispatched to the scene of action. It may be that the fatal example of Pakenham's defeat in his attempt to reach the city by land influenced the arrangements of Welles and Fox. Certain it is that their instructions to Farragut set aside all thought of active use of the troops in the attack. Their simple wording ran (after some preliminary details) thus:—

"When you are completely ready . . . you will proceed up the Mississippi river, and reduce the defences which guard the approaches to New Orleans, when you will appear off that city and take possession of it under the guns of your squadron, and hoist the American flag therein, keeping possession until troops can be sent to you. . . . As you have expressed yourself perfectly satisfied with the force given to you, and as many more powerful vessels will be added before you can commence operations, the department and the country will require of you success."

Such success might have been all but impossible had the Confederate resistance been as perfectly organized as at the time was believed. A full knowledge of the truth as it may be gained from the official reports laid before the Richmond Congress, shows not only that much was left undone in the way of material preparation on the side of the Confederates, but that their commanders were wanting in the unity, vigor, and activity opposed to them by their formidable assailants.

Farragut's earliest reports refer chiefly to the transport of the needful supplies, and to the steps taken for carrying the larger steamers over the bar. The difficulties here encountered were greater than had been anticipated, and it was only on April eighth that the frigates were completely brought over the obstacle, with the exception of the heaviest, the Colorado, which it was found impossible to tow through the mud-banks, however she was lightened. The rest had then to be fully armed and coaled; and in the meanwhile the whole squadron was fitted for the coming conflict, under orders previously prepared by the flag-officer with elaborate care to meet the various contingencies of a battle fought in the contracted space of a river's width. The mere issuing of instructions was by no means the limit of Farragut's care for his command. Imitating, perhaps unconsciously, the scrupulous anxiety of Nelson before the victory of the Nile, he visited every vessel under his flag, and saw that the commander personally comprehended his own share in the work. Thus, too, he was enabled (as his detailed report discovers) to utilize such suggestions as the ingenuity of individuals offered. The first of these was by the engineer of the Richmond, who proposed that the sheet-cables should be stopped up and down the sides in the line of the engines—a plan which was immediately adopted by all the vessels. Then each commander made his own arrangements for preventing the shot from penetrating the boilers or machinery, by hammocks, coal, bags of ashes, bags of sand, clothes bags, and in fact every device imaginable. The bulwarks were lined with hammocks by some, by splinter-nettings made with ropes, by others. Some rubbed their vessels outside with mud, to make their ships less visible, and some whitewashed their decks, to make things more visible during the fight, for the actual conflict was to take place in the night.

While thus consulting in person with his captains, all of whose opinions Farragut heard, that of Commander Porter, was listened to with a deference corresponding to his important charge and the reputation he had already gained, rather than to his relative rank. In his general order of April twentieth the flag-officer freely avowed this, and declared himself to be about to essay an attack which was a combination of two modes suggested by that able and daring officer. The forts were at all risks to be run past in the dark, and the troops to be left behind until a sufficient naval force to protect them was in the river above at a point (called the Quarantine) near to which they might be conveyed by a shallow creek which turned the Confederate main works. The latter could then be effectually besieged, while the bulk of the joint forces moved up along the stream, prepared to operate further by land or water according to the means of resistance, as yet hardly guessed at, which the enemy possessed. This project was in the end not executed in its integrity only because, the forts once passed, opposition practically ceased. The assault was preluded by a bombardment from Porter's heavy mortars. After careful reconnoissance that officer had towed his flotilla within range of the works by the morning of April eighteenth and the work of destruction began by their throwing that day nearly 3,000 large shells about the heads of the garrison.

Those who have wondered at the success obtained at New Orleans need do so no more when they contrast the completeness of the Federal preparations, and the vigor and decision with which Farragut at the proper moment went to work, with the divided counsels and inefficient armaments opposed to them by the Confederates. On March twenty-seventh, General Duncan, a well-known artillerist, who personally commanded the defences, became aware that the enemy's fleet was crossing the bar. Both he and his superior, General Lovell, had previously anticipated this, and had made urgent and repeated applications for a change of armament at the forts, the guns in which were but old 32 and 42-pounders, justly held to be unfit for repelling the steam fleet which threatened the place; while a second line of works nearer to the city mounted but twelve of the former pieces, having been stripped even of the latter "at the urgent request of the naval authorities," who wished to use this part of the armament on some gun-boats fitting for defence of the creeks. That this most serious mistake of not supplying proper ordnance arose from underrating the imminence of the danger on the river side appears plainly from General Lovell's reports. These also show how early in the war the Confederate naval authorities had turned their attention to the use of iron-clad vessels, of which two large specimens, intended both for ramming and carrying guns in shot-proof batteries, were being prepared at New Orleans.

Happily for the success of the Union fleet, the mechanical means which their foes controlled were by no means equal to their powers of conception. This deficiency produced continual delay; while the readiness of Fox and Farragut was so far beyond that anticipated by their professional opponents, that the iron-clads (originally designed for February first) were found unprepared for use when the Federal fleet, three months later, burst its way through to the fated city.

"Immediately" [says General Lovell] "after I assumed command of the department, finding there were no guns of the heaviest calibre, I applied to Richmond, Pensacola, and other points for some 10-inch columbiads and sea-coast mortars, which I considered necessary to the defence of the lower river; but none could be spared, the general impression being that New Orleans would not be attacked by the river; and I was therefore compelled to make the best possible defence with the guns at my disposal. Twelve 42-pounders were sent to Forts Jackson and St. Philip, together with a large additional quantity of powder; and being convinced that with the guns of inferior calibre mounted there we could not hinder steamers from passing, unless they could be detained for some time under the fire of the works, I pushed forward rapidly the construction of a raft which offered a complete obstruction to the passage of vessels."

The personal exertions of an ordnance officer, a relation of the general, did at length procure three ten-inch and three eight-inch columbiad hollow-shot guns and five large mortars, which were mounted just before the bombardment commenced. This was, as before noticed, on April eighteenth: but a week previous to Porter's attack the raft was seriously damaged by a

storm accompanied by a flood, which, according to
General Duncan's statement, "parted the chains, scattered the schooners, and materially affected the character and effectiveness of the raft as an obstruction."

For six long days did the garrisons of the forts endure the pitiless fire which Porter rained on them.
Carefully as the casemates had been constructed, the
thirteen-inch shells inflicted serious damage, and disabled a number of the defenders' guns. The unprotected barracks in the fort were destroyed with all
their contents within the first twelve hours of this tremendous bombardment. The garrison could make
feeble response, owing to the inferiority of range of
most of their pieces; yet the gunners never flinched,
and the enormous expenditure of Federal ammunition
determined Farragut to hurry on the endeavor to
pass the batteries by main force in the hours of darkness on the third night, under cover of a furious fire,
an expedition of two gun-boats, under Captain Bell,
approached the barricade to attempt its destruction by
means of petards or, as they are now called, torpedoes.
"This duty," says Admiral Farragut, "was not thoroughly performed, in consequence of the failure to ig-
nite the petards with the galvanic battery." In fact,
no officer of the American service had at that time
been trained to the use upon or under water of these
powerful engines of destruction. "Still," he continues,
"it was a success, and, under the circumstances, a
highly meritorious one." In fact, the Itasca, under
Lieutenent Caldwell, grappled one of the schooners,
which that officer boarded at once, and detached from
the chains which had secured her to the barricade,
which was thus laid open. His gun-boat was the only

one seen by the look-outs of Duncan, who writes: " A heavy fire was opened upon her, which caused her to retire, but not until she had partially accomplished her purpose. The raft after this could not be regarded as an obstruction."

The following night the garrison was cheered by the descent from New Orleans of one of the two iron-clad rafts, the Louisiana, mounting sixteen heavy guns. By this time the injuries in their defences were very considerable; but under her almost impregnable cover they had hoped to make the necessary repairs. On conferring however with Captain Mitchell, a naval officer who now arrived and assumed charge of all the steamers gathered for the defence, Duncan learnt that her motive power was incomplete, and that so far from taking the offensive against the enemy, his coadjutor was bent on keeping her above the forts until the mechanics had finished their labors. In vain did the general appeal to his chief at New Orleans, and the latter to Commodore Whittle, the successor of Hollins and superior of Captain Mitchell. The commodore's orders were sent indeed to the latter, but with the proviso to execute them only " if in his judgment it was advisable ; " and in consequence, Mitchell held to his determination of keeping the iron-clad for the present out of fire. It is fair to say that his view was supported by those of the naval officers under him. On the other hand, the naval volunteers who chiefly manned the steamers (eight in number, besides the small ram Manasses and a fire-raft flotilla), which had been prepared for co-operation with the forts, were jealous alike of the interference they had at first met with from the generals, and of that to which they now were subjected

when transferred to the rule of their professional brethren.

It is not for us, who inherit the memories of Wal-
cheren, to lean too hardly on the errors which divided
the command of the Confederates at this critical time,
and kept the real chiefs at New Orleans, twenty miles
above the vital point of action. It is enough to say
that the fifth day of bombardment and endurance went
by in vain correspondence and appeals. Not only did
Mitchell refuse to place the Louisiana where her battery might be of use, but the only immediate service
remaining to be performed, the sending down of fire-
ships in the night against Porter's fleet, was left undone,
the tug-boats allotted for that duty being under repair.
" This does not excuse the neglect," says Duncan, " as
there were six boats of the river fleet available for this
service, independent of those alluded to, and fire-barges
were plentiful." More plainly still does General Lovell's report speak of what occurred that night and during the eventful one which followed. " The river-defence
fleet," he writes, " proved a failure, for the very reasons set
forth in my letter to the department of April fifteenth.
Unable to govern themselves, and unwilling to be governed by others, their almost total want of system, vigilance, and discipline rendered them useless and helpless, when the enemy finally dashed upon them suddenly in a dark night. I regret very much that the
department did not think it advisable to grant my
request to place some competent head in charge of
these steamers."

The twenty-third of April broke warm and clear. The
garrisons had now given up hope of immediate aid from
the steamers, and attempted to repair their pressing

damages as they best could under Porter's fire. Before night the latter slackened perceptibly ; and Duncan, struck by this fact (which he correctly enough, as his letter of that evening proves, ascribed to the enemy's growing short of ammunition), and observing movements in the fleet below, once more wrote to Mitchell to urge the Louisiana's being brought into a position to aid at least by her battery in the defence. His request was refused, and when, somewhat later, he communicated the additional news that his suspicions were confirmed by the enemy's boats fixing white flags in the line of their expected advance, he learnt only from Mitchell's reply that the Louisiana would be ready by the next evening. Before that evening had arrived the luckless iron-clad was prepared to be blown up by her captain's own orders. Kept so carefully out of harm's way as she had been, the only damage inflicted by her was that caused by the explosion, to the garrison she had been built to aid.

The anxiety suffered by Duncan and his troops during the early part of the night was enhanced by an increase in the fire of the bomb-vessels which took place when darkness closed, and by their ignorance of what the enemy was doing under cover of Porter's shells ; for, as on the previous night, the promised firerafts were not floated down by the flotilla. Who it was that should be charged specially with this omission it is hard to say. It is clear that Captain Mitchell, though invested nominally with the whole control of the river defence, was unable to make his authority felt by the naval volunteers, whose senior officer, Captain Stevenson, had declared officially three days before, in the name of his force, "it would not be governed by the

regulations of the navy or commanded by naval officers."

At two o'clock on the morning of the twenty-fourth
Farragut gave his pre-arranged signal, two ordinary red
lights, so as not to excite special notice; and the advance began in two columns. That on the right, under
Captain Bailey (Farragut's second in command), was
led by the gun-boat Cayuga, which bore the flag. She
was followed by the steam frigates Pensacola and Mississippi, and five other gun-boats in succession. The
left column, the Admiral's own, was similar in formation, but stronger by a frigate, being led by his fleet-
captain in the gun-boat Scioto, which was followed by
the Hartford (the flag-ship), two other frigates, and five
more gun-boats. The divided counsels of their opponents, the exhaustion of some, the insubordination of
others, the incompleteness of their defences, were all
unknown to the Federals: and how great was their
commander's anxiety as to the issue of his bold advance, and the prospect of passing the forts with a respectable force left, is best shown by his own general
order, sent round a short time before:

"When, in the opinion of the flag-officer, the propitious
time has arrived, the signal will be made to weigh and advance to the conflict. If in his opinion, at the time of arriving at the respective positions of the different divisions of the
fleet, we have the advantage, he will make the signal for close
action, No. 8, and abide the result—conquer or to be conquered—drop anchor or keep under weigh, as in his opinion is
best."

At half-past three the fleet approached the barrier,
the bomb-vessels having also placed themselves so as

11

to fire freely on the forts, and being strengthened for the night by the addition of the sailing corvette Portsmouth, which was towed up within range of Fort Jackson. Severely damaged already, the boom gave way to the rush of the leading gunboats, while at the same moment the forts opened fire, and one of the most fearful scenes began which naval annals record.

"After we had fairly entered into the fight" [writes Farragut], "the density of the smoke from guns and fire-rafts, the scenes passing on board our own ship and around us (for it was as if the artillery of heaven were playing upon earth), were such that it was impossible for the flag-officer to see how each vessel was conducting itself, and he can only judge by the final results and their special reports, which are herewith enclosed. But I feel that I can say with truth that it has rarely been the lot of a commander to be supported by officers of more indomitable courage or higher professional merit."

In short, the darkness of the night, the closeness of the action, and the tremendous calibre of the Federal cannon made it hopeless for any officer to do more than control the movements of a single vessel in the confused uproar which arose. The flag-officer's own was soon in danger so imminent as to task his utmost energies, and we quote from his report only that further portion which speaks of her share:

"I discovered a fire-raft coming down upon us, and in attempting to avoid it ran the ship on shore; and the ram Manasses, which I had not seen, lay on the opposite of it, and pushed it down upon us. Our ship was soon on fire half way up to her tops, but we backed off, and through the good or-

ganization of our fire department, and the great exertions of
Captain Wainwright and his first lieutenant, officers, and crew,
the fire was extinguished.   In the meantime our battery was
never silent, but poured in its missiles of death into fort St.
Philip, opposite to which we had got by this time, and it was
silenced, with the exception of a gun now and then."

Silenced perhaps for the minute ; for the gunners at
such times sought shelter in the casemates close by,
which had preserved them during the preceding bombardment ; yet only to rush forth at every interval of
slackening in the fire of the frigates, and reply with
their feebler pieces to the storm of grape hurled at
them from 9-inch and 11-inch guns.   Their gallantry is
not merely testified to by their own commanders.   More
important witness to it is borne by the detailed reports
of the Federal captains, and especially by those of three
gunboats, the Itasca, Kennebec, and Winona, which
became entangled in portions of the barrier after the
frigates had gone by, and found the fire of the garrison
still so insupportable as to compel them to head down
stream, and thus, for safety, to separate themselves
from the rest of the fleet.

The forts and boom once passed, as well as the
fire-rafts (of which only one, that which struck the
Hartford, did any harm,) the " defence fleet " of
Mitchell had yet to be encountered.   This Farragut
estimated at thirteen gun-boats, and two iron-clads, but
the truth was considerably within this.   The Louisiana
was but a motionless raft, so moored that she could
hardly bring her bow-guns to bear, and fired (it was
said by the garrison) but twelve shots.   The eight gun-
boats had been but poorly fitted, and some of them

mounted but a single large gun, while in weight they were no match even for the enemy's smallest vessels. The action, therefore, was of very brief duration, although gallantly undertaken by the Confederates. Four of their boats had been fitted with iron plates over their bows with the intention of using them as rams, and two of these, the Governor Moore and Quitman, came immediately into collision with the Varuna, which had in the mêlée with the forts got ahead of the rest of the Federal fleet. She was in chase of an unarmed steamer on board of which was General Lovell himself (who had arrived from New Orleans on a visit of inspection just as the firing commenced), when the Governor Moore attacked her boldly, firing a bow-gun which disabled thirteen of the Varuna's hands, and charging her afterwards on the starboard side. The Federals, however, succeeded in bringing an 8-inch gun to bear on the assailant, and disabling her completely in a few minutes; but the Quitman, which had approached the Varuna on the port side at the same time, now butted at her twice, at the second collision driving in her side. In doing this, however, she swung round, and the Federals, before their vessel sank, sent five of their 8-inch shells into their new enemy, and had the satisfaction of seeing her in flames. Of the rest of the " defence fleet " the Defiance was the only one saved under the guns of the fort at daybreak, the others having either been sunk, burnt, or driven ashore, disabled by the overwhelming batteries which the frigates had opened on them. These last had been attacked indeed by the Manasses with a boldness worthy of better success; but her feeble power and small tonnage were found perfectly unavailing to injure the ships through the chain-armor so judiciously prepared. Her encounter with the flag-ship Hartford has been already mentioned. Passing on while the latter was on fire, she charged the Brooklyn full on the starboard gangway, but with little effect, beyond breaking some of the links of the chain and driving in three planks above water line. Wedged in between her huge antagonist and the shore, the ram found herself unable to get up speed for a fresh charge, and was glad to drop down stream. She then crossed over to attack the Mississippi, and struck her with a very partial effect, inflicting injuries similar to those of the Brooklyn, and then passing down to the forts, where she lay for a short while.

The gray of early daylight now succeeded to the flashes of the hostile guns which had lighted up the scene ; and Farragut discovering the completeness of his victory, signalled to discontinue action. His fleet had begun to form and steam slowly upwards when the indomitable little ram was seen singly in pursuit, and preparing to renew her assaults. The admiral at once signalled the Mississippi to turn and attack her ; and Captain Smith, aided by the gun-boats Pinola and Kineo, charged her at once. Captain Warly (who, from her first construction, had commanded the ram), seeing the huge bows of the frigate coming straight towards him, steered to avoid the direct shock, and ran his vessel aground, exposing her to the full broadsides of the enemy. From this helpless position he escaped with his crew to the shore, and the once famous Manasses was fired by the boats of the Mississippi, which had been ordered off to board her. This was the last episode of the battle ; for Farragut, leaving behind him the shattered forts and the relics of the enemy's flotilla, went upward on his path of conquest. Captain Bailey, still leading in the Cayuga, soon came in sight of a small camp of sharp-shooters on the right bank, who, finding their position and line of retreat along the levee under command of the gun-boats, surrendered at once. Near this point known as the Quarantine, the river is approached by the creek before mentioned, as turning (for shallow boats) the forts and barricade. The flag-officer now made use of it to communicate with Porter and General Butler, and leaving two gun-boats to protect the latter's advance from the enemy still remaining at the forts, proceeded on with the rest of the fleet. The farther progress of the Federals occupied all that day and the early part of the twenty-fifth, "owing to the slowness of some of the vessels, and want of knowledge of the river;" but New Orleans was finally approached at ten A. M. on the twenty-sixth. Then came a ten minutes' contest with the inner works, armed, as we know, with but a dozen 32-pounders. The rest of the story of the conquest; the public thanksgiving ordered by the Admiral on board his victorious fleet; the fierce heart-burnings of the proud city, which lay helpless under his guns; the unjust obloquy thrown on General Lovell by the Confederates for not ensuring its destruction by a useless resistance with his petty garrison of 3,000 men; these things, and, above all, the humiliation which followed on Butler's taking possession, are well known. We pass them, therefore, by; citing merely the following paragraph of Farragut's letter, which tells the final history of the forces of Duncan and Mitchell, and observing that the surrender of the former was compelled by the violent insubordination of the same volunteer gunners who had obeyed him with cheerful endurance until their retreat was cut off:

"On the evening of the twenty-ninth, Captain Bailey arrived from below, with the gratifying intelligence that the forts had surrendered to Commander Porter, and had delivered up all public property, and were being paroled ; and that the navy had been made to surrender unconditionally, as they had conducted themselves with bad faith, burning and sinking their vessels while a flag of truce was flying and the forts negotiating for their surrender, and the Louisiana, their great iron-clad battery, being blown up alongside of the vessel where they were negotiating ; hence their officers were not paroled, but sent home to be treated according to the judgment of the government."

With the Louisiana the Confederates had lost their iron-clad frigate Mississippi, the most important naval structure they had undertaken, which was lying unfinished at a wharf near the city, and was burnt on the approach of Farragut, whose victory was thus as complete as any officer commanding afloat could have desired over a combined land and sea force. The garrison of Lovell, and all its stores, should perhaps have been added to the prize ; but the Federals were, strangely enough, not aware that a single ship anchored ten miles above the city would, at the then height of the river, have completely commanded the only exit, which through their ignorance was left open for several days. At the least, however, the success was almost beyond price to the Union Government from its moral importance on both sides of the Atlantic. As to the material advantage won, it may be best judged of by the statement of the well-known Confederate writer Mr. Pollard :—

" The extent of the disaster was not to be disguised. It was a heavy blow to the Confederacy. It annihilated us in Louisiana ; separated us from Texas and Arkansas ; diminished our resources and supplies by the loss of one of the greatest grain and cattle countries within the limits of the Confederacy ; gave to the enemy the Mississippi river, with all its means of navigation, for a base of operations ; and finally led, by plain and irresistible conclusion, to our virtual abandonment of its great and fruitful valley."

" Treachery," was the cry raised by the indignant South at the loss of its commercial capital : and although such a charge against the Confederate commanders bears no inquiry, the fall of New Orleans and its consequences must, as has been shown, be held due in part to the improvident delays and discordant counsels of the defenders, as well as to the want of appreciation in their chosen government of the greatness of the danger which threatened the Confederacy at this vital point. Allowing fully for all these, the highest credit must yet be given to the judgment which planned and the vigor which executed this successful stroke. If the language of Mr. Welles seems a little exaggerated when he says, " It was regarded everywhere, both at home and abroad, as the grandest achievement of the war," no less is it certain that, in calling the capture of New Orleans " one of the most remarkable triumphs in the whole history of naval operations," he is fully justified, both by the daring with which unknown dangers were faced and the vast importance of the victory gained.

The success of Farragut was marred, as has been seen, by the loss of only a single gun-boat ; and comment on the battle won by so hastily formed a fleet would be incomplete indeed if it omitted special notice of the fact that the Varuna *was the only one* of Farragut's gun-boats "converted," from the merchant service, instead of being built expressly for the rougher business of the navy.

"Here let me pause" [says Lieutenant Swasey, in a very clear report of the disaster] "while we reflect upon the unadaptedness of a merchant-built vessel for war purposes, particularly such as the Varuna was called to take part in. Had it been built with that strength which all the other vessels possessed, and the need of which becomes more apparent to the mind of the naval officer each day, we would yet be afloat off the city of New Orleans. Such vessels may perhaps do for the ordinary duties of a blockade, and I think it is yet a question whether they will or not ; but certainly they are not fit to trust lives and property on to engage works of the strongest magnitude."

New Orleans once secured and handed over to General Butler, Farragut pushed up the Mississippi, and in the course of the next two months the Union flag was hoisted at Baton Rouge, Natchez, and every town of importance as high as Vicksburg. This city, strong by its natural position on high bluffs sloping gently landward, and already partly converted into a fortress by intrenchments heavily armed, was now (since the surrender of Memphis on the sixth of June) the only point of importance held by the Confederates on the banks of the great river. It at once, therefore, assumed an importance well warranted by its later history. Summoned on the eighteenth of May to evacuate the place, General. M. L. Smith, who held it, gave a decided refusal ; and Farragut found it necessary to await once more the. arrival of Porter's flotilla, which was not brought up and reported ready until the twenty-seventh of June. On the twenty-eighth a general attack took place, Farragut succeeding in taking two of his three frigates and six gun-boats above the batteries, but producing no effect on the defences. " The enemy leave their guns for the moment," says his hasty report, " but return to them as soon as we have passed, and rake us." About fifty men were killed and wounded on board, and the Brooklyn frigate, with two gun-boats, forced to retreat below the place.

The bombardment continued at intervals, pending an application to General Halleck at Corinth for a corps of his army to aid the fleet, and the result of an experiment (the first of three) made to cut a ship canal through the isthmus opposite Vicksburg, and leave the Federal ships an independent passage. On the fifteenth of July their possession of the river was suddenly challenged by a large ram, the Arkansas, which the Confederates had been fitting on the Yazoo, a considerable stream entering the Mississippi just above Vicksburg. This new enemy was built, in imitation of those destroyed at New Orleans, with a screw-propeller, and iron-clad sides sloping inwards ; and, besides the means of offence offered by her sharp prow, she mounted nine guns. Her plating, however, proved to be weak, and her machinery very defective. Uneasy at the reports of her, Farragut had sent a small river-steamer, the Tyler, to explore the Yazoo, and this probably brought her down incomplete ; for she appeared suddenly, on the evening of the fifteenth, coming into the Mississippi, apparently in chase of the Tyler, and forthwith ran down to take shelter under

the guns of Vicksburg. In passing she received and
returned the broadsides of Farragut's whole squadron ;
and several of the heavier shot crashed through her
armor, tearing up her unplated deck, damaging her
fittings, and killing and wounding some of the crew.
But this was not fully known to the Federals, and her
escape for the time spread alarm as far as the garrison
of Butler at New Orleans. Her history, however, need
not be pursued at length. On her first leaving her
shelter to co-operate with a Confederate land force in
the attack (made August fifteenth) on Bâton Rouge,
her engines broke hopelessly down when yet five miles
from the place, and, drifting to the shore end on, she
fell an easy prey to the shells of the Essex, a large
iron-plated river-boat, whose commander had taken
charge of the Lower Mississippi on the departure of
Farragut. The latter officer, in compliance with orders
from Mr. Welles, had abandoned his contest with the
Vicksburg works on the twentieth of July, and made
down stream for New Orleans, whence he proceeded
with his squadron to carry on operations along the
coast of Texas, where the chief posts were (for the
time) recovered to the Union by his detachments in
the course of a few weeks. " All we want," he wrote
on the fifteenth of October, " is a few soldiers to hold
the places, and we will soon have the whole coast. It
is a more effectual blockade to have the vessels inside
instead of outside." In this simple remark lies the
key to the constantly increasing success of the Unionists in restricting their enemy's trade, a success which
was finally complete when Wilmington fell to Admiral
Porter's and General Terry's combined forces two years
later in the war.

Second only in importance to the exploits of Farragut's fleet during this remarkable year, were the services rendered on the rivers by the squadrons of the Mississippi and Tennessee. Flag-officer Foote (raised to rear-admiral's rank soon afterwards with Farragut) directed their operations with extraordinary activity until disabled by the effects of a wound in May. They were continued for the next four months under Captain Davis, who had succeeded to the temporary charge. In October, however, a new flag-officer appeared in the person of Porter, whose services as lieutenant and commander we have already noticed. The constant approval of Farragut, Bailey, and all with whom he served, had fully justified the early selection of this officer at the opening of the war for high charge by the President; and the latter, proud of so fortunate a choice, took occasion now to advance him *per saltum* to the rank of acting rear-admiral, and to the command left vacant by Foote. Much of the uniform though slow success of the Federal armies in the central states depended henceforth on the activity and energy by which Porter showed himself worthy of his unexampled promotion. But the story of his deeds in that quarter, of Foote's, and of Farragut's, when he appeared a second time in the Mississippi to co-operate in the fall of Vicksburg, forms so essential a part of the campaigns of General Grant, that we prefer to leave it to those writers who have made the progress of the Federal armies in the West their special theme.

The year 1862 and its naval operations have an interest which to many may seem even higher than that which belongs to the subjects we have hitherto treated. The world-famous battle of the Monitor and Merrimack

on April ninth first opened the way to that practical solution of the proper form of iron-clad steamers for special service which no government has attained to as
rapidly as that of the United States. It is as well to
be fully understood on this matter; and the report of
Mr. Welles sets forth in the clearest light the importance of the Monitor's victory, the prescience shown
by his practical adviser, Captain Fox, at the outset of
the war, and the conditions aimed at in the construction of the original vessels built on the turret principle. The details of the battle; the sudden appearance
in Hampton Roads of the Merrimack, heavily plated
with layers of iron, fitted as a ram, and well armed;
her attack and easy destruction of two large wooden
ships of war; the dangerous situation of the blockading steam-frigates, unfitted to cope with and unable to
escape from their antagonist, from whom they were
only saved the first day by her dread of the shallows;
the unlooked-for arrival (in the middle of that anxious
night) of the Monitor, hurried from New York by Captain Fox's exertions to meet and foil the long-threat-
ened design of the Confederates: all these particulars
have been so often and so fully given to the world,
that we forbear to repeat them. At noon next day,
the Merrimack abandoned her attack and retreated to
Norfolk, leaving the honors of her discomfiture to her
diminutive but invulnerable foe.

"Thus terminated" [writes Mr. Welles somewhat grand-
iloquently] "the most remarkable naval combat of modern
times, perhaps of any age. The fiercest and most formidable
naval assault upon the power of the Union which has ever
been made by the insurgents was heroically repelled, and a
new era was opened in the history of maritime warfare."

The defeat and capture by two other Monitors of the Confederate iron-clad Atlanta, prepared with great toil at Savannah, and supposed impregnable until tested on her first essay in June 1863 by the rude shock of 15-inch shells from the new Dahlgren guns, put an end to the last Southern hopes of raising the blockade. Yet the land defences of the other Atlantic ports still defied the navy of the Union. It seemed as though it needed the presence of Farragut or Porter to overcome the prestige of shore batteries. Admiral Dupont, beaten off from the capital of South Carolina, was superseded for declaring that "to renew the attack would be attended with disastrous results, involving the loss of the coast." His views of the strength of Charleston were fully justified by the conduct of his successor. Dahlgren did not repeat the attempt, and his fleet played but a secondary part in the siege conducted by General Gillmore; nor was it until the latter had captured Morris Island that the blockade was made effective by vessels placed in the smooth water near it, and the commerce of the city ceased. Yet so formidable did Fort Sumter, even in its ruins, appear, that so late as the following summer a fresh attempt to force the Monitors between it and Fort Moultrie was discussed and deliberately rejected by the Admiral and his captains assembled in council of war.

The services of Farragut during the year 1863, including his forcing a passage at tremendous risk and loss past Port Hudson, the new Confederate fortress on the Mississippi, and his subsequent co-operation in the all-important conquest of Vicksburg, though of themselves gallant and memorable achievements, are yet, as before mentioned, of a secondary nature, being bound up with the history of Grant's armies, with which Porter also acted throughout the year.

The spring of 1864, however, found the former admiral returning from a brief sick leave, and preparing for a new enterprise, more perilous in appearance than the attack on New Orleans, where well-won success had first raised him to fame. Mobile Bay was one of the few refuges remaining to the blockade-runners at this period of the war. The main entrance to it was guarded by Fort Morgan, a bastioned work of great strength armed with 10-inch hollow shot and rifled 32-pounder guns. The channel was narrow at this part, must be entered by daylight, and was thickly beset by such torpedoes as that which had recently, in spite of Dahlgren's precautions, proved fatal to the steam sloop Housatonic at Charleston, and placed the Ironsides herself in danger. Yet more to be dreaded than fort or torpedo was the ram Tennessee, commanded by Admiral Buchanan, whose courage and ability were well-known to Farragut, and of strength and armament beyond any of those which the Confederates had launched. Her description, given with exactness by deserters, spoke of her as built upon the same principles as the Atlanta, but with the casemate large enough to carry six guns, and plated all over with three layers of two-inch iron, by which additional strength the Confederates hoped to save her from the fate of her model. Her speed was slow, and Farragut declared on his arrival that he would not hesitate to encounter her with his larger wooden ships, but for the fear of her taking refuge in such shallow water as they could not enter. " Wooden vessels," he added, " can do nothing with these iron-clads unless by getting within one hundred or two hundred yards, so as to ram them or pour in a broadside."

Four Monitors being at length supplied him in July, he prepared to test the strength of his enemies without delay, the latter being reported to be striving hard to add other iron-clads to the Tennessee, which alone proved ready for action. She was aided by three wooden gun-boats only, when the Federal fleet entered the channel on August fifth, in great strength, but with much uncertainty as to the issue of the attack. The seven frigates and steam sloops which carried the principal batteries were not only protected by chains stopped up and down, but were lashed each to a gun-boat on the port side, in order that if crippled in the narrow channel they might be towed out of range of Fort Morgan, which was on the starboard hand. The Monitors formed a single line between it and the ships, engaging the work and absorbing its fire as far as possible. Thus covered, the wooden vessels in their double column forced their way up (the admiral most gallantly taking the lead when the first ship, the Brooklyn, hesitated at the sudden appearance of a line of buoys), and found themselves in half an hour above the forts, on which their starboard broadsides had poured such a continuous fire of grape, the missile specially chosen beforehand by Farragut, as the gunners could hardly endure. Not one ship was disabled, and but a hundred of their crews killed and wounded. But the Tecumseh, which led the Monitors, was struck in sight of all by a torpedo, and went down with her crew. Her fate did not prevent her comrades from gallantly carrying out the allotted task; and when the Tennessee sailed from a side channel higher up to as-sail the wooden squadron, the Monitors strove to take share in the general assault Farragut directed to be made on her. He had prepared for this bold movement of Buchanan's by providing false bows of iron to the frigates to charge the ram more effectually as soon as she drew near; and having already cast loose from their respective consorts, they steamed unhesitatingly to meet her. Then began a contest of a completely new order in naval tactics, and in which the ram never as it proved, had a chance of success. Some of her enemies crowded around her sufficiently to impede her motion, while the larger steamers strove to run her down in turn. Steering badly, slow in movement, and close pressed on each side, the Tennessee received in succession the charges of three of her assailants without perceptible damage, " the only effect being to give her a heavy list," and continued to ply her guns for near an hour. The flagship Hartford, after charging under the personal direction of the Admiral (who stood lashed in his main-top), poured a broadside of 9-inch shot at her casemates at a distance of barely ten feet. Two of the Monitors fired their 15-inch guns steadily at her whenever an opening was made; and though one only of their shots damaged the plating of the casemate, another destroyed her steering chains, and her chimney was carried away. The decisive injuries, however, were inflicted by successive damages to the shutters of her gun-ports; and three of these being jammed or made useless by the concentrated fire of the frigates, her reply slackened, and presently a shell entering through one wounded Buchanan dangerously, and caused her immediate surrender. The fall of the forts soon followed, and Mobile, though still itself pro-

12

tected by a shallow bar above, became harmless against the Union: while the victor, whose heroic conduct had won him the personal adoration of his fleet, stood confessed the first seaman of the age. This last achievement won from the grateful Congress the rank of Vice-Admiral, created for Farragut under a special act; a just reward, which placed him on an equal footing with Grant, now raised to be Lieutenant-General of the Union army.

Small as has been the success of the Confederates with their rams, the last brilliant feat of their arms in the war, the capture by Hoke in the spring of 1864 of the forts so long held by the Union forces on Albemarle Sound, was due in great part to the aid of a small vessel of this description, which attacked and drove off the covering gun-boats, sinking the boldest of them with a blow of her prow. This first feat of the Albemarle proved, however, to be her last. In the following October she perished by what may beyond question be called the most daring action of the war, the attack on her at night by a steam-launch carrying a torpedo at the bow. Of the gallant volunteers who undertook this work, two only were saved death or capture, the boat being sunk by the effect of their own engine: but one of these was the young commander, Lieutenant Cushing, already four times thanked for conduct before the enemy, whose new exploit might fairly rank with the boldest deeds of Nelson or Dundonald in their youth. His escape forms an episode of the war, so romantic in itself and so well told by the hero, that we prefer transcribing from his simple narrative:

"A dense mass of water rushed in from the torpedo, filling the launch and completely disabling her. The enemy then continued his fire at fifteen feet range, and demanded our surrender, which I twice refused, ordering the men to save themselves, and removing my own coat and shoes Springing into the river, I swam, with others, into the middle of the stream, the rebels failing to hit us. The most of our party were captured, some drowned, and only one escaped besides myself, and he in a different direction. Acting Mas-ter's Mate Woodman, of the Commodore Hull, I met in the water half a mile below the town, and assisted him as best I could, but failed to get him ashore.

"Completely exhausted, I managed to reach the shore, but was too weak to crawl out of the water until just at day-light, when I managed to creep into the swamp, close to the fort. While hiding a few feet from the path, two of the Al-bemarle's officers passed, and I judged from their conversa-tion that the ship was destroyed. Some hours' travelling in the swamp served to bring me out well below the town, when I sent a negro in to gain information and found that the ram was truly sunk. Proceeding through another swamp, I came to a creek and captured a skiff belonging to a picket of the enemy, and with this, by eleven o'clock the next night, had made my way out and on board the Valley City."

No wonder that this feat procured Cushing not merely his step to commander in the volunteer service, but the special thanks of Mr. Welles under his own hand, with the offer from that statesman of a transfer to the regular navy upon the completion of the requi-site course of study.

The naval operations of the war, which began by Lieutenant Porter's relief of Pensacola with the single frigate available for Union service, in defiance of Bragg's guns, were fitly closed by Admiral Porter's capture of the defences of Wilmington, the last port of the Confederacy, with a fleet of overwhelming strength, before the very eyes of the same general. As nothing was here proved of the iron-clads save their general fitness to share in a steady bombardment of forts of inferior armament, and as we know from undoubted authority that the success of the Federals was assured as much by the fatal indecision of the commander opposed to them (who, though supplied with full means, made no effort to relieve his exhausted garrisons) as by the vast superiority of the fire of the fleet, we do not think it needful to comment on the details.

Long before this affair the efforts of the South by sea had been reduced to what appeared to all the world rather a mere form of revenge than any useful warfare. Failing utterly in the purpose of embroiling the North with any neutral nation, these doings left a seed of bitterness, such as needed much patience to stay from growing into evil fruit in the future. From the fall of Wilmington the advantages of blockade-runners and the mushroom growth of their trade became things of the past. For the rest of the war the Confederate flag only covered what was, after all (if we except the cruise of the iron-clad Stonewall), an ignoble piracy, legalized in default of provision made against it by jurists. The ex-Cabinet of Richmond, which sanctioned this system to the end of their rule, left as a legacy one of the most difficult problems on international duties ever offered for statesmen to solve. But we are more concerned here to point out the urgent necessity which will arise, in case of England's engaging in a war, for our commerce being more efficiently guarded at sea than by iron-clads of 5,000 tons, or first-rate wooden frigates. A class of swift corvettes, carrying two or three heavy guns, with engines so powerful as to enable them to overhaul any ordinary merchant steamers, will be absolutely indispensable, if our trade is to escape ruin in any future naval war while privateering is employed against it. At such a class, Mr. Welles and Captain Fox aimed when they ordered the Kearsage and her consorts; but in this particular service alone did their efforts wholly disappoint expectation. The Alabama, Sumter, and Florida (managed certainly with extraordinary skill under very difficult conditions) roamed unchecked over the ocean. At the close of 1864 the capture of 193 vessels, valued with their cargoes at 13½ millions of dollars, bore testimony to their activity, and to the danger to which, under the new conditions of naval warfare, an unprotected commercial marine is exposed. That these losses were not from expenditure being too narrow, but from the peculiar direction which it had taken under Mr. Welles, is abundantly shown by his report of that date. The navy which four years before had counted but 76 ships, in and out of commission, and of these about one-half sailing vessels, was now increased to a total of 671. Of this number no less than 71 were iron-clads of different classes, 37 of them of formidable strength and carrying heavy Dahlgren guns; and only 112 of the whole were without steam power, these being in fact used for transport purposes.

Whether the fleet thus enumerated was, as Americans openly declared, infinitely beyond any that Europe could at that time show in fighting power, is a question we do not here attempt to decide. Our space does not allow us to do more than indicate some of the more important questions connected with the discussion, and raised by even a cursory view of the performances of the Union navy during the war.

The first of these that naturally occurs is the subject of the exact value and use of monitors. It is clear from Mr. Welles's original report upon these vessels that it was not in England or France alone that official men mistrusted their ever being fitted for sea service. That they were at first much disliked by American naval officers, and were in fact easily disabled in action, the records of Dupont's unsuccessful attack on Charleston abundantly prove. On the other hand, it is certain that Mr. Welles and his adviser after this failure still approved of the construction of Monitors (the Puritan, Dictator, and Roanoke) built specially for sea service ; that the navigation of another large one around to the Pacific has been found by no means so dangerous as was anticipated ; that the crews of these vessels have not found them unhealthy ; and that the experience gained before Charleston has been wonderfully utilized for the improvement of the mechanism of the turret and ports, so that (as is alleged) the shots which then produced so much disabling effect might now be easily endured. The value of these assertions no one was more desirous to see practically tested than Captain Fox himself. Under the special sanction of Congress, he undertook after the war to bring across the Atlantic a large double-turreted vessel, the Miantonomah, for the conviction of the sceptical ship-designers of Europe ; but her being afterwards handed over to Russia for use in the Baltic, as though the return passage were too dangerous to attempt, naturally weakened the then rising belief in the efficacy of the Ericsson system.

Closely connected with this subject is that of the American system of heavy smooth-bore guns; for such as those which won the fight with the Atlantic, and far more, the new 20-inch, are evidently too weighty for any broadside vessel now in use. We know the objection which lies to their moderate charges and the consequent low velocity of their projectiles. On the other hand, it is clear that this may yet be overcome by even a slight improvement on the present Rodman method of casting on a cooled bore, or by the use of wrought iron; while even as they exist, their 450-pound and 990-pound balls, fired with only $\frac{1}{7}$th or $\frac{1}{9}$th charges, are missiles so powerful as none but the highest class of iron-clads could endure. But this subject with the comparison of the American model in power and in their boasted endurance with the huge rifled guns preferred in Europe, would carry us beyond our subject, and we therefore pass it by. For the same reason we do not enter on that part of the torpedo system of defence and assault, to the practical solution of which the American examples served, although dimly and incompletely, to point the way.

There is one deduction which might be made from a hasty survey of the naval annals of the war, against which we desire to give an earnest warning. Some will say—as some have already said—that the chief thing shown is the possibility of creating, from private resources during actual war, all that a great contest at sea may require, without that elaborate preparation and vast expenditure to which in this country we dedicate millions yearly in time of peace. The exam-

ple of the Great Republic and the precepts of the
successful statesmen who carried her safely to a
triumphant reunion prove, when studied conscientious-
ly, the very contrary. It cost them years of toil and
uncertainty and oceans of expenditure before the
naval predominance to which the North had full right
was completely asserted. No minister has ever more
loudly deprecated the relying too much on private
shipyards than Mr. Welles, to whose earnest and
repeated recommendation it is due that the Congress
was soon after the war engaged on the question of
determining the site of a grand depôt for the future
construction of American iron-clads. We in England,
if entering into a struggle for that supremacy of the
seas which involves the very life of our independent
existence, no less than the protection of a vast and
wide-spread commerce, must look to meeting not a raw
seceding province, but Powers who may be swift to
attack, and allow us brief space to prepare. A sufficient fleet must in such event be ready, not waiting the
chances of a hurried creation. Be then the shock
what it may, we doubt not it would be met by hearts
as brave, by heads as cool, and arms as skilful, as those
of the seamen whose exploits we have here briefly
traced. The jealousies of a day, we trust, will die,
while common blood and language will create new
ties: and Englishmen who desire this will not be slow
to recognize as worthy successors of our own great
naval chieftains those names which now fill with pride
the hearts of our kinsfolk on the other side of the
Atlantic.

A NORTHERN RAIDER IN THE CIVIL WAR.

[It needs some apology for introducing here this excerpt from a former work; and its being a detached episode, however striking, in the course of the American Civil War would not of itself be a justification. But the writer has observed that although the struggle has now passed into history, the tendency of our countrymen still often is to exalt isolated feats of arms done by the defeated party, while ignoring what may be called the romantic side of the war on the side of the North, where the same daring spirit in truth existed. Against that tendency the story of Dahlgren was long since written as a protest, and for the same reason it reappears here.]

THE fourth year of the Civil War opened with an attempt by General Butler to surprise the capital of the Confederacy, which was reported to be nearly destitute of a garrison. But after a slight skirmish on February seventh, Butler, finding his advance fully discovered and opposed, retired without further pursuing his project, which had been neither prepared with skill nor executed with vigor. The alarm within the oft-threatened city had been but slight, though there were indeed but few regular troops in its vicinity; nor did any one at this time consider it possible that the Southern capital should be seriously endangered by any expedition of the character of a raid. Yet a month had hardly gone by when its inhabitants were startled by an approach to their walls so daring in design, and by them believed so fell in purpose, that even in its failure it did more to rouse fierce passions and embitter strife than any incident the war had yet witnessed.

Colonel Dahlgren, the real author of the new project, was a man of character in itself so remarkable, and so typical of the deeper passions which stirred the North to its tremendous efforts for the reconquest of the Union, that he well deserves the study of the historian. Born of a good family, and wedded by prescription to the service of his country, in whose navy his father had long been distinguished; he was far from being of those who could view with indifference the lessening of her external power by the proposed separation of the Southern States. By many a thousand of her youth (and among them all there was none of purpose more earnest, or soul more romantic, than Ulric Dahlgren) the vision had been cherished of a mighty democratic power growing up to so fill the western hemisphere with its greatness as to overshadow the whole earth, and shed freedom over its nations. Such a feeling of belief in a country's destiny may be called lust of empire abroad, but it stands for patriotism at home ; and those who boast of England's greatness and "her dominion that the sun never sets on" would do well to examine themselves before they condemn the Young American. To one born and brought up in these convictions of the just future of the Union, its voluntary disruption by the South seemed such a crime as sacrilege could not outdo, and the perpetrators of the act the basest traitors that sword was ever lifted to punish. The very force of the religion which a pious mother had, through his earlier years, instilled into his heart, made him long, like the Puritans of our own revolution, to smite down those who opposed the political faith which to him seemed destined to spread justice and freedom and truth throughout the world. Burning with such thoughts as these, and having just attained to manhood at the out break of the civil war, he threw himself with all the ar- dor of youth and passion into the struggle against secession. Those writers who, content to judge from a superficial view, or led by their own sentiments wholly, have sought to trace the first cause of the uprising of North against South in a national hatred and loathing of slavery, have missed the real motive power which first called twenty millions of free people under arms, and gave to Abolition that growing strength which stern fanaticism wins when it allies its cause with revo- lution. This power it was, this yearning for their country's greatness, and no special love for the negro race, which moved Dahlgren and a thousand others less known than he to offer their lives freely for the unity of their country.

Of daring courage and noted horsemanship, he had soon become sensible of the deficiencies of the Union cavalry, and attempted, as early as the days of M'Clellan, to lead them to a better fame. The breaking up of Hooker's personal staff, of which he had formed one, on the supersession of that general in 1863, gave him his opportunity; and he applied for the command of a detachment of horse, with which he volunteered to harass the rear of the Confederates. Twenty dragoons only were granted him at first; but his almost imme- diate capture of an orderly, bringing dispatches to Lee from Richmond, brought him into notice, and after the battle of Gettysburg he moved, with 100 of the sixth New York Cavalry placed under his orders, to attack

the retreating trains and their escorts.   In this service,
and the series of skirmishes near Hagerstown, he effected as much real havoc as Kilpatrick or Gregg with their
whole divisions of horse; but on July sixth he was
badly wounded in the leg, in covering some of his
captures from a superior force.   Amputation proved
necessary, and his career for some time was closed by
the illness that followed ; but his name as a dashing
leader (added possibly to the great services of his
father to the Union) caused the President to console
him with a flattering letter from the War Secretary, en-
closing his brevet of colonel, bestowed without passing
through the usual grades.   Recovering by slow degrees,
and musing much, no doubt, upon the high career
which seemed open to him—who now held rank such
as Napoleon had not reached at the age of twenty-one
—he returned to the Army of the Potomac in its winter
quarters, when hard weather and enforced idleness
made the sufferings of the Northern prisoners at Richmond seem doubly near to all.   There were known
to be about 10,000 Federal soldiers there confined in
the Belle Isle prison on the James, while the garrison
of the city was but weak.   The prisoners crowded in
this island complained much of their treatment ; and
although receiving the same rations as were issued to
the Confederate soldiers, these were so scanty that
those who could not eke them out by private means
fared but ill compared to their well-supplied comrades
in the field.   It is not surprising that many plans were
canvassed for their release by surprise ; and that to
Dahlgren, whose feelings led him to believe the worst
of the Confederate Government, the enterprise however carried out, seemed the holiest of duties, as well

as a swift road to further honors. Forthwith an expedition was arranged, under the nominal conduct of General Kilpatrick, who felt the urgent need, after the autumn failures, of doing something to retrieve the reputation which was slipping from him. The more dangerous part of the design—and no forlorn hope was ever mustered for more perilous work—was undertaken by Dahlgren. This consisted in a proposed attempt to cross with a detached force to the south side of the James, and move on Richmond by that bank, where an enemy would naturally be but little expected, and near which the prison lay. Kilpatrick, with the main column, was to make a simultaneous demonstration against the works to the north of the city ; and it was hoped that, under cover of this, Dahlgren's men might break their way into the prisons and release the captives. Once free, it was even supposed that the number of these, and their desperation, might enable them to master the surprised capital, and perhaps hold it until Butler's forces, which were to advance at the same time up the peninsula, should come to their aid. It is significant of the determined character of the man, that the chief who was thus to guide his dragoons into the heart of a hostile city was still suffering from the debility of fever, and unable to move on foot without crutches.

On the night of February twenty-eighth, after a part of the Army of the Potomac had made a feint on Lee's flank, the expedition left Meade's lines for Ely's Ford, far beyond the Confederate left. It was composed originally of 3,800 cavalry, with three light guns, the whole being formed of selected detachments of well-mounted men of various regiments. Crossing the Rap-

idan unopposed, they pushed on through the wooded
district south of Chancellorsville, called the Wilderness
(soon to be the scene of a series of deadly struggles
enduring half the length of a European campaign), to
Spottsylvania Court-house, where Dahlgren, with 500
volunteers, left the main column on the twenty-ninth for
his separate march, which lay southward direct to the
James, which he hoped to gain in the vicinity of the
threatened city, and yet far enough from the works to
prevent his arrival being discovered.

Kilpatrick, continuing his south-eastward course,
struck the railroad to Richmond not far from the well-
known junction at Orange; and pausing only to do as
much damage to the line as was consistent with a
somewhat rapid march, rested for the night some miles
farther on, near the southern branch of the Pamunkey.
A detachment of 400 men was sent eastward before
daylight, with intent to destroy the railroad bridge
over the stream, but retreated on finding it protected
by a party of infantry; and the whole force was soon
on its way towards Richmond, now but twenty miles
distant, in the hope of finding its way into an unde-
fended capital. Early in the afternoon an outer line
of redoubts was reached and passed through without
resistance; but the advance had been made known by
the telegraph some hours before, and a heavy fire from
works within upon the cavalry of General Davies,
which supported the advanced guard, soon proved that
the movement was discovered and prepared for. Davies at once dismounted his men and deployed them
as skirmishers, after the fashion adopted by the Northern cavalry, and in days long past by the extinct dra-
goon of the European armies. But Kilpatrick, seeing

the redoubts before him to be strong and apparent'y
well manned (though there were in truth but a few
hundred troops, with some city militia within them),
and hearing nothing of Dahlgren's expected attack on
the other side, grew alarmed at his own position, and
drew his men off before dark, moving westward across
the Chickahominy to Mechanicsville. Here he en
camped for the night; but General Wade Hampton,
who arrived that evening at Richmond after a rapid
march with 400 Southern horse, learning the enemy's
position, resolved to attempt a surprise, which was so
far successful that he captured a hundred of their number, and broke up the encampment, forcing them to retreat down the river. In the morning however Kilpatrick discovered how small was the number of the pursuers, and his rear-guard under Davies drove them off
with ease. Passing thence, he was met at the close
of the day by the force from the peninsula under Butler, which had been intended to co-operate with him;
and which, by some unexplained misconception, had
moved just a day too late to be of any effectual assistance. Two days later the united column was joined
by the greater part of Dahlgren's command, coming
southward after circling round Richmond; but their
enterprise had yet more completely miscarried, and
their leader had paid for his share in it with his life.

He had parted from Kilpatrick, as before stated,
at Spottsylvania, and had reached Frederickshall, his
next point, early in the day. Having here destroyed
the railroad station with some stores, but missed a
park of artillery which he had hoped to capture, he
proceeded onward to the James. A negro fugitive of
the district had undertaken to conduct the party to

the desired ford not far from Richmond: but through
treachery or ignorance he missed his way, and at midnight the Federals, after much wandering, found themselves a day's march higher up the stream than the
point they sought. The wretched guide was sacrificed
on the spot to their fury, and the course of the river
followed down towards the city; but the latter was
now only attained on its guarded side; and that at
dark, twenty-four hours after Kilpatrick had retreated.
Driven off in a vain attempt to surprise the nearest
work, Dahlgren marched northward through the darkness, seeking for the present only to save his column,
which he strove to guide in person; but at dawn he
found himself with but a hundred dragoons following
him, the rest having wandered from him on the way at
some turning of the by-roads he pursued. That day
he crossed the Pamunkey and Mattapony rivers in
succession, inclining eastward in hopes to find some
road open towards York River. But the country was
now beset by armed parties of excited citizens and
militia in chase of the invaders; and in attempting to
continue his march in the dark, he fell into an ambush
at midnight, and was shot down with some of his men,
the rest surrendering. That his body was stripped
and plundered, and a ring cut from his hand, was but
natural under the circumstances, and no uncommon
fate in war: but the order found upon his person, directing his men "to exhort the released prisoners to
destroy and burn the hateful city, and not allow the
rebel leader Davis and his traitorous crew to escape,"
was made the pretext for such an act of savage retali-
ation as the war had not yet witnessed; the exposing
his corpse to the common gaze as that of a murderer

slain in the midst of his felon deed. His family denied
the authenticity of this document : but their charge
of forgery against the Richmond Government was
scarcely supported by evidence or probability, though
the local journals gave color to it, by their folly in
printing as if true whatever exaggeration added to the
original words in the excitement of the hour. However the exact truth may be, certain it is that the
attempt on her capital envenomed to the utmost the
feelings of the South : as the insult to the remains of
the gallant dead, and the virulent assault on his memory made subsequently in an official report of the
Confederate Secretary for War, served to enhance the
bitterness of the Unionists against the Seceded States.
Is it to be wondered at that a new generation is needed to reunite in heart the two sections, the hopes of
whose bravest youth led to such fierce purpose and
such bloody end as Ulric Dahlgren's ? What freedom,
what greatness, can close the wounds made among
the homes of the recovered Union by a thousand lives
and deaths like his ?

DE FEZENSAC'S RECOLLECTIONS OF THE GRAND ARMY.*

No subjects have created wider differences between critics than the military genius and system of Napoleon. To some few of those who have considered them, the admiration usually lavished upon them appears fulsome and indiscriminate. This section regards the French Emperor as nothing more than a bold and unscrupulous adventurer, seizing the reins of power by political intrigue, and then using his authority to collect and throw into the field unheard-of masses of men, to whose numbers and courage, opposed to feebler adversaries, his long train of imperial conquest was due. Such men balance Acre against Toulon, Aspern against Austerlitz, Leipsic and Waterloo against Friedland and Wagram; and confident in the fact that they find weaknesses and flaws in the object pressed on them as perfect, refuse to recognize any strength or brilliancy in it. A far larger class there is (we speak with all respect of one that has Thiers for its representative and Napier in its ranks) who err almost equally in the opposite direction. To these Napoleon, regarded simply as a general, appears faultless. His administrative arrangements only failed by lack of care in others;

---

* *Souvenirs Militaires de* 1804 *à* 1814. Par M. le Duc de Fezensac Général de Division.

his strategy never erred ; his tactics were to the last superior to those of his foes. Climate, diplomacy, the deficiencies of his lieutenants, the envy of his allies, even his own want of political judgment and moderation, may have caused his disasters; but they are never to be attributed to want of foresight in his arrangements for the field, or mistaken views of the military events around him. Let any evidence be rejected, and any supposition entertained, rather than believe that he was ever wanting to his army, or his army to its chief.

A third school of critics has of late arisen, who pursue a simpler and more truthful method, the only one worthy a sound writer of military history. This is to lay aside, as far as may be, all prepossession for or against the man, and look only at what the general did. Take nothing for granted in what, after all, are mere matters of evidence and fact. Accept no one-sided statement from any national historian who rejects what is distasteful in his authorities, and uses only what suits his own theory. Believe not that any man ever lived who, in so dark and uncertain a science as war, had the gift of infallibility. Gather carefully from actual witnesses, high and low, such original material as they offer for the construction of the narrative. This once being safely formed, judge critically and calmly what was the conduct of the chief actor; how far his insight, calmness, personal control over others, and right use of his means were concerned in the result. This plan is that which Clausewitz has pursued with the campaign of 1812, Cathcart with that of 1813, and Charras, with singular success, in throwing light on the great struggle of Waterloo.

The work of the latter has left but little that is new to be added as regards his special subject, and his untimely death alone prevented his repeating this literary triumph by carrying his researches further back. The fragment published posthumously of his intended "Guerre de 1813" shows the same industry and clearness which distinguished his former writings. Had he lived, we may believe he would have laid bare the inner details of the gigantic struggle in Germany with the same thoroughness which had placed him already at the head of all French writers who have treated of Napoleon's latest campaign.

For this high class of military history, which aims at truth, and seeks first to know what was done, before delivering judgment on the action, all genuine narratives of eyewitnesses have a peculiar value. Many such have already served to illustrate the history of Napoleon's wars ; but there has hitherto been wanting an account by some writer who had held every rank in the Grand Army from the private to the general, had intelligence enough to reason from its details up to its general action, and who could admire the genius of Napoleon, without in any way being identified with the system which he founded. The memoirs of no marshal, chamberlain, or grand equerry meet these conditions. They could be found only in a man who had rank independent of Imperialism, education outside the Lycée, and patriotism superior to party.

Such a man was the Duke de Fezensac, whose death, at a most venerable age, the third Napoleon noticed in a public letter addressed to his family. His "Military Recollections," will for ever occupy one of the highest places among the literature that illustrates

the Napoleonic era. That portion which bears upon
the campaign in Russia was published long ago, and
seems to have won its way but slowly to the notice it
merited ; for an interval of more than ten years elapsed
before the author was emboldened to offer to the world
the complete work. There needed not the apology of
his modest preface to make this acceptable. The personal details which abound in it do, as he truly says,
paint the very manners and spirit of the times. Let
us add that they paint the true features of the system
of war which the author observed from its midst with a
force and accuracy, which gives this unpretending volume a genuine historical value far above that of the
brilliant pages of " The Consulate and Empire," which
M. de Fezensac, like many other loyal Frenchmen, rates
higher than their worth. To tell plainly and without
exaggeration or concealment the truth with regard to
Napoleon's method of war; to show how great it was
on some fit occasions, how full of shortcomings it
proved when overstrained ; to trace the effect of its
deficiencies in the vain efforts of the great conqueror
to stem the European tide when it once turned full
against him ; to do all this with the spirit of a keen-
eyed observer, yet of an honest soldier of France : this
is no trifling task to have accomplished. Moreover, M.
de Fezensac has taken pains to throw his personal
memoirs into an historical form by adding here and
there outlines of the general course of events connected
with the war ; yet has carefully distinguished between
what he saw and what he only gives from report.
Where he differs broadly from the usual authorities as
to the actual working of Napoleon's army, he does so
in the most modest way, and gives good reason for his

own sounder opinion.   In short, the reader who visits
under his guidance the camp of Boulogne, follows him
thence through the brilliant strategy of 1805, 1806 and
1807, in Germany and Poland, passes on with him to
Napoleon's own brief personal command in Spain in
1808, and later, makes the disastrous campaigns of 1812
and 1813 in his company, will know more of what the
warriors of the Grand Army really were and did, at
these successive periods, than could be learnt by a lifelong study of popular French works on the subject.
M. de Fezensac does not indeed pretend to tell us what
went on in the German and Russian camps during
epochs so glorious and so fatal to the pride of France.
In this he shows no special ignorance, but much superior honesty to French historians of the vulgar class
who take no trouble to search any records but those
of their own nation, as well as to those who, like M.
Thiers, never use any records, save when they seem to
corroborate their own prepossessions.   The campaigns
above mentioned do not include all the service which
the author saw, but special circumstances prevented his
keeping personal notes of the gigantic struggle between
Napoleon and the Archduke Charles in 1809; and
although he witnessed the great events of Eckmühl,
Aspern, and Wagram, he modestly mentions his omission to record them, and dismisses them in a page.
Through the other portions of his narrative we now
purpose to follow him, not with the intent to rewrite
the story of well-known marches and battles, but to
show how much the popular histories which delight
the worshippers of Napoleon lack a reality to be found
in the observations of one single-hearted individual of
his million soldiers.

The book opens with the camp at Boulogne, where the author, then a youth of twenty, went to join his regiment. He was already too old for a military college; for his parents had long withheld their consent to his entering the army of one whom they, as members of the old French aristocracy, regarded as a low-born usurper. "Like all the young fellows," he first thought of the cavalry; but a friend of the family who commanded the 59th regiment of the line, persuaded him to enter under his tutelage into that arm —a step, he assures us, never afterwards repented of. In the capacity of a private soldier therefore, he first became acquainted with the vast machine by which Napoleon's busy brain was preparing to intimidate England in the first place, and, when this failed, to strike Germany prostrate. "If I consulted only my attachment to you and to your family," said his friend Colonel Lacuée, " I would make you my secretary and keep you personally about me. But for the sake of your own career, you must learn to know those whom you will one day command; and the way to do that is to live among them."· "*By doing this,*" he added, "*you will learn to know their virtues ; otherwise you will only know their vices.*" The author italicises these words, as implying that he considers them the key to the whole relation between officers and men. Such was, at any rate, the creed of the republican soldiers who furnished Napoleon with his materials, of whom Colonel Lacuée was a fair specimen. A favorite at one time with the First Consul, he had shown, in common with a vast number of the higher officers, a sympathy with Moreau which the new ruler of France could not brook. One must look deeply into the history of the time to understand how widely this feeling of sympathy extended through the ranks of the army, and how bitterly Napoleon resented all manifestations of military respect and of personal regard towards the great general who more than rivalled him (according to the candid statement of his own favorite, Dumas) in its affections.

Lecourbe in exile, Dessoles pining in neglect, Richepanse sacrificed in an obscure expedition in the tropics, testified to the animosity with which he pursued the more distinguished members of Moreau's staff. Lesser men felt it only in a less degree ; and Colonel Lacuée, being among those who had shown an interest in the fallen general, was dismissed from snug employment on the staff, and ordered to take the command of a regiment which Napoleon told him as he left, was one of the worst in the army, and which from its ill appearance had gained the soubriquet of the Royal Tatters (*Royal Décousu*). The 59th had had for their last colonel an officer who did not scruple to embezzle from the regimental chest ; a fact the author mentions as though it were no extraordinary occurrence in that *ci-devant* republican army, of whose severe purity so much has been written. Lacuée was at least a gentleman, though ignorant it seems of the duties assigned to him as the head of a regiment. He had contented himself with acquiring the power of manœuvring his battalions and enforcing discipline, leaving in the hands of the quartermaster the more vulgar care of improving the ill condition of the clothing which had made the regiment so notorious. This good colonel, with his aristocratic habits and republican theories, was of a disposition much superior to the troops he commanded, and his rough subordinates hardly understood though they learnt to like him. M. de Fezensac has traced the lineaments of his character with a loving hand, and leaves them as clearly drawn in these opening pages as though he sought to tempt some future novelist with a ready-made hero.

Handed over by Lacuée after a few days' holiday to the captain of his company, the young aspirant began his new life by laughing at the eccentricity of his uniform, a compromise between the stiff republican garb of the expiring age and the imperial extravagance of the future. From a full description of this dress, with its three-cornered hat, black gaiters, and long powdered hair, we pass to an admirable account of the life of the camp at Boulogne, as seen in the winter of 1804–5. Here he at once digresses, to show us how different practice is from theory, even in the most elaborately formed army. We hear of various regulations which, as in certain other services, exist only to be broken. Of these infractions the most striking in an army constituted as the French up to that time had been, relates to the sergeants, those important links between the officers and their men. The rule was that they should live among the latter; the practice was that they had a separate hut to themselves in each company. " This arrangement," says the author, " had its good and its bad side. The sergeants being separated from the soldiers, could not exercise so active a watch over them. During my apprenticeship as private and corporal, I saw many things escape them. But they were the more respected for being the less often seen, and I believe, to speak decidedly, that this is the more important matter." Theorists who would construct an ideal British army, upon the model of some French or Prussian Book of Regulations may here learn how little mere written rules signify when they conflict with the spirit and habits of the service. Those who have judged the separation enforced in our own army between non-commissioned officers and men to be the mere product of aristocratic prejudice may find their lesson and reproof in this disinterested opinion.

Placed as M. de Fezensac was for the next few weeks in the position of a private soldier, it is interesting to see how far a young man of fortune seeking promotion through the ranks of Napoleon's army, had to submit to real hardships, and in what his lot differed from that of the ordinary recruit. In some matters, it seems from the details afforded, the French gentleman private was destitute of the special advantages of a Prussian *advantageur*, or an Austrian regimental cadet. He ate, sat, and slept with the other privates, could occupy no separate lodging, employ no recognized servant from among his comrades, nor escape being nominally detailed by his sergeant for the most repulsive duties of the camp. On the other hand, when closely looked at, his service as a private was little different from that required of the young German noble, except in the matter of his enforced companionship with those of a different class of life. His comrades paid him to the full the respect due to one who, in their soldier's phrase, " had a louis a day to eat of his own," and could give a dinner to forty of them at a time. For a few sous any of them would take his turn at sweeping and cooking. The hairdresser of the company connived at his avoiding the growth of the obnoxious and antiquated cue. The corporal who placed him on the only turn of sentinel duty that was ever allotted him, connived at his quitting his post before the proper time for relief. In fine, if brought further from the level of his personal rank for a few weeks, he had the advantage over the volunteer private of other armies in the quick promotion which rewarded his endurance. Having only left Paris in the month of September, he gained his first step of corporal on the eighteenth of October. Of this he frankly tells us he proved hardly worthy, receiving various reprimands for his irregularity in his new duties, to which it was possibly owing that he was allowed to continue in this rank until midwinter, finding his life, still spent among the men, at times intolerably irksome. Ordered to go in January with a guard detachment on board one of the gun-boats which Nelson kept imprisoned in Etaples harbour, he murmured openly to his friend the colonel, and finding no comfort in the cool reply, "You must learn to be put out," went off in sad humor with his new duty, which was to last a month. Lacuée was, however, merely testing his patience by this service, and on the fifth day he was summoned back to camp on promotion to the rank of sergeant, a step which raised him out of immediate contact with the rough privates with whom he had now been for four months herded. None of these, it would seem, showed any jealousy of the elevation of their aristocratic messmate, for birth, wealth, and education had become as sure passports to promotion in the army of the Consulate as in that of the most ancient monarchies. Two months had not passed over the new sergeant's head when he was brought before the colonel, charged with a dereliction of duty; but his supposed offence being shown to be but an ordinary practice, though irregular enough, the color-sergeant (or company sergeant-major, according to French grade) was broken for not reporting it, and the cause of his disgrace promoted in his stead. At six months' service young de Fezensac thus found himself in a position which gave him practical charge of a company, and which was, as it still is, the recognized stepping-stone of the deserving soldier to a commission.

The sergeant-major of that day differed little from the subaltern in social condition. The officers had all passed through this rank, and all who then held it were entitled, if qualified, to look for the epaulette of a sub-lieutenant in their turn. Many, however, were not thus classed, for a certain degree of education and some small means were in practice necessary for further promotion. As this last qualification sounds like an anomaly in a service where merit has been commonly supposed the sole road to advancement, the autobiographer has taken pains to explain his mention of it. It seems that in those days the captain of the company left to his sergeant-major the charge of the accounts, subject only to a quarterly settlement; and as the pay of the latter was actually insufficient for his wants, it followed that, if he could not eke it out by other means, he usually had recourse to petty dishonesty. Where this was exercised only against the government, it was very lightly regarded. The captains only said they should be glad to know of the little resources which their accountants managed to get hold of. The soldiers were well aware when their pay for days of absence or sickness was charged to the public, and had their professional jest ready; "The sergeant-major's arithmetic—put down nought and carry nine:" but this indulgence by no means extended to the plunder of individuals; and a case of unfair stoppages from a conscript would ruin the author of it, if detected. Always ready, as M. de Fezensac more than once tells us, to suspect every one of cheating them, from their Minister of War down to the sergeant-major, they watched narrowly to see that no advantage was taken by him of themselves; and moreover they expected for their connivance at his other peculations a forbearance for their own petty impositions on the hucksters who served the camp, and their forays on the neighboring forest for firewood. Napoleon, the author tells us, issued in vain the most severe orders against this last abuse. Such was his characteristic way of dealing with the like difficulties, and it answered to some extent, but only when the army was directly under his own eye: an explanation which helps us to understand how in after years the bonds of discipline snapped under the test of service in Russia. His successors have taken the more rational mode of paying the soldier fairly, and, as M. de Fezensac remarks, have a right to be more strict.

Very coarse and bare was the soldier's life here depicted, with its mixed good-humor, grumbling, and dishonesty; its wearisome evenings, spent in bed for lack of candle; its cold dark mornings, enlivened only by the chance of a glass of brandy and a roll. Yet the reader looks naturally to the camp of Boulogne with respect, as the nursery of the Grand Army which carried its eagles from Madrid to Moscow. Surely we may assume that the professional aspect of the gather

ing was always kept in sight, and that the military
spirit was here developed at least as high as a time of
peace can allow.   Those writers can hardly be wrong
who, in unvarying chorus, ascribe the success which
followed, to the vast pains with which Napoleon's staff
used the camp to improve the tactics bequeathed by
the revolutionary wars.   Indeed that the weapon was
here actually forged before which no other army could
stand, has been asserted in plain terms by French
writers of authority, from Marshal Marmont down to
Baron Ambert.   We ourselves were led formerly to
adopt the same language, being misled by authors of
such critical pretension as Trochu and the Duc
d'Aumale.   But M. de Fezensac's personal experience
caused him to take a totally different view of the
Boulogne army; and as he dissents in the broadest
terms from the class of writers just cited, we quote his
evidence entire, that the reader may judge what the
general assertions are worth which have long deceived
the world :

"The camp of Boulogne, of which that of Montreuil
[held by Ney's corps, in which the author served] formed the
left, has left deep memories in our history of that age.   The
advantage of gathering troops into camps of instruction is
known to all military men.   To that of Boulogne is attributed the honor of the successes which we gained in the following campaigns, and we are supposed to have been always
occupied with manœuvres, military works, and exercises of
all kinds.   I shall astonish my readers therefore, by telling
them how very little, at the camp of Montreuil, our chiefs
occupied themselves with instructing us, how ill they profited
by this precious time.   Marshal Ney commanded two grand
field-days in the autumn of 1804, and as many in 1805 ; I

was present at them as a private soldier first, and then as officer. There was a general upsetting and excessive fatigue. We started before daybreak after taking our soup, and did not get back till night, having had nothing during the day but a dram of brandy. General Malher, who succeeded Partonneaux in command of the division, hardly brought it together three times, and handled it then very badly. Brigade drill there was none, for the brigadier did not even come to the camp. Each colonel taught his regiment in his own fashion. There was some slight theoretical instruction and drilling of conscripts, and in the spring the non-commissioned officers had all to go through their drill afresh, beginning with 'the extension motions'. . . . This instruction was carried up to battalion-drill, but the regiment was rarely manœuvred in a line. There were a few marchings out for a short single day's stage, and some target practice without any method ; but no skirmishing, nor bayonet, nor fencing exercise. No field-works were thrown up, nor was any officer employed in any kind of instruction. Regimental schools might easily have been established, but no one had thought of them in those days. It was better to get drunk when one had money, and to sleep when one had none. The other regiments did no more. . . . At the beginning of March each company was allotted a small garden to cultivate ; but at this the men grumbled, such charms had idleness. Soldiers are like children ; it is necessary to do them good against their own will.

What then were all these young men about at times when not under exercise, nor cleaning their arms and persons ? Nothing at all, I may safely say. To sleep a part of the day after having slept all night, to sing songs, tell stories, quarrel sometimes without knowing why, and read such few bad books as were procurable. Such were the daily lives of sergeants as well as men, of officers as well as sergeants.

Yet, on the whole, their morals were not so bad as might be supposed."

If any of the recruits of that day had been brought up in those religious habits which the Revolution had, for the most part, banished from France, they found little encouragement for their devotions at the camp. No mass was celebrated for Napoleon's troops, except when they chanced to be quartered in towns. " I do not want a bigoted army," M. de Fezensac quotes as a saying of the Emperor, who had abundant cause to be satisfied on this head. He adds his own opinion, that the moral tone of the whole service was lowered by this omission of customary religious observance.

In thus exposing the waste by Napoleon and his lieutenants of their opportunities at Boulogne, the critic is careful to point out how far this great assemblage was practically useful. Two chief advantages were obtained by it. In the first place, the rough life of the camp, devoid alike of comfort or diversion, prepared all ranks for those inconveniences of the campaign which they were soon to taste to the full. They often found the night bivouac of the next winter more endurable than the huts of Boulogne. A more important use of their training lay in the gain to all ranks from their knowledge of those with whom they were to be associated in the rough trials of war. To the staff and superior officers this was especially valuable. Marshal Ney, the author instances, was thus enabled throughout the coming operations to confine his attention to the points that required it, knowing exactly which of his subalterns might be trusted to take care of themselves. Moreover, there was a high military spirit in certain regiments which had done great services in the revolutionary campaigns, and this spread by emulation among those brigaded with them, who longea for like opportunities of winning the respect of the army. On the whole therefore, despite the grievous shortcomings he lays bare, M. de Fezensac judges the camp life to have contributed much to the success which followed it.

If he is severe on the mistakes and omissions of his seniors, he is not less plainspoken as to his own faults. Although at first proud of his advancement to sergeant-major, he was disgusted to find his new rank laden with liabilities beyond his means, due to his predecessor's carelessness or dishonesty, and he soon got so out of heart with his duties as to neglect them openly, and incur a reprimand. At this juncture, happily for the prospects of the young soldier, a vacancy occurred as sub-lieutenant. It was one of the special steps still reserved for election, in accordance with the practice of the old Republican army, soon afterwards abolished. The choice lay, in the first place, with the sub-lieutenants of the corps, who presented three names to the lieutenants, and the latter selected one of the three for the step. The popular notions of the French service of that era would picture such an election as the very model of rude honor and martial integrity. In this case the aristocratic candidate had the special disadvantages of his recent known carelessness, and of considerable jealousy on the part of the subalterns at his rapid progress from the ranks. Some of them also had personal friends, men who had seen hard service, among his competitors. Against this, however, was the simple fact that young de Fezensac had not yet lost his

14

colonel's favor, and that it was known that Lacuée desired him to receive his step by election, as more hon orable than to wait for a nomination vacancy. The desire of pleasing the commanding officer outweighed merit, service, and friendship, and the choice fell on the young Parisian lounger of eight months before, rather than on either of the veterans of Marengo, who were the other competitors. Before the imperial confirmation could be obtained, the sub-lieutenant elect was startled by a decree—aimed at such families as his own, whose sons avoided the military schools of the Empire—requiring four years' service in every non-commissioned officer promoted. Happily for de Fezensac the imminence of a general war rescued him from this new difficulty, and after a few weeks' delay he received a provisional commission, which was never revoked.

This was on July second, 1805, a day unfortunate at its close in our hero's annals. One of the sham embarkations, which were still practised, was to take place next day, and brought some guests into the huts of the 59th. This double fête was too much for the newly-made officer, who signalized his promotion by getting drunk, and by using insubordinate language to the captain of police, thus drawing on himself the colonel's displeasure and a close arrest for a fortnight. A chief part of this childish punishment (for such in our service it would be regarded) was the fee to the sentry stationed at the door, who received a perquisite of three francs a day for his extra duty. No friends were nominally to be received by the culprit; but as two brother-subalterns shared his hut, he had the full advantage of their guests, if his leisure proved wearisome.

No discipline in fact could be less effectual than this sort of compromise between the severity of a court-martial and the minor penalties inflicted on the rank and file ; for one of the other subalterns is in the same page described as under a succession of these arrests half his time, behaving in fact very much as an ill-conditioned cadet of seventeen at Woolwich or St. Cyr. M. de Fezensac felt the inconvenience little, but the displeasure of his colonel much, until a frank avowal of contrition to the latter, with a confession to his parents of his sorrow at having offended so good a friend, restored him to the favor which he thenceforward took more care to deserve.

The ideas and customs of his brother-officers were found by the new subaltern to be in no way superior to those of the class he had now left. All had seen service ; but very few had had a decent education, and fewer still had used their leisure to improve it. " Their manners were vulgar," he tells us, "their politeness the politeness of the soldier." For this the reader may very possibly have been prepared ; but it is more startling to learn how rarely such men rose to any eminence in their profession, notwithstanding the constant succession of wars in which their master engaged. Of all the long list of officers on the strength of the 59th when de Fezensac entered it, but one became a general, and the most distinguished soldier of them all never was more than colonel of a light-infantry regiment. Such must of necessity be the lot of ordinary men in any service where promotion goes chiefly by selection, and that selection depends wholly on a superior's will. Where one man is advanced by sole discernment of his merits, a dozen others will owe the

like advantage to some personal acquaintance with
those near the fountain of power. The interest which
as we shall see, pushed de Fezensac himself from his
first commission to the rank of general of brigade in
eight years, like that which in as many months had
passed him on from the recruit-squad to the officer's
epaulette, could only be exercised at the cost of men
less known, and probably enough too, less fitted for
high rank.

The summer of 1805 was passed by the soldiers of
Boulogne in wondering whether the evolutions practiced by the troops and flotilla were but a feint or seriously designed to lead to an embarkation. Some of
de Fezensac's brother-subalterns prophesied a speedy
conquest of the insolent islanders; some declared the
whole a ruse of the Emperor's, preluding a sudden attack on Germany; none feared any event so much as
another winter passed in the same dreary purposeless
existence as the last. Neither section of these military
prophets was wholly wrong or right. Napoleon's own
correspondence has fully revealed the real truth to be that
the invasion was his first and darling object, and was
abandoned only when he found his admirals fail utterly in their share of the task. On August twenty-sixth,
it was known in the camp that Villeneuve had gone
back to Cadiz, leaving the English fleet in undisturbed
possession of the Channel. " Happily," as our author
with a soldier's *naïveté* says, "the new coalition permitted Napoleon to substitute for the expedition, so
often and so vainly announced, a general European
war." On September first, the three divisions of Marshal Ney were on their march for Strasburg, and with
them moved the new-made subaltern. His provisional

commission had never been confirmed by the Minister
of War; but on this point he now felt easy, feeling
that rank was more likely to be won than withdrawn
on actual service. Burdened with nothing but his
sword, he no longer regretted his choice of the infantry, and trudged gaily along at the side of his platoon.
Like his own, the spirit of his comrades ran high, and
made the constant onward move seem easy. He bears
special testimony to the exceptional order of this three
weeks' march, on which the officers never quitted their
companies without a reprimand. He himself incurred
an arrest from his major the first day for a brief delay
in appearing on parade, a reproof from his captain
somewhat later for spending more time over his break-
fast than the men, and a sharp remonstrance from his
colonel for over-politeness to a fatigued vivandière
which threatened to cost him his promised trip to
Paris, where his parents expected to see him for a few
hours. Once more Lacuée proved kinder in action
than in word to his young protégé, and the desired permission to quit the regiment for a brief space being
granted, the young soldier posted rapidly the necessary
hundred miles, embraced his family, took one brief
glance at those joys of Parisian existence on which he
had often looked back regretfully during the past
year and then turned his face once more to the Rhine.
Borne back to his regiment with all the speed the post
would allow, de Fezensac contrived to miss the outfit
which kind hands had dispatched beforehand by the
diligence, and with a borrowed sword and epaulette,
passed the great frontier stream on September twenty-
seventh, near Lauterburg, and plunged with his regiment into the defiles of the Black Forest beyond, a

unit in the legions which were to tear the crown of
the Western Empire from the house of Hapsburg.

We are not about to follow the author through his
narrative of the great events which led to the shameful
disaster of Mack at Ulm. They have been illustrated
with marvellous freshness in the well-known work of
Colonel Hamley, who has so clearly analyzed the
strategy of Napoleon's design as to make the stupen-
dous events of that October as plain as they can appear regarded from the victor's side alone. Those who
would understand them in their strictly German aspect,
and know the details of the miserable delusions and
vacillations which ruined the Austrian theorist, must
go to the exhaustive work of Rüstow on this campaign,
which is as remarkable for its industry as for its general impartiality. We have another task here specially
before us, which is to show from unexceptionable testimony how little to be relied on was the so-called system by which Napoleon supplied his army in such
movements. In this the first week of its first campaign,
fresh from camp discipline, full of patriotic spirit and
confidence in its great head, scarce clear of the borders
of its own fair land, the Grand Army is found, upon
the first difficulty it had to encounter, resolving itself
into a host of armed and violent marauders. We give
M. de Fezensac's account of the affair in his own words,
the simple force of which it would be difficult to improve :

"On the evening of the fifth, before reaching Geislingen,
our division turned to the left to follow the movement of the
other corps towards the Lower Danube. We marched
through the whole of the night and the day following, with

only a few moments for rest, and without any food. The Emperor had ordered that the soldiers should carry bread for four days, and that the wagons should have four more day's rations of biscuit. I do not know what happened in the other corps. *As for us, we had nothing,* and as the 59th marched in the rear, according to its number, it was nightfall when we got to our bivouac near Giengen, the town where General Malher, our division commander, had his quarters. The colonel reported to him the arrival of the regiment after their six-and-thirty hours' march, and asked permission to make a requisition for rations. The general refused, having promised to spare the town; but the result was to authorize every sort of disorder, for the villages around were sacked, and the first day of bivouac became the first day of pillage. The colonel, almost famishing himself, found some grenadiers roasting a pig. His appearance at first caused some confusion, but a moment later one of the privates, more bold than his fellows, offered him a share of the repast, which was heartily accepted, and pillage thus became officially sanctioned."

Thus initiated into the the new system of "making war with the legs," Colonel Lacuée pressed his regiment on to the Danube, and fell at the passage of the bridge of Gunzburg three days later, the first officer of rank the French lost in the campaign.

M. de Fezensac, who came up with the reserve of the 59th after the first part of the fight, takes the opportunity of recounting this his first action, to point out, by the simple process of telling the exact truth, how wofully short of the language of bulletins and dispatches was the conduct and discipline of his regiment.

"This day did our regiment much honor ; but to speak the truth, I do not think the enemy's attacks had been very severe. I found the officers agitated and restless, occupying themselves with encouraging the soldiers, and trying to restore order ; for the companies had become mixed, having, as I said, passed the bridge singly, and on getting to the plain beyond, received the enemy without having time to throw themselves into proper order for defence. I am persuaded that there was a moment when a bayonet attack and a charge of cavalry on our flank could have thrown us back, and forced us into the Danube. In this situation the two reserve companies ought to have been of great value ; but the captains, in their hurry to get to the field of battle, would not take time to form them after passing the bridge, and the regiment involved them in its disorder. Happily darkness was falling, and the Austrians were ignorant of our little strength. Nevertheless we passed the night under arms, and did not venture to make fires."

During the night M. de Fezensac learnt that he had lost his kind friend and colonel, whose last words to an officer who caught him as he fell were to "leave him, and go back to the fight." Very different stories were heard by the young subaltern of other regimental acquaintances, new to the proof of war.

"One sergeant whom I knew (afterwards a good officer, and killed in action) hid himself, nor was he the only one. Each company had a similar anecdote to relate. These night affairs are very convenient. You may lose yourself in the wood, or tumble into the brook at your pleasure. I have had occasion throughout my military career to admire the skill of men who are always missing at the moment of danger but never so as to be compromised by their absence."

The narrative of the surrender of Ulm which follows is worth studying for its own sake, and for its
vivid picture of a well-known difference between Ney
and Murat, which ended in the former publicly challenging the other, before Napoleon and the imperial
staff, to follow him under fire. This, too, was when all
was going well with the Grand Army. A less prescient
mind than Napoleon's might have foreseen in such dis-
putes at critical moments the germs of disaster in after
days, when the tide of fortune should turn against the
commanders whose jealousies their master's presence
could hardly restrain.

M. de Fezensac has not failed to record his opinion,
very different from that usually accepted, of the system which in this instance placed 30,000 prisoners at a
stroke in the hands of the Grand Army. We quote,
with some omissions, his comments on the means
which led to this success, reminding our readers that
it is no holiday soldier who thus speaks:

"This short campaign was, as it were, an epitome of
those that followed. Excess of fatigue, want of provisions,
severity of weather, disorders and marauding, nothing was
wanting to it; and in that month I first felt what I was
destined to experience throughout my career. Brigades, and
even regiments, being sometimes dispersed [for subsistence,
sake, the author means], the order for concentration would
come late, having to pass through a number of different
channels. From this it followed that the men had to march
day and night, falling asleep on their way, and arrived at the
place assigned without having eaten anything, or finding any
victuals there. Marshal Berthier used to write, ' *In the war
of invasion that the Emperor is making, there are no magazines.
It is for the generals to find their own means of subsistence in*

the country that they traverse.' But the generals had neither time nor means to procure regularly the wherewithal to feed so numerous an army.   Pillage, therefore, became authorized, and the districts which we passed through suffered cruelly, *yet we were not the less famished throughout the campaign. . . .* Bad weather made our suffering still more severe.   A cold rain fell, or rather a half-melted snow, in which we plunged deep, while the wind prevented our lighting fires.   On October sixteenth, the day whe͏͏ ͏͏ilip Segur bore the first summons to Mack, the weather was so frightful that no one kept his post.   There was no grand guard or sentry, the very artillery was left unwatched, and each man sheltered himself as best he could.   I never, except in the campaign of Russia, suffered so much, never saw the army in the like disorder."

Is this fairly written in the histories of the great campaign around Ulm? The French writers slight it ;* the more accurate Germans, as Rüstow, have failed to correct them in a matter exclusively French.   As far as we are aware, the truth would have been universally slurred over but for the following notice, which shows that history has in this respect submitted to be blinded in her gaze by the sun of Napoleon's genius, and has actually gone back in truth since the publication in the year 1810 in London of a pamphlet in French by an unknown Russian officer whom we shall here quote. In it the actual truth was told, as now vividly re-

---

* The bad weather is mentioned by the various French writers and their followers ; but no reference is made by any of them to the starvation which accompanied it. Dumas, indeed, expressly says that Marmont's men suffered from the weight of the rations they had to carry. As Marmont's corps came in by a separate route through a plain country, it is quite possible that it escaped the destitution which the rest of the army, crossing the Black Forest and Suabian Alps in rapid succession, naturally experienced.

produced by M. de Fezensac. The author appears to have been on the staff of Kutusoff in 1805, or to have had his information direct from those that were:

"To surround Ulm it was necessary to concentrate. Numerous columns defiled upon the same road, appeared at the same point. 100,000 men, fatigued by long marches, destitute of provisions, come to take up a position which grows more and more confined. They are now no more allowed to straggle from their post, for then the whole enterprise would fail. What a critical moment! The resources of the country occupied by this mass are consumed in an hour.

"To enhance the difficulty, the heavens seem to dissolve. A heavy rain, continuing for many days, floods the country. The streams burst their banks. The roads are frightful, and in more than one place altogether disappear. The army marches in mud, and bivouacks in water ; it is ready to perish with misery and hunger ; discouragement and murmuring spread through it. What is to be done ? A proclamation [of October twelfth ; see Napo. Corresp.] is read at the head of each column, which praises, flatters, aud caresses the army, pours eulogy on its constancy, tells it the enemy is enclosed, and that only a few moments more of perseverance are needed. Thus the soldiers are kept quiet ; but as they must have bread, active and intelligent officers are sent through all the neighboring districts, to obtain it by threats, if requests fail. All yields to the power of requisition, and in twenty-four hours bread is procured, and the horses and vehicles of the inhabitants are used to bring it in . . . . Ulm is invested, blockaded, capitulates, and the French army reaps the fruit of its endurance and of its incredible activity."

The writer of this essay had evidently nearly

reached the truth which French military writers have obscured, but which de Fezensac's narrative enables us to grasp. In fact, a general carrying on war on the system which Napoleon adopted clearly does it at tremendous risk. The object to be gained may justify him in a military sense for the time, but, on the other hand, an unexpected detention on the way, a week of bad weather, a slight check from the enemy, may ruin the spirits of his army beyond recall. What is more important still to note is this. The system of living by requisition bears within it its own Nemesis in the demoralization which it spreads through all ranks of the army, and in the sure preparation thus made, even in the midst of success, for the day when defeat shall become irreparable disaster. As this truth is admirably summed up by M. de Fezensac at the close of the first part of his work, we quote his words, themselves the best condemnation of the popular historians of his country, and the plain proof that the organization of plunder is, even in the strongest hands, a deception and a blunder:

"All these causes developed insubordination, want of discipline, and the habit of marauding. When at such a time soldiers went to a village to look for rations, they found themselves tempted to stay there. Thus the number of stragglers wandering through the country became considerable. The inhabitants met with every sort of annoyance from them, and wounded officers who sought to bring them to order were answered with threats. *All these details are unknown to those who read the history of our campaign,* where there is only to be seen a valiant army of devoted soldiers emulating the glory of their officers. No one knows what sufferings are often the price of the most brilliant successes, nor how ex-

amples of selfishness and cowardice are mingled with traits
of generosity and courage."

Can those who read this, wonder any longer at the utter destruction of the Grand Army in Russia, and the
still more marvellous dissolution of the Cohorts of 1813 ?

Ulm taken, the army pressed on to occupy Vienna,
and conquer at Austerlitz ; but in these triumphs the
corps of Ney had no share, being left to guard Bavaria
and keep the Tyrol in check. The peace of Presburg
sent the 59th Regiment into four months' cantonments near Salzburg, where the sojourn of de Fezensac himself was extremely agreeable, and was the origin of a lifelong friendship with the Austrian family on
whom he was quartered. Why he became thus en-
deared to his involuntary hosts is clear enough when
we recollect that he was a gentleman by birth and feeling, and that the ordinary occupation of his comrades,
even in his own friendly coloring, is shown to have
been alternately to bully the male inhabitants, and to
pay unsought civilities to the females of their respective billets. Two anecdotes out of many are enough
to describe the miserable condition of things, of which
M. de Fezensac declares that, apart from the troubles
connected with the victualling and lodging of the troops,
the local authorities were often treated with wanton
disrespect :

"If a discussion arose, the soldier was always right, and
the inhabitant always wrong. A private of the sixth company declared that thirty francs had been stolen from him,
and his captain, without any inquiry, ordered that it should
be made good . . . . The officers, often too far away, could
not stop these abuses ; besides the greater part of them gave

an example of exaction. If any one wanted to go anywhere, he made requisition for a carriage and horse, but offered no payment. An officer of high rank wished to go in this way to Schaffhausen, and was to have four relays ready, from post to post. At one of these he was kept waiting, and by way of punishment, sent twenty-five men extra to be quartered on the village."

To impress the government post service for every kind of private journey seems to have been the universal practice, even with those who, like de Fezensac himself, abstained from and condemned all personal plunder. And it would have been, concludes the writer with his usual truth and force, better for their discipline to find the soldiers in regular rations than to quarter them individually on the peasants. But these were stripped, while the army was left without pay, and even without clothing, in order that the stores in France might be left untouched. Such was that economy of Napoleon's military administration of which so much praise has been written by certain panegyrists.

From its cantonments in the Hereditary States and Suabia the army at length was moving slowly towards France, when Napoleon halted it, to await the pending rupture and war with Prussia. Meanwhile, de Fezensac's family had not forgotten him; and feeling that his regimental prospects would naturally suffer by the death of Colonel Lacuée, they had made interest at Paris with the friends of various generals high in command to have him transferred to the staff. Refused in more than one quarter, their wish had found favor with Ney; and on October sixth, two days before the campaign of Jena began, the sub-lieutenant left

his regiment to report himself at the Marshal's headquarters in his new capacity of extra aide-de-camp.
From this date, until suddenly made colonel of a
regiment at Borodino, his service lay wholly with the
staff.

M. de Fezensac, at this point, digresses slightly
from his narrative to speak of the essential differences
which separate the mind and knowledge of the regimental from that of the staff officer. The latter, he
says, is often as ignorant of the habits of the soldier
and of the details of duty as the former of the purport
of the movements he is executing. Hence he concludes that to form a good general officer, or even a
good commander of a regiment,* a man should have
served in both departments. In this view he follows
strictly that of Napoleon, who abolished—in name, at
least—the practice of promoting officers on the staff
from one grade to another, and ordered that a captain,
to win rank as a field officer, must return to do duty
with a regiment. This rule was but nominal in the
case of a man of interest like our writer, who in spite
of it, received the rank of major of cavalry for services
done as a captain on Berthier's personal staff; but its
existence served, as Jomini, who was strongly prejudiced against it, has particularly noticed, to drive
young men of energy and promise from the staff into
the line, and thus in his view to disorganize what he
declares to be the soul of a well-ordered army. The
system of Napoleon was abandoned by his successors
in French military administration, who restored and

---

* The colonel of a continental regiment, be it remembered, has
two, three, or even four battalions to superintend, and his duties in
many respects are those which we assign to the head of a brigade.

completed the plan by which the staff is first selected out of, and then kept altogether distinct from the other services. This reform, the creation of a distinct Staff Corps, has been supported by writers who, with Jomini, declare that the plan of Napoleon failed to give a sufficient supply of intelligent officers for the higher posts. It has further been adopted in other services, the Austrian especially; and its non-existence in our own has been often alleged as a defect by those who see its advantages without all its drawbacks. The effect of the French system is necessarily to draw so strong a line between the staff and the body of the army as to deprive the one of all sympathy with the other, and to take away from the general mass of officers all rational motives for studying the higher branches of their profession. This last result may not seriously matter where most of them are so little educated that they would in vain strive to raise their minds above the petty details of the regiment, nor the former where occupation for a large Staff Corps can be found in time of peace. With us these conditions are reversed; and to copy the French in this matter was neither necessary nor expedient, however desirable it might be to avoid the chance method of Napoleon. Our own new system, imitated almost unconsciously from Prussia before Prussian practice in matters military became the fashion, opens to every intelligent young officer in the service the means of obtaining by study and merit a qualification for the staff, and his turn of five years' service in an appointment; and it seems in every way better suited to our circumstances. It needs but to be thoroughly and impartially applied to give us a supply of instructed soldiers for our future needs at a cost far less than that of the smallest Staff Corps of supernumerary officers.

In Napoleon's army (as is still the case in our own) all the personal staff of a general was selected from private considerations; and when M. de Fezensac joined that of Marshal Ney before Nuremburg, no one asked if he had even the moderate qualifications of service and knowledge which an aide-de-camp with us must possess. The army was already in motion for Jena, and M. de Fezensac having spent his whole means on a single sorry horse, started with it. During the next few days he had abundant practice in his new duties as messenger, and arrived on the famous field with his marshal early in the day that ruined Prussia, and gave the death-blow to the tactics bequeathed by Frederic. Here he saw Ney expose his person in the reckless way which earned for him the title of "the bravest of the brave," a fashion which on this occasion cost two of his staff, wounds got at his side. The subsequent pursuit of the Prussians is ordinarily remembered only for the rapidity with which it was carried on. M. de Fezensac, while giving the army full credit for the activity displayed by chiefs and men, shows us another and a darker side of the picture. " Pillage was never carried further than on this march, and disorder reached the height of insubordination." On the way the young aide-de-camp was thrown into company with Jomini, then simply a colonel on the staff, yet already a man of mark ; for before joining for this campaign he had indicated Jena as the point where the decisive battle would be fought. At Nordhausen they were both nearly murdered by soldiers whose excesses they sought to stop, and were only saved by drawing sword and

15

riding through these mutineers; for "our subordina
tion," says the author, "does not rest on bases as solid
as that of other armies." This state of things caused
Ney to apply to the Emperor for special powers to arrest and punish the stragglers; but it was checked for
the time by the halt of the corps to form the blockade
of Magdeburg, while the rest of the army completed
the pursuit and destruction of the Prussians.

The young aide-de-camp had (as already stated)
kept near to his chief on the field of Jena, but, except
on that occasion, saw little of him throughout the campaign; for the new-made marshal was terribly afraid of
compromising his dignity in the eyes of his staff, the
more so, perhaps, as some of them were of the older
aristocracy of birth:

"Marshal Ney kept us at a great distance. During the
marches he went on alone in front, and never addressed a
word to us, unless obliged. The aide-de-camp in waiting
never entered his room, save in the course of duty or by special summons, and it was the rarest of events to see the marshal conversing with any one of us. He ate alone, and never
gave an aide-de-camp an invitation. This apparent haughti-
ness arose from the desire to maintain his position. The
transition was sudden from the days of 1796, when Augereau
had reproved his officers for allowing themselves to be addressed as *Monsieur*. A few years later the Republican generals of that date had become marshals, dukes, princes.
This change embarrassed Ney, who besides had reason
sometimes to believe that his elevation made others envious
of him; so he thought to make himself respected by the
hauteur of his bearing, and sometimes carried it too far."

Before leaving the subject of the conquest of Prus-

sia, it should be remarked that this narrative effectually
dispels certain common illusions as to the perfection of
the details of the system on which the Grand Army
worked. One, which some of the best of French military writers have unfortunately propagated and confirmed, relates to the personnel of the higher officers.
So far from these being invariably the efficient and
well-trained leaders they have been represented, in
Ney's own corps one of the divisions changed hands
twice during the two months; once because the general (Vandamme) was of so proud and violent a temper
that he could not brook Ney as his superior; and again
because his successor proved so worn out as to be
physically and morally unfit for active service, so that
the marshal took upon himself the responsibility, a
great one for a lieutenant of Napoleon, of dismissing
him from his charge. Another relates to the care
which these rough, practical soldiers gave to the details
of their duty. What would Wellington have said, had
any division commander of the army, during one of
his sieges, changed his own quarters three times for
considerable distances, without notifying the fact to
headquarters? Yet this was done under Ney, during
the blockade of Magdeburg, by the general of a dra-
goon division; and so little was such an irregularity
regarded, that when brought by his staff to the marshal's notice, he only shrugged his shoulders, and said,
" *What a way to carry on duty !* " As to the internal
service of the staff, for which at one time Napoleon
got great credit, the truth, as told by M. de Fezensac,
enables us to fill up the outline suggested by certain
hints of Jomini in his narrative of the subsequent campaign of Poland, which imply that the army then

already felt deeply the deficiencies which their master discovered too late.

"Long journeys on duty were made in carriages charged at the post rate ; but some officers put the money in their pockets and obtained horses by requisition. This was a bad plan in every view, for apart from the dishonesty, they were ill served, and lost valuable time. As for messages taken on horseback, I have already said that no person took the pains to inquire if we had a horse that could walk, even when it was necessary to go at a gallop, or if we knew the country, or had a map. The order must be executed without waiting for the means, as I shall show in some special instances. This habit of attempting everything with the most feeble instruments, this wish to overlook impossibilities, this unbounded assurance of success, which at first helped to win us advantages, in the end became our destruction."

From reflections thus darkened with the shadow of the future, the author carries us forward into Poland, whither Napoleon now transferred the scene of conquest, determined, in his own phrase, " to win back on land the colonies France had lost."

Here M. de Fezensac places the turning point of Napoleon's career. The first entrance into Poland brought the French into collision with Benningsen's army ; and although the Russians had to retreat after the battle of Pultusk, they did so without disorder or loss, for " the time of half-successes, of incomplete triumphs, had arrived. Then also began the miseries of the army, the want of forage and provisions, the privations of every kind which I shall afterwards have to detail." Here the course of duty threw the young aide-de-camp into the company of Bernadotte, with whose courtesy he was much impressed, and whom he suspects, from the excessive interest taken by him in the people of Poland, to have already conceived hopes of an elective throne. Losing his way a few days later in the search for one of Ney's generals (who, like the cavalry commander previously mentioned, had shifted his quarters without informing the marshal), he fell in again with Jomini, and was directed rightly by that officer, from whom he learnt that the Russians were suddenly advancing. The short winter campaign had begun, which was to end in the desperate encounter of Eylau, the first check that befell the Grand Army and its master.

Who does not know how bloody and indecisive was the struggle of that day? Genius has reflected the whole story in the ghastly picture at the entrance of the Louvre. The idlest traveller turns arrested, in spite of personal insensibility or national coldness, to gaze on the sheet of snow, the burning villages, the agonized group of wounded in the foreground, and above them the pallor-stricken face of a man at whose bidding all this misery was wrought, and who felt at that moment (so the artist seems to tell us) some presage of Borodino's useless slaughter, the fires of Moscow, and the ruin that followed. On this occasion Benningsen's firmness was insufficient to maintain the equality his army had asserted, and he slowly withdrew next morning, leaving the ground to the enemy. M. de Fezensac's share in the events of the day was an important one, for he bore to Ney the message which was to bring his corps to take share in the fight. His horse was already worn out when he got his orders at eight A. M., and with difficulty could he, being fortunately in funds, buy a restive animal to carry him.   He knew nothing of the roads, and had no guide.   " To ask for an escort would have been of no more use than to ask for a horse.   An officer had always an excellent horse, knew the country, was never taken, met no accident, and got rapidly to his destination ; and of all this there was so little doubt that often a second message was thought unnecessary."   This want of proper precaution was near costing the Emperor dear, for his orders did not reach Ney till two P. M. ; and the corps only came up at the end of the day.   Bernadotte's was wholly absent, and that, as Jomini assures us, solely for want of a good system of messengers.   What, then, are we to think of the assertion of M. Thiers (which M. de Fezensac quotes to flatly contradict it as regards Ney) that Napoleon sent off seven officers *the evening before* to press the two missing marshals to come up ?   What are we to think, may it not be further asked, of certain apocryphal messages sent to Grouchy in the Waterloo crisis ; messages taken as historical facts by M. Thiers, though their receipt has been consistently denied from the first, and no record of their dispatch exists, save in the St. Helena " Mémoires," an exile's apology for his disasters, interesting no doubt for its ability, but hardly fit material for serious history.

The battle of Eylau produced a four months' cessation of hostilities, during which the Russians suffered much, but their enemies still more.   Sixty thousand stragglers, M. de Fezensac assures us, were missing from the French muster-rolls, and the greater part of these were mere marauders, who stripped the country of the supplies which should have been brought up and husbanded by the commissariat.

" Never were more orders " [he adds] " given than by Napoleon to insure subsistence to his army ; never were any
worse executed. Some of them indeed were wholly imprac-
ticable. There might be traced in them the illusions or char-
latanism of him who, in later days, ordered his troops *to protect the peasants who brought provisions into the markets of Moscow.* To discover the hidden stocks, to bring them into
Warsaw, to repair the mills, to make regular issues of rations,
were all very well on paper ; but those who made the campaign knew what it all came to. It is wrong then to say " [the
writer has here M. Thiers and others of his class in view]
"that the army had enough, and sometimes even more. I can
declare, on the contrary, that with all these fine orders so
given in January, our army was dying with hunger in March."

In the latter month M. de Fezensac was captured
when on a message ; and having thus an unsought
opportunity of seeing how the enemy fared, gives his
evidence as follows :

" M. Thiers speaks of the sufferings of the Russian army
of Cossacks asking bread of our soldiers. I do not dispute
the matter, but at their headquarters appearances gave the lie
to this assertion. I saw the staff living in abundance, the soldiers well clothed, the horses in good condition. Assuredly
the comparison was not in our favor."

Refused an exchange, as having seen too much of
the camp thus described, he was sent into Russia, and
remained a prisoner until the battle of Friedland and
peace of Tilsit released him.

Thus restored at last to Paris and the society in
which he had been brought up, M. de Fezensac met
and married the daughter of Clarke, Duc de Feltre, the

Minister of War.   It is no reflection on an honest sol
dier to say, that he thus secured his military fortunes
more certainly than if he had followed Ney in the
famous échelon attack at Friedland, which overthrew
that army whose condition he had lately admired, and
which Benningsen too confidently exposed.   Soon
afterwards he was entering Spain, once more on the
Marshal's staff, and with him pursued Moore's army to
Corunna.   He had here just time to observe the bitter
enmity of the Spaniards to their conquerors, and the
ill working of the Napoleonic system of requisition in
a poor and hostile country, when he was recalled, with
many of the staff, to Paris.   Napoleon was about to
carry the Grand Army once more into Germany.   In
the fifth year of his service, and now holding the rank
of captain and the enviable position of aide-de-camp to
Berthier himself, M. de Fezensac followed the eagles to
Vienna and received a slight wound at Aspern, which
procured him his grade as major and a pension, with
the title of baron—" rather for what I would have
done than for what I did," adds the narrator, modestly.
His journal here was but a record of headquarter movements, and he has forborne to publish it.   A short mission to Spain, with some intructions to Macdonald,
composed the rest of his service until the fatal invasion
of Russia was begun, and he passed once more east
ward through Germany on Berthier's staff.

No part of the work is more interesting than that
which follows.   In almost immediate attendance upon
Napoleon up to the day of Borodino, M. de Fezensac
was named three days later to the command of the
fourth regiment of the line, which had lost its colonel
in the fight, and thenceforward served through the

rest of the Russian tragedy in his new capacity, and in the corps of his old chief, Ney. Of the whole library of histories and memoirs devoted to the eventful retreat from Moscow, there is no account more valuable than his. A natural devotion to the responsibilities of his new duty made him sympathize to the full with the sufferings of his regiment; while his six years' service on the staff enabled him to discern how much of these were due to the shortcomings at headquarters. The system of requisition alternated with pillage, which we have seen him denounce for its inherent unsoundness, had at last broken down altogether, and left the army helpless and starving in wastes of mud and snow. The bonds of organization and of regimental discipline, imperfect in the day of victory, had snapped asunder at this great disaster, leaving all ranks levelled into a helpless selfishness, until the Grand Army, so long the terror of Europe, became in its turn the sport and booty of an avenging peasantry. One bright spot only illumines the dark picture as M. de Fezensac has painted it. The noble self-denial and inexhaustible energy of Ney had never had such full justice done to them before. No one who reads this narrative can doubt that the marshal united in his person, to a degree no other man has rivalled, the true physical and moral qualifications for the rear-guard commander of a retreating army. On this portion of the " Souvenirs," we forbear to dwell further. It was not only published (as before stated) many years before the remainder, but to many English readers is especially known by the excellent version of Sir W. Knollys, who has completed his private translation of the original narrative care fully from other sources, and thus made so complete a handbook of the campaign, as to cause regret that his labor has never been offered to the general public. For our present purpose it is sufficient to say that of the 3,000 men who originally composed the fourth regiment, 200 only recrossed the Vistula after the retreat, and of the missing number only 100 ever reappeared from captivity; exactly nine tenths had been sacrificed to Napoleon's spirit of adventure. The officers naturally suffered less in proportion than the men; yet of their original strength of 109, sixty perished, and fourteen only escaped unhurt. M. de Fezensac conducted the remnant of his corps to Nancy at the end of the winter, bearing from Ney the short but honorable testimony (in a letter to General Clarke): "This young man has constantly proved superior to the critical circumstances in which he was placed. I present him to you as a true knight, and you may fairly look on him henceforth as a veteran French colonel." His father-in-law did not take the hint himself, but Ney's recommendation reached the Emperor through others- and while M. de Fezensac was in Paris soliciting promotion for his subalterns, he was himself gazetted general of brigade; the Minister declaring himself as much surprised as any one at his son-in-law's good fortune. Soon afterwards he was on his way to Bremen, appointed to a newly raised Army Corps, of which Vandamme had assumed the charge, and in which the author found the officers, almost without exception, composed of two classes; boys from the cadet-school and worn-out middle-aged men. The serviceable officers had for the most part disappeared, or attained higher rank. Such was the confusion in the War Bureau that a lieutenant of the 59th soliciting a company was forthwith gazetted, by mistake, to a major's rank in another corps. When the error was found out, it was not thought worth while to correct it, and the new major took command of his battalion, at the head of which he fell. Of trustworthy soldiers in any capacity Napoleon began to feel the need, for he wrote to Marshal Davoust, after sending him to command in the north of Germany: "Take care and treat Vandamme well: men who understand war are getting scarce." This advice, according to M. de Fezensac, came not a whit too soon, for the violent temper of the general soon after caused an explosion in the presence of the whole staff upon some point of military etiquette, which tried Davoust's patience to the utmost. The war now recommenced, and while the Grand Army was winning Lutzen and Bautzen successively, causing Napoleon vainly to fancy himself once more the arbiter of Europe, Davoust recovered Hamburg and the Lower Elbe in a series of well-managed, though not very difficult manœuvres. Vandamme here won much credit, and General de Fezensac, who was often detached and acting on his own responsibility, was highly praised by his new chief; so that when the latter, during the ensuing armistice, was ordered to the Emperor's headquarters, his brigadier followed him and again obtained a command in his corps. Vandamme's manner, he tells us, though unbearable to his superiors, was by no means harsh to his own staff; and the energy and vigor of the man, who was known to be ambitious beyond all things of such distinction as should place him on a level with more fortunate rivals, gave promise of brilliant opportunities to the force he led, numbered as the First Corps of the newly raised levies with which Napoleon vainly hoped to revive the glories of the Grand Army whose name they had assumed.

M. de Fezensac found in his new brigade a better supply of officers than he had hoped; for many, invalided in the spring, had now rejoined the eagles. On the other hand, the ranks were full of young untrained recruits, and the non-commissioned officers were ignorant of the very elements of their duties. The dispersion of the force during the armistice for subsistence' sake rendered it the harder to complete the necessary instruction, and the more impossible to enforce discipline. "We were to fight all Europe," he sums up his description, "and yet never was there a more untrained force than ours." "All the world knows," it is significantly added, "how the countries we occupied suffered; in this respect, at least, our young army was quite as knowing as its predecessors. Under pretext of looking after the comfort of the men various officers ransacked town and country, made requisitions, and allowed themselves afterwards to be bribed off." From such pursuits as these, and with unfinished training in its proper trade, the Grand Army was roused by the termination of the armistice. Austria had thrown her slow but heavy sword into the balance, and France and her conscripts were hopelessly over-weighted.

There has been much discussion as to the exact force brought to bear on either side in the new campaign, which exceeded in its dimensions any other the world had seen. It seems to us more important to note fully what has been here revealed to us of the composition of Napoleon's army, and to remember that no reinforcement of any importance reached it. We may then well understand how its body and substance melted away under the disasters that ensued, more rapidly than the historian can trace. For a moment the brilliant victory of Dresden, enhanced by the mortal wound of his old rival Moreau from a French shot on his first exposure, led Napoleon to believe that the star of victory had risen on him once more : but in the same week that this triumph was won, his dreams of restored empire were rudely shattered into ruin by three tremendous blows. Oudinot's Army of the North was defeated decisively within sight of the hated city of Berlin, which it had been detached to threaten. Macdonald in Silesia received a fatal check on the Katzbach, which so loosened the discipline of his conscripts that the three days' retreat that followed cost him ten times the number lost in the really trifling action : the real cause being revealed in an intercepted letter to Macdonald from General Puthod, who speaks of his division, *before the combat,* as quite unmanageable in the existing want and bad weather. These two misfortunes the Emperor's panegyrists charge to his lieutenants, forgetting that he was solely and wholly responsible for the choice he had made of them. The third, however, that of Vandamme's corps at Culm, has been so completely and unequivocally fixed upon his own mismanagement by concurrent testimony, that even M. Thiers scarce endeavors to disprove it, and admits as true the charge against his hero, of striving to excuse himself at first by blackening the memory of his general, then reported to be slain.

M. de Fezensac shared, of course, in all the events of that terrible disaster. He rejoiced at the outset in the bold movement which threw the First Corps into

the rear of the vast mass of enemies retreating from
Dresden. He became anxious with others when it was
found that all connection with the other French corps
was lost. He felt anxiety change into alarm when
Vandamme, on the night before the battle, left his
corps exposed to be attacked by vastly larger forces in
the plain before Teplitz, while the heights behind him
were unoccupied, and no friends heard of in any quarter. " No one partook his illusions," says M. de Fezensac, who regretted then, no doubt, his choice of a leader. " Generals, officers, and soldiers alike wanted confidence. That is a bad feeling with which to enter
into action." When 40,000 troops in such condition,
and so placed, are suddenly attacked in front and rear
by forces double their own, the result cannot be doubtful. In two hours Vandamme's corps was either taken
or scattered in panic flight through the wooded emi-
nences by which the Prussians had come behind it.
Acting on a maxim of Ney's, that "you should never
surrender till they take you by the throat," M. de
Fezensac forced his way through the enemy's skirmishers and escaped, finding one-third of his brigade
remaining, when he rallied it under cover of Saint Cyr's
troops on the Dresden side of the hills. Less fortunate
than his brigadier, Vandamme was long ere that time
a prisoner in the market-place of Teplitz, his tall form
a show to triumphant townfolk, and his loud voice ap-
pealing in vain for punishment on the excited soldiery,
who had plundered and threatened him with violence ;
for his harsh treatment of Silesia when quartered there
had made his name infamous throughout Germany.

" The moral effect of this defeat " [M. de Fezensac observes] "was worse than the numerical. Its result was a discouragement that lasted to the end of the campaign. Young soldiers require success ; only old ones can bear up against reverses. We saw no more those men who, the day before, had so boldly attacked the enemy. On the morning of the twenty-ninth, the First corps numbered 40,000 brave fellows ; on the night of the thirtieth, 20,000 disheartened soldiers."

The spirits of the enemy rose proportionately, and an officer dispatched next day to seek exchange of prisoners, was refused reception at their headquarters.

Cheered by successes on all sides, the Allies now set themselves firmly to the task of ridding Germany of the French. Jealousies and divisions were laid aside for the common good, and the personal ambition of powerful monarchs sacrificed to the political object. Alexander himself set the example of self-denial, by refusing the supreme command, pressed on him by our Prince Regent, on the plea that, without Moreau's aid the task would over-weight him. From that time forward Napoleon's struggle was hopeless. Hemmed in the basin of the Elbe by his false strategy, straightened from the first, and soon starved, his young legions melted away in the Saxon autumn as fast as their predecessors in the Russian winter, until the time came when their enemies, better fed, in better heart, and with recruited numbers, closed in and gave them the final blow at Leipsic. The First Corps, now under Count Lobau, saw little of all this, being placed in Dresden to recover its condition, and finally abandoned there by one of the many mistakes Napoleon made in this campaign. His retreat from Germany of course compelled the surrender of the force thus isolated, and M. de Frezensac, again a prisoner, drew his sword no more.   Those who follow his " Recollections " ever so carelessly throughout will understand the mingled feeling with which he heard the abdication of his chief, whose genius he had admired, though never blind to his faults.   He accepted the Restoration as the best hope for the future of France ; and the tricolored cockade, which he doffed after ten years' wear, was laid by as his simple souvenir of the Grand Army.   Few saw so plainly what strength and weakness met in that vast machine ; none have better told the story of its triumphs and its fall.

HENRY VON BRANDT, A GERMAN SOLDIER
OF THE FIRST EMPIRE.*

IN 1806 Prussia had enjoyed ten years of the
ignoble peace purchased by the Treaty of Basle.   Her
king, though entering warmly at first into the coalition
against revolutionary France, had soon tired of a war
in which defeat would fall heavily on Prussia and
success would but strengthen her German rival by the
re-establishment of Austrian dominion in Belgium.
The campaigns of 1792-3 had added no lustre to Prussian arms.   Long disuse of the practice of war had
unfitted for the field the stiff machines which in outward show alone represented the warriors of the Great
Frederic.   Battalions in which each captain bought
recruits for his company from crimps at the cheapest
rate had proved as unequal to the proof of a campaign
as the untrained staff and commissariat which attempted with them the invasion of France.   Military
pedantry had long had sway in the service, and combined with bad administration to cause the soldier's
trade to be shunned by all who could choose one for
themselves; nor had a war undertaken nominally to
restore the Bourbons awakened the latent patriotism
of the Northern German.   Peace, therefore, was
popular with all classes, and prince and people were

* *Aus dem Leben des Generals (Dr.) Heinrich von Brandt.*   Berlin :
1868—9.

alike content to withdraw from the inglorious struggle
to a not less inglorious neutrality, leaving Austria to
defend single-handed the integrity of the Empire over
which she nominally presided.

While the unequal contest went on from year to
year between revolutionary ardor and Hapsburg
obstinacy; while worn-out veterans, failing on either
side, gave way to abler men; while modern strategy
from the feeble warfare of 1792-3 rose suddenly, under
Napoleon and the Archduke Charles, to the highest
stage the art reached before the days of steam;
Prussia, tranquil in her avoidance of the storm which
shook her neighbors, applied all her power to consolidate the acquisitions made not long before as her share
of the partition of Poland. The struggle carried on
for centuries along the lower Vistula between the
Teuton and the Sclave had ended in the triumph of
the former. German capital flowed over to fertilize
Polish territory; to farm a Polish estate was at once
the most profitable and aristocratic of employments
for the Prussian noblesse; and the process of amalgamation and absorption had fairly set in which has continued steadily down to the present day, disturbed
only for a short season by the era of Napoleonic conquest of which we are presently to speak. The old
university of Königsberg in East Prussia was frequented
by the youth of both races alike in the first years of
this century. Among these was our autobiographer,
Henry von Brandt, one of a large and wealthy family
of noble race, who had cast their lot in the new territories acquired by the House of Brandenburg; and so
little, he tells us, was independence sought by the
Polish students of 1805, that it was the fashion for

them to mix freely with the Germans in class-room and in sport, and to call themselves " South-Prussians," as the others were Brandenburgers or East-Prussians.

This tranquil process of amalgamation was not to last long. Events were at hand which would shake the foundations of prescriptive authority throughout Europe, and change for a season the aspirations, fashions, and even the names, of doubtful nationalities. Napoleon in his camp at Boulogne was already the object of attention to the whole civilized world ; and young Brandt, like most of his fellow-students, paid more attention to French than to his proper study of law, and read the journals more diligently than the works on jurisprudence which his professor recommended. Bonaparte (for by his family name the Emperor of the French was then universally known), unmatched as administrator and general, elected sovereign of a mighty people, yet not many years before a friendless collegian, an unknown subaltern, was the object of romantic admiration on the part of the simple students of Königsberg. Some of these would have made an actual idol of their favorite hero, but that the sudden execution of the Duc d'Enghein just before the coronation of his slayer, threw a damp over the ardor of many who, until that dark deed, had counted Napoleon as good as great, and had regarded his self-exaltation to supreme power as the truest act of patriotism to a distracted country.

Germany and her people were soon to be undeceived as to the purity of his motives. Foiled in his designs upon England, Napoleon turned his arms eastward, seeking to fix a quarrel first upon the hereditary

enemy of France. A war with Austria was easy to
provoke, certain to be popular, and gave promise of
further results than a mere fresh humiliation of the
twice-vanquished Court of Vienna. The word was
given to pass the Rhine, and that campaign of Ulm
began in which (as De Fezensac has clearly shown) the
shortcomings of the grand army proved to be great,
even after its Boulogne training ; but which led to
successes so vast that all shortcomings were forgotten.
Russia came late to the aid of her threatened neighbor,
only to add to the triumph of the victor on the decisive field of Austerlitz. Prussia, on the other hand, had
long been trained to look coolly on at the defeats of
Austria, and would have regarded this fresh reverse
with complacency but for the sudden violation of her
own territory made for French advantage by Bernadotte's corps at the outset of the campaign. This outrage at once raised her spirit against Napoleon, and all
Northern Germany doubted the wisdom of the policy
of isolation which had given the French their recent advantage. Like the rest of the Prussian youth, the
Königsberg students cried out for satisfaction ; but,
like others, were easily appeased by the annexation of
Hanover, offered their country as a sop by the wily
invader, who thus sought to gain time to concentrate
his army on his new base on the Main. He had gathered 190,000 men there ready to crush their independence, while they were yet, as Brandt honestly tells us,
blindly rejoicing over the new addition to the " strength
of their fatherland." Then, indeed, the mask was
thrown off, and the struggle for the national life they
held dear was seen to have been but deferred at the
invader's pleasure.

"I can still most vividly remember," says our writer, "the astonishment which fell upon all when the news of our defeats reached Königsberg." Citizens and students had shared to the full the singular delusion entertained by high officers of the army, and even published by General Rüchel in a general order to his corps at the outset of the campaign, that the French successes of which they had heard had been won against inferior enemies in spite of a bad system, such as must inevitably fail when tested against the better-trained battalions of Prussia. Jena has been usually looked upon as the crucial shock in which the old tactics handed down by Frederic were suddenly found wanting; but, in truth, the proof of their inadequacy to meet the more rapid and lighter movements of the enemy, was furnished abundantly at the very first collision of the armies four days before on the little plain of Saalfeld. On the other side came Lannes, Napoleon's own favorite marshal, the best handler of troops in action, according to his master's judgment, of all the quick tacticians that followed the Imperial Eagles. On the other was Prince Louis of Prussia, chief of the war party in the Berlin Councils, "a man," says the greatest of all German military writers, "now thirty-three years of age, of vehement courage but dissipated habits, burning for military fame but unversed in the practice of war, and counting on his own personal valor to redeem every error of judgment." Lannes had with him Suchet's division, veterans long trained to war on the light method bequeathed by the Revolutionary armies, and perfected by practice: and these officered by men who had all won their posts in real service. The Prussians opposed to them were not

much fewer in number, drilled with an exact pedantry
now unknown, confident in the hereditary reputation
of their army, but slow and unready in movement, and
led by officers of little but parade-ground practice.
The French division, pouring through a pass into the
plain in which the Prussians were drawn up, extended
swiftly to its left till it embraced the whole front of
the enemy, and then prepared to advance in columns
covered by the usual swarm of skirmishers thrown out
around the head of each. These the Prussian troops
at once began to fire heavily on, either mistaking them
for an attack in force, or irritated by their boldness;
but the well-dressed lines and serried ranks of Louis
were vain against the crouching scattered foe, whose
deadly dropping shots his battalions returned in vain.
The Prussians fell thick and fast, until Lannes observing his foe already shaken, and having placed his columns so as to seize readily each point of vantage
offered by the ground, threw them on swiftly to the
attack. Before the Prussian lines could change front,
they found the enemy penetrating between them and
gaining their unprotected flanks. In vain did Louis
ride from side to side encouraging his men; in vain
did he try too late to use the slow infantry of the line
to support his few riflemen against the skirmishers
whose fire was mowing down his close formation. In
an hour from the time of the attack his force was in
flight, and he himself lay weltering in his blood in the
track of the fugitives, cut down by a French sergeant
after a brief summons to surrender, a vain sacrifice to
the long-cherished notion of the invincibility of the
tactics of a by-gone age.

Such, though in lesser detail, was the first intelligence from the field of war that rang through Prussia. Then came the fearful news of the defeats of Jena and Auerstadt. The army had been all but destroyed, three of the four chiefs taken or slain, the king was in hasty flight. The defeat by Bernadotte of the last reserves upon the Saal soon followed, the investment of Magdeburg, the defection of the Saxons, the fall of Berlin, the capture of Blücher and his flying cavalry. The evil now thickened day by day, and accusations of rashness, of treachery, of imbecility, of cowardice, were repeated whenever civilians spoke of the once admired national army. At Königsberg, and wherever the German Sclavonic elements had met closely, there was a sudden division of sentiment and separation of society. The Polish fellow-students of Brandt had naturally but little sympathy for the sufferings of Prussia. They felt not the shame of her defeats; they looked with curious and not unfriendly eyes to the great conqueror who already turned his arms towards their enslaved country. After the first positive news of the course of the campaign, they withdrew from mixing with the Germans, and forgetting their former assumption of Teutonism, called themselves Poles or Lithuanians. Even the students from Dantsic, Brandt tells us, kept apart from the genuine Prussians, among whom the misfortunes of their country awoke a warlike spirit which foreshadowed the glorious rising of 1813. All were crying out for arms; and when a royal aide-de-camp reached the city with orders to form new corps of provisional battalions, a crowd of well-born young men came forward to offer their services. Brandt was one of those accepted for an ensign's duty in one of eighteen battalions to be raised in East Prussia, the

ranks of which were to be filled by conscripts or discharged soldiers called back to service. Little but misery could be expected in such quarters as he now found
himself, placed in a semi-Polish village for winter training, under a government whose warlike means were
exhausted or in the enemy's hands, and with small
knowledge on the part of most of the officers and men
of the profession they had suddenly adopted. Cold,
dirt, and scanty rations were the chief features of the
life of the new ensign and his brother-soldiers, and the
only military necessary of which there was abundance
was the drill, which went on unceasingly. The training
was at first by companies, but these were soon formed
into battalions, and the latter before long were completed and tolerably instructed. Probably the Prussian Government had not the means of putting them
into the field, for through the long spring of 1807 they
were left unemployed, not without murmuring on the
part of the officers, who envied the brave deeds of their
comrades at Eylau, and believed that a reinforcement
to Lestocq's corps before the battle might have made
of the indecisive struggle a glorious victory. Young
Brandt meanwhile did not waste his leisure, but gave
his spare hours to the study of the small library he had
brought with him, and almost learnt by heart Cæsar's
" Commentaries," the " Seven Years War," and Vol-
taire's " Charles XII.," in the intervals of drill, finding
this easier, he frankly says, than to command his squad
with the full confidence necessary in an inefficient officer. At length an order reached the battalion to
march upon Tilsit, which was received with joy until
news came of the cause. Prussia's hitherto faithful
ally, the Czar Alexander, had seen his chosen general

Benningsen throw away the whole advantage of a long and able defensive campaign by the one morning of rashness that brought on the battle of Friedland. Hoping vainly to surprise a French detachment, he risked an army, inferior in numbers and less easily moved than the French, in face of the enemy and with a deep river in its rear. Napoleon seized on his advantage with a readiness worthy of his young days of Italy, and the victory which followed, though more easily won than those of Marengo and Austerlitz, was as striking and decisive as either. Russia abandoned her ally a few days later, and the victor was able to dictate his own terms to the prostrate monarchy of the Hohenzollerns. Prussia came out of the struggle shorn of half her territories, and a mere helpless vassal of the French Empire. Among her losses were the recent acquisitions of Polish soil, and her boundaries were so freely clipped to make the new Grand Duchy of Warsaw formidable, that some hundreds of thousands of pure Germans were transferred to the latter, and became in all but name, subjects of France. Among those thus abruptly handed over was the family of Brandt, and the young ensign was ordered forthwith to lay aside his Prussian commission and repair to his home. His discharge bore on its face the official endorsement of its purpose, being "granted in order not to withdraw the bearer from the service of the new authorities of his country."

Following out the instructions handed him, the ex-ensign made his way to Warsaw and presenting himself to the commandant, was sent on to appear personally before Davoust, who held a sway, almost absolute at that period of military rule, over the newly-formed

Grand Duchy, of which he was Governor-General. The young Prussian, after some waiting, was ushered suddenly into the presence of the redoubtable marshal. He found leaning against a door-post a middle-sized, strongly-built man, somewhat under forty years old, of stern, hard features and thoroughly military bearing, dressed in a simple uniform, with jack-boots and a plain officer's sword, his rank being denoted only by the silver baton embroidered on his epaulets. "You are from the Memel," he asked, at once of Brandt; "did you see the Queen there?" "Yes, your Excellency, I saw her but the day before I came away." "Was she in trouble? Did she look sorrowful?" were the next questions put rapidly by the interrogator. "I only saw her walking on the beach with the two eldest princes," was the reply, which produced a sharp "Answer me my question; did she look as if she were in trouble?" "Yes, indeed," replied Brandt more boldly; "and she had good cause, for they have taken half his country away from the King." "And whose fault is that?" went on the marshal, without showing any anger at the Prussian sympathies of his hearer, but seeking apparently to work up his own feelings of hostility to the injured royal house; "was it not she who forced the poor King into danger? Did not she compel him to throw down the glove to the Emperor? Was not she herself at Jena, haranguing the regiments in uniform? But for her intrigues and the bluster of the officers of the guard, the King would have now been in alliance with us, and the monarchy of the Great Frederic not have been dashed to pieces. However," he suddenly added, recollecting himself, "all this is no business of yours. Go back to your own home, and be henceforward a faithful subject of your new lord."

Brandt went, but only to find that all the comfort and prosperity of his father's house was destroyed by the waste of war. The exactions of the French commissariat had almost ruined his own family, while all around them there reigned the confusion of revolution, for the Prussian functionaries had been removed and their places were not yet supplied. Feeling his presence at home to be but an additional burden on means already overtaxed, and burning to put his lately acquired knowledge to some use, Brandt resolved, in spite of Davoust's warning, to seek entrance once more into the Prussian army. His father had once been acquainted with Blücher, who was at that time stationed near the Polish frontier of Prussia ; and armed with a letter to the veteran, even then a distinguished officer, young Brandt made his way to his quarters. The general read carelessly the introduction handed him, and roughly told the applicant that he knew already of too many in the same case, and could do nothing for him. The coarse, sharp manner with which Brandt's suit was rejected, struck him all the more after a visit made on quitting Blücher to the heroic and ill-fated Schill, whose personal courage and warm patriotism had made him known in Prussia far better than most officers of higher rank. He had already come to be looked upon by many as the future champion of their suffering country, and Brandt's friends had advised him to try what an interview there would do for him in case he failed to find aid in Blücher. Schill, though already the centre of a movement which gave birth afterwards to the famous *Tugendbund,* could

promise nothing for the young man who sought his
interest; but his manner was in pleasing contrast to
that of the old general, and the writer pays our nation
the compliment of finding no word so suited to express
his admiration of it, as that of *gentlemanlike*, borrowed
into his text from our tongue.

Heart-sick with disappointments and weary with his
journey, Brandt once more gained the Polish town of
Sochaczew, near which his parents lived. He found
here an ex-Prussian officer and friend of his father's
who had been appointed to the nominal command
merely for the purpose of making him responsible for
the supplies of a French division which was in camp
not far off. French officials in the characters of town-
major and government secretary ruled the district
through the Commandant, and led the the poor man,
who knew but little of their tongue, a life of misery;
while he dared not resign his post for fear some successor should be appointed, less reluctant than himself
to spare the inhabitants as much as possible from further exactions. Brandt offered his assistance in the
Commandant's office, and was gladly accepted, being
appointed, as the only equivalent his friend could give
to the rank of corporal unattached. Two months passed away in this fashion, the young man's zeal and attention making him more and more useful, when there
reached the place a Polish major employed in gathering recruits for the troops then being raised for French
use on the banks of the Vistula. He applied to the
Commandant for the aid of a temporary adjutant, and
obtained the loan of the services of young Brandt, who
received his warm thanks, when he left the place a few
days later, for the assiduity and activity which had

enabled him to finish his business with unhoped-fo₁
speed. But this officer, it soon appeared, had not contented himself with empty praise. Though he had
held out no promise of helping Brandt to a better position, he remembered him to some purpose when he
reached Warsaw. Three weeks after his departure, a
French gendarme reached the Commandant's office at
Sochaczew, with a dispatch addressed to " M. Brandt,
late ensign in the Prussian service." Opening it, he
found, to his astonishment, that Marshal Davoust had
appointed him sub-lieutenant in the " Legion of the
Vistula," under authority granted to the Governor-
General to fill up the vacant commissions in the new
corps, and now directed him to proceed to the depôt
of the regiment, which was to be located at Sedan,
then an almost forgotten fortress left far within the
frontiers of the new Empire, but destined to a sad
celebrity in later days, when the heritage of that Empire should be dashed to pieces before its walls. The
young Prussian was too well trained in submission to
local authority and too desirous of employment to do
more than cast one glance of regret at his lost chance
of fighting for his native country. In a few days more
he was on his march through it with 500 Polish recruits,
and ere long, traversing the great road by which Napoleon was to flee ruined from Leipsic six years later,
arrived upon the Rhine at Mayence, and crossed the
river into France.

Marching in that country he found more pleasant
than in Germany, where the political circumstances of
the time had made the Poles peculiarly obnoxious.
"They left off calling us barbarians, and rascally
Chinese," he says, "though our village quarters were

still rough and unpleasant enough." Arrived at Sedan, the new recruits were properly shoed, dressed, and after a very brief delay, ordered forward to join the armies gathering at the gate of the Pyrenees. Napoleon's first Spanish adventure had disastrously failed, through the incompetency of Dupont, hitherto a favorite and distinguished general. Europe had heard with astonishment of 20,000 disciplined French troops laying down their arms to a mere mob of hasty levies. All Spain had risen. English gold and arms were pouring in to the aid of the insurgent Juntas. Moreover, the French in Portugal had been completely defeated about the same time by a young British general, one Arthur Wellesley, hitherto unknown to European fame, and had evacuated that country altogether. A small corner only of the Peninsula was left to the king whom Napoleon had named to the throne of which he had laid treacherous hold, under guise of friendly intervention. Europe had witnessed the new turn of events with astonishment, and there were not wanting prophets to declare that the hour of Napoleon's fall was near, and that fortune had for ever abandoned the man who had used her favors so ill. But the Emperor took better measure of the calibre of his enemies and the immediate circumstances of the time, and prepared deliberately to enter Spain in person with resistless strength, little dreaming of the tenacity of the national resistance which was before him, or of the fatal wound to his strength which "the Spanish ulcer" was little by little hereafter to inflict. A quarter of a million soldiers were passing the Pyrenees to avenge the disaster of Baylen, and among them young Brandt, and his squad of Polish recruits, left Bordeaux after a brief halt to take their part in the great Peninsular campaign of the autumn of 1808. He had time to mark the true Southern looseness of manners which showed itself in forms repulsive to his stricter sentiment, as his detachment made its last marches to the Pyrenean frontier of France; to observe the strange likeness of the sandy wastes and fir-clad heaths of the Landes to the Polish plains in which his childhood had been passed; to gaze wonderingly at the building at Bayonne, where the Emperor had meditated on and fixed the fate of the Spanish princes who had trusted themselves to his keeping; to glance at the baths of Biarritz lately used by Napoleon himself, while the cavalry of the guard formed a chain of videttes from sea to sea, circling round the bathing-place for the protection of his sacred person; to call up to memory the mysterious legends of the stony pass of Fuenterabia into which the column next plunged; to see at every stage the individuality of the Polish depôt melting away in the gathering military stream in which it formed but a drop; and so the young subaltern found himself in Spain, marching as already in the enemy's presence, with van and rear-guard, and side patrols, searching closely every lurking-place, and his illusions as to the romance of the country vanishing as the promised land of beauty resolved itself into a succession of paltry villages of closely fastened houses, tenanted chiefly by hideous old women, with here and there a few peasants, dirty and degraded, but still defiant of the invaders.

Brandt's first Spanish quarters proved more agreeable than the outer aspect of the house, a close-barred decayed mansion, had promised. The host, a genuine

hidalgo in birth and manners, did his best to converse
with his unbidden guests, " which, as he did not understand either French or German, and spoke chiefly on
religious subjects," was not at first an easy matter.
Having made out the tenor of his questions to concern
the faith of the strangers, Brandt wrote out for him in
Latin the Apostles' Creed, which not only satisfied the
Spaniard of the soundness of their tenets, but led to
his raking up, for present use, the stock of that language he had brought many years before from the
University of Huesca, where he had studied with intent
to take orders. A conversation in this medium followed, turning on the politics of the crisis, the host declining to give Napoleon the rank of " Cæsar" or
" Imperator," and allowing him no more honor than
was implied in the title of " Supremus Dux Franco-Gal-
lorum." When, on further questioning, the guest declared himself not a Catholic but a Lutheran, and assured the host that in Germany people of the two churches
could meet together, live together, and even marry one
another, the good Spaniard declined to give ear to
such wondrous stories, but declared that for him any
one who used the Apostles' Creed was a good Catholic
and no heretic, and as such he would welcome him.
" The conversation," adds the memoir, " affords such
an excellent illustration of the state of the land in which
I was to pass the next few years, that I have purposely
dwelt on its details." The next stage brought him to
Pampeluna, where he found leisure to visit the works
of the citadel and examine the entrance where a party
of French soldiers, from an encampment outside, had
surprised the place in the preceding winter under cover
of a pretended snow-ball match, the players and spec-

tators having their arms at hand in a bread-cart. St. Sebastian and Barcelona, with other lesser places, had been occupied in a like treacherous manner, and their seizure by a pretended ally, according to our writer, had much to do with the hatred which brought on the subsequent insurrection.

The campaign had fairly opened when Brandt reached Pampeluna. It is not necessary for us to follow out in detail the childish strategy with which the Spanish leaders, intoxicated by the success of Baylen, sought to surround and cut off Napoleon's concentrated masses. Against such imbecility the Emperor would have triumphed with ease, even had he not wielded armies superior in numbers as well as training to the ill-organized bodies which were scattered on his front and flanks. An English reader may well take comfort in the thought that the only exception to the faults of Napoleon's enemies in that fatal autumn, was the gallant blow by which Moore, striking on the conqueror's communications, released Madrid for a while from pressure, and gave the remnant of the Spanish forces time to recover from their first disasters. When Brandt came on the scene, and joined his regiment, the armies of Estremadura and Galicia had been already scattered by the French, and Lannes was marching against those of Andalusia and Arragon, which formed the western part of the great arc which the Spanish had formed round their enemy. Despite the misfortunes of their comrades, the two commanders, Castanas and Palafox, had too much jealousy or over-confidence to unite, although both were close to Tudela and within sight of each other. Lannes paused, according to his orders, for a day or two, to give Ney, who was co-op-

17

erating to the westward, time to cut the foe off from
Madrid, and then moved his columns against them.   He
was suffering at the time from a severe accident, yet
exerted himself personally to reconnoitre the Spanish
positions, and discovered the two armies just so far
apart as to give him the opportunity, which he eagerly
seized, of beating them in detail.   Turning first against
Palafox, whose troops were drawn up in a line so long
as to be far beyond their commander's power to manœuvre, he rapidly attacked the Spanish centre with the
division of Mathieu, supported by the brigade of Habert, of which Brandt's regiment formed part.   The
Spanish regiments menaced gave way at once, and
Lannes pouring his cavalry through the opening, the
whole army of Arragon was soon in ignominious confusion and retreat.   Lannes then executed a rapid
change of front to his right to move against Castanos;
but the troops of the latter were so intimidated by the
spectacle of the defeat of their comrades, that they
moved off without even waiting to receive the attack,
bringing on their commander by this conduct the vulgar charge of treason, with which the generals of revolutionary armies are for ever assailed when unsuccessful.   Brandt relates but briefly the events of this
important day, in which the imaginary strength of
Spain finally collapsed ; and his account of it is chiefly
given from notes made long after, partaking thus
rather of the historical than the personal view.   In
fact, his own battalion being held in reserve, never approached the enemy at all, and but that a cannon-shot
or two went over his head, he could with difficulty believe
he had shared in the great action, in which the enemy
left behind them 4,000 killed (including many drowned

in the attempt to escape over the Ebro) and thirty guns. The whole event seemed like a dream to the young subaltern, who never saw the Spaniards distinctly, and though continually advancing with his regiment, only heard the shots getting more and more faint in the distance, as the retreat changed into rapid and unresisting flight. His corps, the third, which had done most of the work, had apparently reason enough to despise their adversaries ; but were soon to learn the old lesson, that troops contemptible in the field, may yet fight desperately under cover. The remains of Palafox's army sought refuge in Saragossa, and recovering heart when they found themselves unpursued by Moncey (who now commanded in Lannes' place), prepared for that defence which has made the city for ever famous in the history of patriotism. Moncey was thought but poorly of by his soldiers, who from the first instinctively felt him to be but a slow and feeble successor to the brilliant victor of Tudela. Although the battle was won on November twenty-third, not two days' march from Saragossa, it was a week before the French commander came in sight of the city ; and when fairly before it, want of means, or dread of repeating the failure made earlier in the war, held him back from any attempt to take the place by a coup-de-main : nor was it until he had received a regular park of heavy guns, and been reinforced by the whole corps of Mortier, that he commenced, about the middle of December, after several vain summonses to Palafox, the first operations of the memorable siege.

The story of that heroic struggle has never been so agreeably told as in the memoirs of the young German whose career we are following. Brandt was, indeed,

unfortunate enough to be detached at its opening to
Alagon, where the hospitals of the army had been
opened after the late victory, and to fall ill of an in-
fectious fever which was fatal to hundreds of the
wounded soldiers whose lives the Spanish bullets would
have spared. But after looking closely at death in a
form more frightful to the soldier than the worst to be
met on a battle-field, after wandering from his quarters
in a delirium, and unconsciously taking possession of a
bed in a ward full of dying privates, the young Prussian
fell into the hands of a rough but kind-hearted doctor
of his own regiment, and speedily recovered. In January he was again at the camp, and soon afterwards
ready to take his turn of the most severe duty that
subaltern was ever taxed with; for Grandjean's division
(to which Habert's brigade belonged) was charged with
the principal attack, and no regiments were more distinguished than those of the Vistula Legion, whose
chief, Colonel Chlopicki, here first earned the high
name which he kept to the end of his career.

Brandt found his battalion regularly quartered with
others in some former gardens of the suburbs. The
field officers and staff were, for the most part, housed
in the ruins of some sheltered building; but the bulk
of officers and men alike were living in narrow excava-
tions covered over with earth laid on branches, and
supplied with slender rations, eked out chiefly by food
purchased from certain adventurous suttlers of the
French side of the Pyrenees, who had swarmed across
the mountains—the roads into France being then tolerably safe—to trade on the wants of their countrymen.
The soldiers would in general have been poor custom-
ers, but for irregular resources not recognized in the

imperial pay-lists. The chief of these during the early part of the siege was the plunder of the pockets of the Spaniards slain in the continuous skirmishing by which the French carried the suburbs and olive-yards around the city after a contest of many days. At that time the defenders were frequently more numerous than the assailants, and among them were a large proportion of patriotic volunteers who had flocked into Saragossa from the country, bringing all their little worldly wealth upon their persons. There were in Brandt's regiment many gamekeepers and foresters from the woods of East Prussia, accustomed to shoot from their youth, who found the prospect of such human quarry so much to their taste, that they were never so pleased, during this part of the siege, as when it fell to the turn of their battalion to furnish pickets for the front.

The work became closer and more serious about the time that Brandt resumed duty. Under the guidance of a veteran sergeant who had fought in former days in Italy, Austria, and Poland, he learned all the mysteries of loopholing to advantage, so as to keep his own men under cover, at the same time, as far as possible, observing the enemy. Attacks now went on unceasingly, and before long the besiegers made good a lodgement in the city: but their real work still remained to be done, for Saragossa was crowded with massive stone buildings, convents for the most part, with walls of such portentous thickness as to make of each a separate fortalice; while the narrow, devious streets were so wholly commanded by the windows or loopholed openings used by the defenders, that they were almost useless for purposes of approach. The French were reduced to winning their way to the heart

of the place by the slow process of mine and sap, varied
by sharp assaults upon the strong buildings successively
breached by their explosions, and in each case obsti-
nately defended. Thus week passed after week, with
constant losses, frequent displays of individual heroism,
and a regular though often very slow advance ; for
Lannes had returned to take command of the army,
and his energetic spirit breathed itself through all below
him. Lacoste, the general of engineers, who had
become known in person to every soldier of the attacking force, fell a sacrifice to a needless exposure of his
person on a subaltern's duty ; but Rogniat, in later
days the severest critic of his imperial master's method
of war, took up the work with zeal, and it went forward
steadily, each lodgement in a building newly gained
being thoroughly strengthened by Lannes' own orders
before a new one was made : until, on the eighteenth
of February, the University buildings, which commanded the junction of the two principal streets, and
had resisted all attempts at assaults, were blown in
with 1,500 lbs. of powder, and the column of attack
that followed the explosion safely lodged within. Palafox then at once wisely treated, and three days afterwards the remains of his once formidable garrison
defiled before the French army and laid down their
weapons. The imperial soldiers viewed with some
indignation the cortége of about 10,000 ill-clad irregulars who appeared. Their ranks were full of gray-
bearded men and lads, their discipline was nominal,
their uniform for the most part confined, except for the
officers, to a gray cloak and red cockade, these volunteers being clad otherwise just as they had left their
distant homes, in peasants' or artisans' dress. The

French soldiers murmured audibly that they should be drawn up in parade order to receive so mean a set of prisoners ; but the Spaniards (our writer judges) looked on their defenders with very different eyes, and the spirit of earnest resistance which began at Saragossa kindled at every opening, and made the subjugation of the Ebro provinces the hardest task a French marshal ever accomplished.

There is nothing novel in the admiration extorted from Brandt by the obstinacy of the defence ; but he shows us that there is another less popular but equally true side to the story of Saragossa, which is that the resistance made by Palafox reflects not less credit to those who had to overcome it, and involved losses to the gallant Spaniards out of all proportion to their number. The glory, he says, which the world has bestowed upon the latter, should by right belong first to their conquerors. Deducting the divisions detached to watch against attempts made to relieve the place, Lannes had but about 15,000 men available for the actual attack. Of these nearly a third succumbed to the enemy's fire, or the more dreaded typhus ; but they managed to hold within their works a fighting force estimated at the outset at 30,000 soldiers and irregulars, and to destroy or take the whole. The service was naturally unpopular as well as severe. " Why did not I fall at Eylau or Friedland," said a dying officer of grenadiers to Brandt, " where we were fighting against a worthy enemy ? " It was only the devotion of the higher staff which maintained in the soldiers for weary months the necessary zeal and fire. Brandt himself on various occasions saw not only his brigadier, Habert, but Junot and Lannes, take up a musket in the trenches,

and exchange shots with the enemy's marksmen. The
latter exposed himself repeatedly like the meanest soldier, and on one occasion Brandt watched him continuing to fire, until the enemy, annoyed at the persis-
tence of the unknown skirmisher, deliberately trained
a howitzer on the portion of parapet behind which he
stood, the first shell from which killed a captain of
engineers at the marshal's side. Junot was more reck-
less still than his chief, fully justifying his reputation
won at Toulon, where he first owed Napoleon's notice
to this quality of daring. He delighted apparently in
sitting coolly under a hot fire, discussing the proceed-
ings around him in rough soldier's phrase with any one
who was near ; and it was after such a conversation, at
a time of special danger, that Brandt heard a veteran
major near him grumble forth, " Is it possible that this
man, who is so hopelessly mad, can be kept at the head
of an Army Corps? "

At times it needed something more than cool conduct towards the enemy to preserve the sway of these
rough leaders over the rougher elements they ruled.
General Habert, a tall, powerful man, a type of the
coarse but daring officer of the Republican era, was
stooping one day to gain cover as he passed along a
trench by a party of recruits who had just joined one
of his French regiments. " Ha ! your generals are afraid
sometimes, then," cried one of the coarse jesters who
are to be found in every company of common soldiers.
Foaming with sudden anger, the brigadier turned upon
the daring speaker, seized him by the collar, and pull-
ing him out of his cover, held him on the top of the
parapet, standing himself by his side. A volley was
poured on them at once by the enemy, and the

unhappy joker fell dead, while the general escaped with a slight flesh wound in the arm. " It serves the conscript right," was the only comment made by the comrades of the slain soldier, " for speaking like that of such a general as ours." And to the end of the seige, the brigadier, despite other outbreaks of violence, was as popular as ever with those whose perils he shared.

For some months after the fall of Saragossa the campaign in Arragon languished. General Habert was unfortunate enough to fail—thanks partly to his own fierce temper—in the only operation of importance entrusted to his brigade ; and the failure was a significant proof of the difficulties nature had placed in the way of the conquest of that rugged country. The general was engaged in crossing the Cinca river, which he had approached by a forced march, and hurrying on the passage of the advance guard of his brigade in the only two skiffs available, when he was interrupted by one of the boatmen, who was seen by Brandt to rush up and hastily accost him, as though remonstrating at the continuance of the attempt. The Spaniard was repelled with a loud curse, accompanied by a kick, for his interference, and the passage went on for a brief space, until the eight flank companies of the brigade and a small detachment of horse were safely across. Then the wisdom of the warning became apparent. The river suddenly rose, as the boatman had predicted, and poured down its bed in a few seconds in a raging torrent, which at once forbade all thoughts of further crossing. The companies already sent over were cut off from the bulk of the force, and the noise of the stream prevented all attempts at com-

municating with them. The flood showing no signs
of abating, and no orders from their chief being likely
to reach them, they were seen to move off, and disappeared from the sight of their comrades, no one knew
whither, while General Habert, after vainly trying to
pass at other points, and waiting the whole day in
hopes of communicating with them, returned the next
morning to Barbastro, from which he had marched.
Two days later the lost cavalry suddenly appeared,
but only to bring the ill news that the whole of the
infantry that had passed, the picked troops of the brigade, had fallen into the enemy's hands.   Their senior
officer had formed the idea, on discovering his isolated
condition, that his safest course was to march due eastward through the Pyrenees into France; but the
Spanish garrison of Lerida, with the aid of the guerillas who swarmed in that district, had headed his
column off on every side, until, worn out with fatigue
and hunger, it had been compelled to surrender.   Habert, who had forced them into peril, and been unable
to devise means for their succour, was in despair over
the loss of his favorite companies.   The rough soldier
was seen to burst into tears, exclaiming frantically,
" *Oh! mes pauvres grenadiers! mes braves voltigeurs!* "
with genuine self-reproach for his own want of precaution.   Suchet has not omitted to note the disaster in
his memoirs, nor to remark that for ages this river
Cinca had been noted for the sudden and dangerous
floods which sweep down its bed from the mountains
without warning.

   This failure, and some others less important, had
seriously depressed the spirits of the third corps, which
had been left under Junot after Saragossa fell; but the

advent of Suchet, who was appointed to the command in the summer of 1809, soon worked a wondrous change. Then was seen to the full how completely, in time of active service, the character of a chief is infused through the army placed under him, and influences even its lowest ranks. The new general won the respect of his troops at once by the practical skill with which he examined their appointments in his first inspection, and their affection by the praise he bestowed freely where officers and men deserved it. Each private felt from that time that he had over him a general who cared honestly for his wants, and exacted from him no unnecessary toil, though the enemy were to feel his activity against them to be unsparing when activity was of service. Discipline was rigidly enforced, and the country people so fully protected from all individual exaction, that Brandt tells us of a soldier being sent before a court-martial for robbing a peasant of a few eggs. Hence trade forthwith resumed its natural course wherever not interrupted by the guerillas and the presence of these became more dreaded than that of a French garrison. The regular taxes, aided by forced rations for troops on the march, sufficed for the fair wants of the army, and supplied means for the series of operations which the new chief soon began, and which was continued, with almost unvaried success, until his sway was extended over a third of Spain. In these campaigns, of which Suchet himself has ably written, Brandt shared to the full. The young Prussian subaltern came to be personally known to the marshal; had the command throughout the years 1810–11 of a picked company of skirmishers; and saw Blake's army driven out of the field, shut up in Valen-

cia, and finally forced to surrender to a force but very
little exceeding its own numbers. Two years and a
half had then passed by in the operations which caused
Napoleon to declare Suchet the best general he possessed, and which left the marshal, at the opening of
1812, in almost undisturbed possession of all that part
of Spain which Wellington's operations could not reach.
Brandt judges Suchet rather to have been a man of
exceeding energy in action and carefulness in preparation, than a soldier of great genius. He lived with
remarkable simplicity even when ruling absolutely three
large provinces; and although his wife was with him
whenever he halted, his table was invariably of the
plainest description. "Vegetables of the country and
the inevitable mutton cutlet, the whole consumed in a
quarter of an hour," formed the simple entertainment,
at which Brandt, in his capacity of officer on guard at
headquarters, was often present. He had gained the
marshal's confidence by this time very specially for
one of his rank, and had received from him the Cross
of the Legion of Honor after a second wound, with a
promise of promotion, which however accident withheld from him for some time after. He was therefore
but little surprised when sent for by his chief, and told
that he was selected to escort the captive Spanish general on the first stages of his journey towards France.
At this his last interview with his renowned leader,
Brandt could observe plainly a depression ill corresponding to the recent triumph that had rewarded such long
toils, and believed it to be the consequence of the news
which had just reached the army of a fresh outbreak
of the insurrectionary spirit of Arragon, extending to
the very gates of Saragossa. Possibly the marshal, in

the midst of his successes, foresaw the day when the faults of others would undo all the advantages he had won for France, and force her to abandon his hardly-won conquests. ".Marmont calls him a mediocre officer —not one of those special men who grow greater with danger," observes our writer justly ; " but for all that he was the only French general in Spain who uniformly succeeded in all his undertakings." The marshal gave his instructions as to Blake in the few significant words, "Treat him like a commander-in-chief, but watch him as you would a rascal ; " renewed his promise of obtaining Brandt his early promotion, and dismissed him to his new duty with the kindly expressed hope of seeing him soon again in Valencia—a hope not destined to fulfilment, for the young lieutenant was never again to meet the chief under whose teaching he had been trained into a practised soldier.

The escort set out on its way, and Brandt, before his task was ended, found good reason to remember the marshal's caution. The frontier of the province of Valencia had not long been passed when he found himself compelled to halt at Uldecona, a small place which had been vacated for some reason by the French garrison. This being the first time he had been compelled to trust to his own detachment for security through the night, and the vicinity being thickly wooded, he spent the evening in placing his posts so carefully as if possible to guard against surprise from without or escape from within. Some steps from the balcony of General Blake's chamber led direct into the garden, and near this point the anxious lieutenant not only placed a special post, but visited it repeatedly after darkness came on. It was an hour after midnight that he was thus inspecting his watch, when he heard a door open quietly on the balcony, and saw the general appear full dressed. Finding himself however observed by Brandt, who now ascended from below, the Spaniard asked who was there, and receiving the reply, " The commander of your Excellency's guard," retired either disconcerted from his attempt or annoyed at the appearance of suspicion. Although the exercise of this vigilance by Suchet's orders towards a high officer on his parole might seem at first unjustifiable, it must be remembered that Generals O'Donoghue and Renovales had just before disappeared from similar custody, violating their words of honor under pretence that these were made void by a guerilla attack upon their escort.

Next day the party arrived at Tortosa, but on the way were joined by a Colonel Pépé, a Neapolitan in the French service, who had been appointed to conduct the Spanish commander thence into France. Blake having complained to Pépé of the surveillance under which he had been placed the night before, the colonel took, or pretended to take, the captive's part, and reproached Brandt roundly, even threatening to report him, although the latter showed that he had but carried out Suchet's orders. The subaltern was not sorry when a slight return of an old fever came on him at Tortosa, and gave a fair excuse of his leaving his detachment for the time, and with it the obnoxious duty. This was his last employment in Spain; for making his way on recovery to his battalion, he found it under sudden orders for France with the rest of the Vistula Legion. The spring of 1812, had now set in. Napoleon's gigantic scheme for completing the subjugation of continental Europe was about to be put in execution; and Polish troops could least of all be spared from this greater design to share any longer in the Spanish struggle which he deemed of such minor importance. Yet Wellington had now wrested Portugal a second time from the grasp of the Imperial Eagles, and, firmly established on its strong eastern frontier, was preparing to pierce the barrier of fortresses which separated him from Spain, and to win fresh triumphs from the divided armies of Joseph in the new year's campaign. The spring was to give him Ciudad Rodrigo and Badajos; the summer to behold him scattering in rout the army of Napoleon's favorite marshal at Salamanca; the autumn to find the French authority tottering throughout the Peninsula in every province save those held by Suchet. But this year, destined to be so fatal to his armies in Spain, was selected by the Emperor for throwing the bulk of his forces to the very opposite extremity of Europe, thus leaving his brother's marshals wholly beyond reach of succor, if fortune should declare itself for the patient and watchful enemy who had just baffled them in Portugal. Such rashness was not unnoticed by those in the French army to whom a long course of training under the Eagles had left an independent thought. Murmurs were audible among the officers ordered from Spain, and the thoughts of many were put into plain words by Chlopicki, the favorite chief of the Polish Legion, whose saying, " Our good Napoleon has lighted his candle at both ends, and will be burning his fingers very soon," expressed pithily the doubts of the hour, and reads now with all the force of fulfilled prophecy.

Although expecting soon to revisit their own coun-

try, and possibly to assist in restoring her past glories,
the Polish soldiery had many regrets in leaving Spain.
Hard as their service had been (for Suchet's campaigns
were in fact a series of sieges, varied by marches and
combats), it had had its alleviations. The character of
the commander had caused his troops to be everywhere
respected. Except where the professional guerillas,
little better often than bandits on a grand scale, held
sway over a district, Suchet's forces had of late met
with but little of that persistent hostility with which
the French had to struggle in other parts of Spain.
They had advanced gradually in the career of conquest
from the rugged districts of Arragon and Catalonia into
the smiling plains of Valencia, which Brandt declares
to have struck him as worthy of the Spanish saying
which makes of them "a Paradise," though he will not
admit that the violent passions of the natives, though
remarkable enough even in Spain, deserve the qualification which the proverb adds, "peopled with devils."
The rough Polish soldiery fully appreciated the produc-
tiveness, if not the scenery, of their late quarters, and
a veteran sergeant, as he turned his back on the last
view of the district, was heard to declare, what was no
uncommon sentiment, "One can live better there by
soldiering than by hard work in our country;" words
which clothe with reality the old tale of the avidity
with which the barbarian invaders of the Roman Empire poured down upon the sunny lands of Southern
Europe.

Brandt himself had his personal regrets as he turned
his face towards the Pyrenees. The mountains shut
from the young man's gaze a spot to him sacred, which
he was never more to revisit, the small town of Cata-

layud, where, two years before, he had passed through what he terms the "Idyll of my Life," an innocent love passage with the young ex-novice. All the sentiment of a true German lover is poured forth in his description of his short acquaintance with the fair Inez, whose guardian, a hard uncle of the true Spanish type and deep hater of French rule, removed her suddenly from the place during one of the absences on duty of her young adorer. Brandt from that day never saw nor heard more of his Inez. Happy for them both as he admits this separation to have been (since there could have been no good issue to such an attachment, and their one hope, to escape from her family and get married in France, was practically a dream), yet the sorrow of that loss he declares to have dwelt with him through fifty years of prosperous after-life and a long and happy marriage with one of his own rank and nation. No other love, he will have it, is so deeply tender and unselfish as that of a Spanish maiden ; and in reading his picture of the simple grace and loveliness of the fair girl of Catalayud, one may realize the truth and beauty of those minor romances of Cervantes, which are so much less known than the world-admired "Don Quixote," though hardly less picturesque or less illustrative of the people of whom he wrote.

Brandt found his march through France, when fairly entered on, an agreeable change enough. The Poles were everywhere looked on as good friends and worthy soldiers, and the Cross of Honor, borne by the young sub-lieutenant, attracted constant notice. The decoration was in those days not easily earned. It was something, he says, that men turned round to look at ; and princes would do well to remember how vastly

18

the indiscriminate distribution of such honors de-
teriorates their practical use as genuine yet cheap
rewards of faithful service.   Readers of the " Fezensac
Souvenirs" will remember how rapidly promotion in
the Grand Army fell upon those who had good military
connections.   It speaks volumes for the difficulty of
obtaining it without such help that Brandt, after having been chosen before the enemy for the command
of a flank company (for such, with its full complement
of officers and men, his charge had been), leading it
constantly in a succession of combats and sieges for
two years, and winning favorable notice and special
military honors from a marshal of France, yet left
Spain still a sub-lieutenant, though he was soon, as we
shall see, to receive his long promised step.   The
Legion marched leisurely at first, but was hurried forward through Central France, and at Montlieu the
commanding officers of battalions received sudden
orders to send their men forward in country carts.
The account of the whole march speaks ill enough for
the internal discipline under pressure of the Imperial
regiments.   The colonel was never seen by the men;
the battalion leaders only appeared now and then,
instead of sharing the march step by step; and when
the carts were provided, for want of any proper supervision, parties were allowed to fill each and drive off
just as they chose, and to straggle at night from their
already dispersed quarters.   It was not surprising that
from three to four hundred men were absent when the
Legion mustered at Versailles, many of whom did not
rejoin their standards until the regiment was marching
from Paris some days later.

On March twenty-second, 1812, the Legion entered

the capital, and as it stood waiting for orders on the Place Vendome, Brandt heard his name called out, and saw his colonel holding a paper, which proved to be his long-expected brevet of lieutenant. It was dated on March twenty-fifth, 1812, an obvious mistake as he judged, for that day year had been the date from which Suchet had recommended him, as that on which he had specially distinguished himself by suppressing with his company a serious émeute in the battalion against an unpopular major. Moreover, the commission was a duplicate copy, and the original had of course been sent to his late headquarters in Spain. But before Brandt had had full time to discover the mistake, much less to take steps to have it rectified, he was on his way to Russia, where the ravages of the dreadful campaign that followed were to give him further well-earned promotion. He was yet therefore in the first flush of unalloyed pleasure when the regiment was ordered to move on to the Tuileries, and making its way with difficulty through the crowd of vehicles which even in those days choked the Rue St.-Honoré, turned into the Place du Carrousel, where the Emperor was in the act of reviewing a large mass of troops. There was little attempt at show; the divisions were drawn up in column; and the Polish Legion took the place assigned to it near the Guard in a very confused state, for it was only by degrees that its ranks were brought out of the disorder caused by hurrying through the crowded streets. But the purpose of the day was not mere parade, nor even the evolutions with which commanders of peace armies are wont to act dramas hardly possible in war. The troops had been summoned together for the special object,

more important than these in Napoleon's eye, of bring
ing his own person into that familiar contact with his
soldiery which he had long proved a most powerful
means of calling forth their ardor at the commencement of some great undertaking. The Polish Legion
waited its turn for inspection patiently, while above
them in a gallery a party of gaily-dressed spectators
made comments on the scene below. Among them
one gentleman was conspicuous for the marked indifference with which he turned his back on the review,
while keeping up a lively conversation with the ladies
he accompanied; and some of Brandt's Polish comrades recognized by his uniform the Russian ambassador, not yet dismissed from the Court already openly
hostile to his master. In fact, that last exchange of
diplomatic forms was still in progress, by which great
nations bent on war strive to hide from the world their
willingness to enter on the contest, and to throw on
their opponents as much as possible the responsibility
of the evils which it must needs bring in its train.

A half-hour or more had thus passed, when a sudden call from their commander brought the Legion to
attention; and in a few minutes more the historic form,
which was recognized by all as soon as seen, approached the head of the regiment. The Emperor was on
foot, with but a few attendants; and among them were
Chlopicki, some time since made general, and one or
two other well-known Polish officers, to whom he first
expressed his general satisfaction with the conduct of
the Legion. Then he walked slowly down the side
of the column, and, stopping suddenly every now and
then, interrogated the oldest looking captain as to his
exact country and length of service, inquired the

cause of the absence of another whose place with his
company was filled by a junior officer, asked Brandt
himself sharply how often he had been wounded to get
that cross, and, satisfied with the reply, added, "You
are young enough still; you will be a captain in good
time." Then he pulled from a private's haversack a
piece of his morning's ration of bread which was projecting, tasted it, and with an emphatic "*Pas mal*,"
passed on. His eye falling next on a man of the light
company who was exceptionably obese, he told the
Polish general to question him as to where he had contrived to get so fat, and having the answer re-transla-
ted, "Since I got back to France," ordered him to be
told, "You are quite right to take good care of yourself now; you may be obliged to fast by-and-bye."
Passing on, the Emperor indicated one or two men to
be called out and show their packs and cartridge-
boxes, and expressing his satisfaction with the condition of these, told them to fall in again. Had he
unrolled the great-coats, Brandt adds, he might have
seen that they were in a miserable condition, the hasty
march of seventeen days which had brought the regiment to Paris having ruined those which the Spanish
bivouacs had spared ; but this discovery was spared
the colonel, whom Napoleon complimented by declaring loudly that his regiment did not the least show the
effects of the hard campaign it had just shared. Before passing from it, he selected a veteran sergeant out
of those he saw decorated with the Polish medal (the
ordinary reward of good conduct in the Legion) to
question him publicly as to his services, and finding
him to have been five times in the list of the wounded,
ordered him the coveted distinction of the Cross of

Honor. This last stroke done, he left the regiment, telling the colonel to express officially for him his pleasure at its condition. That afternoon at their quarters an order was read out, conferring a number of decorations on officers and men, those of the former carrying the title of Knight of the Empire and pensions varying from 500 to 3,000 francs. The payment of these, however, was not charged upon the military chest which the Emperor watched so closely, but on certain taxes on the trade of the Rhine, or on the newly conquered districts of Valencia. Prize-agents forthwith appeared, who in those days made a regular traffic of buying up such donations; and the officers who had the Rhenish pensions found no difficulty in obtaining advances: but even Suchet's successes had not made Spanish securities marketable, and the few recipients who lived through the coming campaign found the value of the Valencian grants limited to the accompanying title of Chevalier.

Brandt, with about five thousand other officers, was that night invited to a huge banquet to be given by the Emperor, at which, however, the Imperial presence was represented vicariously by Marshal Bessières. The scene was confusing enough, and seemed suited rather to the headquarters of a conquering army than to an emperor's court. Loud bands, rough soldier waiters, and coarse crockery, all strangely smacking of the canteen, were intermingled with choice wines and viands of true Parisian excellence. The music of the instruments, and the clatter of the French voices (none but Frenchmen could be heard, says Brandt, in such a din) ceased for a few seconds after the meal was over, and a loud *Vive l' Empereur* to the single toast of the night resounded through the building. Then the assembly dispersed through the city to seek amusement elsewhere. Brandt and his party found places at the theatre, where the Œdipus Coloneus was performed in a French dress; but, except the acting of Talma (which was well suited to the tragic part of Sophocles's unhappy hero), the taste of the young Prussian, trained to the classic original in his student days, found the whole representation unreal and almost grotesque.

A long inspection by Marmont, who had not yet left Paris for the duel with Wellington which was to ruin his rising fame, occupied the next morning, the whole interior economy of the regiment being looked into by the marshal in his capacity as Inspector-General of Reviews. Then followed hasty visits to the chief sights of Paris, among which it is strange to note that, despite the presence of Imperialism which pervaded the atmosphere, the death-place of the slaughtered D'Enghien was especially sought out by curious Polish and German eyes, and its site found to be already made a show-place. Three days later, the regiment was on its march to Sedan, where its depôt had been stationed ever since the Legion was raised. One only of the four brother officers who had left the place for Bordeaux with Brandt four years before, came back to it again, so severe had been the demands of the Spanish war. The regiment was now, with some others of the Legion, assigned to a newly formed division, and the Emperor lost all the popularity he had gained among them on his late inspection, when the Poles heard that their beloved chief Chlopicki had been passed over in favor of a French general, Claparède, one noted too for

an overbearing brutality of manner, uncommon even
in those of the rough school of the Revolutionary
armies in which he had been trained. "We shall find
him," said the old adjutant-major, "a very unpleasant
comrade, a perfect roaring lion, seeking whom he may
devour;" while another officer bitterly remarked that
Napoleon was imitating with the Polish Legion what
the allies had done with their country, Poland; tearing
it in pieces, and distributing it out to foreigners. The
soldiers were as little pleased as their officers, nor had
they as solid consolation as the latter, who, on the
same day that gave them their new commander, received through him the Imperial order for the instant
formation of the skeleton of a third battalion to the
regiment, an order repeated throughout the Legion.

This augmentation of the strength of the corps was
carried out with the celerity which probably in no
other service but that of Napoleon has ever been attained consistently with the least approach to efficiency.
The promotion of all the junior ranks was made over
to the colonel, who forthwith told off a sub-lieutenant
to take temporary charge of each of the new companies, whose commission as lieutenant was to follow as
matter of course. Similarly a non-commissioned officer
was selected for each to act as sub-lieutenant, to be
confirmed in the rank after a short trial. The higher
commissions, however, were reserved, and Brandt
found himself for the present in command of the new
light company, composed, besides its three officers, of
a few picked corporals, and some recruits from the
depôt. A few hours later, he had drawn up his charge
for Claparède's inspection, and had to face the sneer
with which his new general expressed his doubts

whether so young a man could really have deserved the decorations he bore. A warm retort from the lieutenant, declaring that he had won what he wore under Marshal Suchet's own eyes, produced no more apology than the coarse advice, " Don't get hot about it, Mister Officer ; " but the rest of the inspection went on quietly enough ; and as the new battalion marched early next morning in advance of the rest of the regiment, Brandt was for the time freed from any disagreeable consequence of the collision. Claparède's conduct it may be observed, at the head of the division, fully justified the reports that had been heard of his character ; but his brutal severity fell oftener during the campaign upon luckless peasants and others who came by chance within his grasp than upon his own soldiery. It is in time of peace, or in the comparative leisure of a garrison, that the exactions of the martinet press most odiously on those he commands. On the march or before the enemy, there is less opportunity for the exercise of petty tyranny ; and soldiers will then forgive much that would be obnoxious within the barrack-walls in a general who shows himself fertile in resource and fearless in peril in the field.

In joining his new battalion Brandt had parted from the more educated part of his comrades, and so found little companionship in what would have been otherwise a most interesting journey to one whose records at every step show him to have been an intellectual observer of scenery and manners. At Metz, however, he was fortunate in a fleeting acquaintance with a young artillery officer, who escorted him over the works of the great fortress, and in whom modesty and knowledge seemed, his German listener thought, strangely

mingled for one just emerged from cadethood, and
joining the most renowned and successful army the
world had ever seen.   The controversy not yet wholly
settled in our own country as to the value of practical
or theoretical training for officers, even then occupied
men's minds in some degree ; for Brandt's new friend
lamented the length of the time he had been compelled
to pass in studying exact sciences, as so much deduct-
ed from that in which he might have been traversing
the world with his regiment, and perhaps witnessing,
instead of reading of, deeds of arms.   The young men
parted next day, but they were destined to meet once
again.   In the crisis of the great battle of Borodino,
when Brandt's division was ordered to hold the great
redoubt just carried from the Russians, it was flanked
by a battery of artillery which had lost all its officers
but one young subaltern, whose valor and exertions
awoke admiring comment from Berthier, Davoust, and
the Viceroy Eugene, who were all near the scene, and
opposite the Russian centre.   Seeing him suddenly
struck by a cannon-shot towards the close of the fight,
the Viceroy desired Brandt to take a surgeon to the
spot, and in the dying youth, who was fearfully man-
gled, our writer recognized the newly-commissioned
artillerist of Metz, and thought sadly of the aspirations
for real service which were so soon to be fatally real-
ized.

The Legion recrossed the Rhine, marching steadily eastward.   The smiling plains of Saxony and the
rougher districts of Silesia were passed in turn; Brandt
giving his few leisure hours to the study of a Russian
grammar which he had bought upon the way.   The
roads grew sandier and heavier as the Oder was ap-

proached, until the march was so toilsome that wagons were furnished, contrary to the usual practice, to carry the knapsacks and rations, so that the soldiers should be weighted with nothing but their arms. The villages now grew dirtier and more poverty-stricken at every stage, until the German frontier was fairly passed, and the Poles found themselves once more in their own country under the shadow of the White Eagle, which everywhere marked the spurious sovereignty of that hybrid creation, neither province nor kingdom, the Grand Duchy of Warsaw. French protection had indeed done little for the physical aspect of the country. Focus of Napoleonic intrigue, debateable land between the aggressive Frank and unyielding Muscovite, Poland had had for years to bear much of the pressure of war without its excitement or its glories; and now, as forming the base from which the Grand Army was to move to its greatest enterprise, the burden lay doubly heavy upon her. Yet no one complained of the government, or threw the odium of crushed trade and exhausted means on French domination. No one expressed a wish to have the Prussian rule restored in Posen. No one, amid all the poverty and misery of the land, murmured at anything more than the general hardness of the times. The Grand Ducal Government was national and popular, because it was felt to sympathize with its subjects. This is strange testimony to gather from a Prussian pen ; but it is more striking still, and may bring a lesson to other rulers than the counsellors of the Hohenzollern, to find from such unbiassed authority that the reasons of this strange and complete acquiescence of the Poles in the revolution which had overthrown their late masters, lay in the intense dislike entertained towards the Prussian officials, with their cold, rigid measurement of Polish inferiority, their zeal for forcing improvements and education of a strictly North-German type upon a country unprepared to receive them—in short, what Brandt, seeking for a single words, terms the *Borussomania,* which had led his countrymen, during their years of possession, to strive to bring the whole of the institutions of their conquest into the exact mould of their own. It was not what Prussia had desired to do for Poland, but the manner of her doing it, which had made her government so obnoxious that amid the standing exactions caused by protracted preparations for war, none regretted the change of rulers; none, at least, except the few who, like Brandt's own family, born and bred Germans, had settled in Posen, and thus been severed by the political circumstances of the time from the land which still held their affections. For these Prussian settlers, representatives of the Teutonic civilization which, with the sword in one hand and the spade in the other, had in the struggle of long centuries been winning the broad basin of the Vistula from the Pole, now suffered no less in property than sentiment by the conditions of the struggle in which Napoleon had embarked. "You have come to a beggar's house," was Brandt's father's salutation, as he clasped the young lieutenant in his arms; and their greeting was not ended when word was brought that the foragers of a passing French column were taking the very crop off the ground for their horses. "What am I to do?" said their commander, in answer to Brandt's remonstrance. "I will give the *bons*" (the orders for repayment of the supplies by the commissariat). "I make myself responsible to the

Emperor for all I take. But I must carry out my instructions, and collect whatever is really necessary for my party. And I find the magazines all cleared already." Empty they were, indeed, those stores which in Brandt's early years had expanded only to grow fuller year by year. Ney and his whole staff had been lodging here for days not long before. The Crown Prince of Wurtemburg and his retinue had succeeded closely the marshal and his attendants; and the roomy mansion was no sooner freed from the pressure of this uninvited presence of royalty, when it became the quarters of a battalion of French infantry. Brandt's visit to his former home was necessarily short, and, with a saddened heart and much anxiety for his parents' future, he turned his back on Sochaczew, and made his way to rejoin his battalion near Thorn.

Early experience had skilled Brandt in his present duty of training Polish recruits rapidly for the field. Supplies of the necessary clothing and arms were abundant and freely dispensed, most of the former having been prepared near the frontier ready for the design which Napoleon had framed long before. Brandt saw the Emperor but once at this period, when he rode hastily on to the ground at the close of a brief review held for him by Mortier, and called sharply for the prefect to complain of the youth of the Polish conscripts, adding, "Young lads do nothing but keep the hospitals full"—words which he must have had a hundred occasions to repeat when the wild enterprise in which he was embarking had left him to struggle during the year following against united Europe with armies built up of the youthful material he thought so ill of.

Anecdotes of the Emperor's sayings and doings

abounded at this era among the vivacious Poles, and
circulated freely through the motley force which was
gathering at his orders. Brandt repeats as one of the
most prominent of these the well-known address of
Napoleon to the Polish deputies, in which he declared
himself that in place of court dress he would have
desired to see them "booted and spurred like their
ancestors in presence of a threatened Tartar invasion."

This story has been often told before; but the overbearing manner of the Emperor to his allies is better
illustrated by his personal treatment of certain distinguished individuals who attended his levées. Among
these came the Count Szoldrecki, the richest land-owner
of Poland, whose name Napoleon mistaking for some
manufacturer of whom he had heard, addressed him
with the abrupt interrogatory, "How many hands do
you employ in your works?" Receiving no reply from
the puzzled nobleman, he added sharply, "You own
porcelain factories, do you not?" and when the prefect, horrified at the mistake, whispered who the Count
really was, his questioner, far from apologizing, merely
turned away with an "*Ah! c'est très-bien,*" and spoke
to the next comer. So at a special reception of the
Polish ladies, he addressed to a young noble-woman of
rather gross proportions the startling words, "How
many children have you?" "None, sire," was the
reply. "What, then, are you a *divorcée?*" "I am
not married at all," said the lady. "Better not take
long in choosing; you have not much time to lose,"
was the gallant reply which closed the conversation.
There were even severer stories than these afloat; and
Brandt meeting an old friend who moved in the best
Warsaw society, heard that the impression made by

Napoleon was of the most unpleasant character. " His
manners are thought bad, his voice sharp and creaking,
his address imperious and overbearing." There was
current at this time everywhere an epigram on the new
ruler of Poland by a nobleman who had been well
known for his intimacy with the former king, Stanislaus,
and who gave his verdict on the head of the newly
revived Court in the sententious Latin words, *Nec
affabilis, nec amabilis, nec adibilis.* In fact, the singular
elevation which Napoleon had reached, his sense of the
enormous means of offence he wielded, the servility of
the vassal princes who obeyed his edicts, had altogether
blinded his eyes to the insecurity of his position. The
muttered threats of hatred and vengeance which had
followed his triumphal progress through Europe were
unheard by its dictator. The growing dimensions of
the Spanish war which threatened his rear, the activity
of the *Tugendbund*, which spread its ramifications across
the vast territory that lay between him and his faithful
France, was unknown or unheeded. Even in Poland
his policy was suspected, and the strength which that
still powerful country might have put forth against his
enemies, lay dormant because he lacked the political
courage to promise, as the price of victory, her longed-
for independence. To pledge himself to this, it is true,
might have cost him the half-hearted support of an
ally; but the secresy with which he preferred to veil
his future policy was sufficiently alarming to Austria to
prevent her from exerting herself heartily for the overthrow of Russian power, while it checked the beating
of the national pulse of Poland, and made the enterprise seem to be for the aggrandisement of an individual rather than the liberation of a people. The most

eminent of the many writers who servilely worship
Napoleon's genius as a chief, has pointed out, in an
eloquent passage of " The Consulate and Empire,"
that this political error, at the very crisis of his fortunes, was an irremediable misfortune to his cause.
It has been said of late that he lost his last campaign
mainly for want of boldness and decision.   The historian who cannot credit his idol's having in the least
degree been found wanting in those qualities on the
plains of Belgium, condemns their absence in his Polish
policy with severity as bitter as any hostile critic could
employ ; and this opinion of M. Thiers is fully supported by that of General Brandt, reviewing, in the
long years of calm that followed, the stormy scenes in
which he had borne a part.

We should need space for a volume rather than an
essay were we to attempt to follow our author through
the story of the last six months of 1812.   No passage
of history has been more brilliantly or abundantly
illustrated by the actors in it than the fatal invasion of
Russia ; and yet it is not too much to say that no
commentary on its details, nor any narrative of its successive phases, has ever been given to the world sur-
passing that of General Brandt in vivid interest.   We
may add that the future critic or historian of Napoleon's great disaster can hardly accomplish his task
completely without viewing the expedition as it appeared to one who has combined in his description a
personal sympathy with the Grand Army with the unbiassed judgment of a foreigner on its shortcomings ;
and who being by education a German, by country a
Pole, and by profession a Frenchman, was able to
regard the whole struggle of the eventful year without

sharing the delirium of national passions amid which Europe arose to tear off the chains that had bound her. Without entering here into any discussion of the general causes of Napoleon's failure, it may be said that, in Brandt's opinion, the aggravated sufferings and vast losses of the retreat from Moscow were due almost entirely to the shameful lack of discipline which had crept into the Grand Army. Probably the very dimensions of his overgrown force prevented Napoleon from knowing its disorderly condition. When the frost had once set in with its attendant miseries, it was altogether too late, in Brandt's opinion, to attempt to restore control: but had the staff not previously lost the respect of the soldiers by avoiding its share of the hardships of the campaign, had the same energetic means of punishing stragglers been resorted to as in the equally severe winter of 1806–7, order might have been retained through the most trying periods that followed. A few examples of corporal punishment, such as were administered on the bloody field of Eylau to the absentees who came in after the battle, an execution or two at the head of each column of the first men who wilfully threw away their arms after turning their faces homeward: and the retreating army might have preserved its cohesion. The stores formed upon the road would then have been properly distributed, instead of being dissipated by plunder and waste, leaving those who came late to starve even where plenty had been laid up for all. Supplied with food, the combatants might have held together, and, by showing a good front, have obtained rest for themselves and given time for the staff to collect and organize the stragglers. But all order had fled before the frost set in and found thou-

19

sands of unarmed soldiers and disorderly followers, mixed with equipages laden with plunder, impeding and confusing the columns of march. The cold and suffering that ensued only completed the demoralization of the army which lax discipline had begun. As to the part played by the Russians, General Brandt asserts that but for their faults no single Frenchman should have recrossed the Beresina, much less have made his way safely, as he did himself, though suffering from a wound, back into Poland, where he was received and nursed to recovery at his father's house. It was not until the end of May 1813 that he was able to rejoin the Legion, now shrunk into a single regiment, with the well-won rank of captain and senior adjutant.

The eventful autumn which followed saw Napoleon, after temporary successes, expelled from Germany by a succession of disasters which only the greater dimensions of those endured the year before in Russia have cast into the shade. Brandt shared to the full in the last and worst of these reverses, and at Leipsic fell desperately wounded into Russian hands. His memoirs, if continued to this point, would have been invaluable to the student of the War of Independence; but his capture and subsequent illness prevented his preserving even the most fugitive notes of the events of 1813, and as far as the military portion of the work is concerned, it closes at the escape of the author from Russia. When next the life of the veteran of Spain and Moscow is continued in detail, we find him once more serving under the flag beneath which the young student of Königsberg had been enrolled ten years before in the hour of Prussia's calamity. It was the policy of the victorious House of Hohenzollern to show that Prussia's late temporary losses of territory had been the mere consequences of military calamity, and to ignore the attendant political circumstances now that military success had restored the kingdom to its former dignity and possessions. The involuntary transfer of allegiance which had placed Brandt beneath the Imperial Eagles found easy pardon, and he was received on his own application into the Prussian service, resigning with pleasure the commission proffered him in the Polish army, now absorbed into that of Russia. The remainder of the long and varied career we have too briefly reviewed was passed in honorable employment under his legitimate sovereign. He lived to serve under Gneisenau and Clausewitz as a confidential staff officer, during the armed neutrality which Prussia maintained upon her eastern frontier in the Polish Revolution of 1831. He became noted as a military essayist, his pen attracting such attention as to single him out by royal choice to defend the Prussian administration against certain virulent attacks made on it by the Paris journals in the early days of Louis Philippe's reign. His ability thus becoming fully known to his sovereign, it was a natural choice which sent him soon after, as the Military Commissioner of Prussia, to report on the condition of the French army under the new *régime*. At the camp of Compiègne, where the chief force of the Citizen King was then exercised, Brandt met on equal terms many ex-Napoleonist generals whose names had been historic when he was yet serving as a subaltern under Suchet; he discussed Prussian organization with Marshal Soult, and was introduced to Thiers, then in the early prime of par-

liamentary power, and to the Duke of Orleans, study
ing hard his part for the crown he was never destined
to wear. Among the incidents of the chief review he
attended, Brandt observed a young aide-de-camp twice
thrown from his horse, yet remounting each time to
pursue his duties as actively as if refreshed by his fall.
He asked and noted the name of this energetic officer,
then Lieutenant Macmahon of the 1st Cuirassiers,
and before closing his own memoirs lived to recognize in him the victor of Magenta and favorite marshal
of France. That these memoirs were not published
until after the writer's decease, is sufficiently explained
by the outspoken views they express on Prussian policy in Poland. As a record of the achievements of
Marshal Suchet in Spain, as a contribution to our
knowledge of the ever-fresh tragedy of the Russian invasion, as an impartial criticism of the process by which
Northern Germany absorbed the Sclavonic provinces
on her borders, these volumes are of deep importance
to the student of the stormy period with which this
century opened. But above all these in interest, in
the eyes of many, will be the author's description of
the realities of military life under the First Empire.
It is hardly too much to say that the study of this
work, following that of the Fezensac "Souvenirs,"
throws more light upon the details of the Grand
Army, and upon the working of the system which all
but enslaved the world, than had been shed by all
the national histories and official biographies with
which Europe has been deluged these sixty years
past.

CORNWALLIS AND THE INDIAN SERVICES.*

To rule a subject empire with wisdom, vigor, and purity; to make the name of England respected throughout the decaying empires of Asia; to infuse into the stagnant material of Oriental civilization the life that springs from European progress; such have been some of the tasks which our supremacy in India has imposed upon those who there serve the state. Great missions often seem to call forth great men; or if these are not always to be found, at least the highest qualities of those employed are brought out and nourished by the very difficulties of their task. Thus it has happened, that if in India the baser elements of the ruling race have not failed sometimes to take advantage of the ductility of the subject, England has, on the whole, good cause to be proud of the services to whom her charge has been confided. From the time of Lord Cornwallis to the present day, it may truly be affirmed that Indian officials, as a body, would bear favorable comparison for energy and purity with the public men of any empire in the world. More than this; as the personal conduct of the administrator may there influence the destiny of millions, so the chivalrous side of the dominant race has found an opportunity denied in the close atmosphere of European

* *Lives of Indian Officers, illustrative of the History of the Civil and Military Services of India.* By Sir John Kaye.

politics.   The services of India have had in their ranks
men of such saintly lives and heroic action as mediæval
writers dreamed of, if they did not see.   But that the
names of men of this type, and of others eminent
under the Company's rule, have become household
words in the land that sent them forth, is due chiefly
to the special knowledge of a small band of writers.
Those only who themselves are acquainted with the
East can make the conditions of life there, and especially those that affect our rule, of interest to far-off
British readers.   And among them none has done so
much to bring the scenes of modern Indian history,
and the figures that move among them, home to his
countrymen as the veteran author Sir J. Kaye.   In his
more important works he has made familiar among
English families the deeds of their kinsmen who have
lived and died to preserve and consolidate our empire.
In his " Lives of Indian Officers" he presents us with
a gallery of portraits of characters, of various types
indeed, but of all of whom their countrymen may well
speak with pride.

Cornwallis, statesman and soldier, forms a worthy
foreground to the group selected from the civil and
military services which owe their high character to
him.   A great man and a good, his heart was in his
work, and his work lives after him.   His success in
Indian administration contrasts so strongly with the
sad story of his American enterprises as to justify those
who attribute the failure of the latter to any cause
rather than want of zeal or judgment.   We could have
wished to avoid following Sir J. Kaye into the history
of the difference between General Clinton and his great
lieutenant.   This, and the military events with which

it is interwoven, are rather touched upon than written
in the work before us; and for its purpose it would
have been better to have kept to that Indian ground
where the biographer treads more safely than in the
swamps of Carolina and Virginia. It would certainly
have been juster to Cornwallis. His name is of necessity so connected with the disasters which closed
the Revolutionary War of America, that an imperfect
notice of these is in the very nature of things almost
an injury to him. Nor is this repaired by extracts
given us from one or two of the less important letters
of the series relating to the occupation and defence of
Yorktown. This correspondence, published originally
by Cornwallis himself in 1783, should be read as a
whole by those interested. Thus treated, it proves
abundantly what he asserts in his introduction : " When
the arrival of the French fleet, and the approval of
General Washington, were made known to Sir Henry
Clinton, it will appear that his promises of relief in
person were uniform, without giving me the smallest
particle of discretionary power, different from holding
the posts that I occupied." That he did not attempt
to break out of the toils in the early part of the investment, is thus explained by Cornwallis with a clearness
which seems to defy contradiction : " The enemy were
in a strong position and considerably superior in number, but I should have attacked them without hesitation if I had thought myself at liberty, after a victory,
to escape into the Carolinas [from whence, be it observed, he had but lately marched triumphantly] with
the troops that were able to move. No other object
appeared sufficient to justify this measure. But a
defeat would probably have been followed with the

immediate loss of our post, which until the end of September was in a most defenceless state : and *as I could never have proved that I should not have been relieved*, I should have been exposed to public execration, as a man who, having reason to expect the early arrival of the Commander-in-Chief to supersede him in his command, had, in hopes of personal reputation from a victory, sacrificed the essential interest of his country."

Thus much in justice to a great man who struggled manfully against the fates that bore him down, and with him the last hope of recovering America by the sword. Bülow, the Prussian military writer, a man of genius as brilliant as his fate was unhappy, witnessed the struggle in person, and has borne disinterested evidence that these hopes were not as chimerical as it is now the fashion to assert. From the day, however, that Britain lost the control of the ocean which divided her from her revolted colonies, the war could have had but one result. A success on Cornwallis's part in Virginia might have added to his laurels already gained in New Jersey and the Carolinas, but would have only delayed the issue for a little space. Such a free communication as the Federal fleets had along the coast of the revolted states during the Civil War was equally needed in our case. Without it Sherman's overland march from Savannah, made eighty years afterwards, might have had little better issue than that of Cornwallis through precisely the same district. With such aid the modern commander established his fame, as the elder, for lack of it, came nigh to ruin his reputation. Happily the discussion of the circumstances of the Yorktown surrender produced a clearer impression in Cornwallis's favor among the statesmen of the time than Sir J. Kaye's narrative will, we fear, among his readers. Hardly was the American War concluded, when we find both Fox and Pitt, amid the acrimony of the Indian debates, looking to Cornwallis as the man who best might wield supreme control in our new great dependency. "The name of such a man," said the former, "might make Parliament consent to the vesting of such powers in a Governor-General; but certain I am that nothing but the character of that noble Lord could ever induce the legislature to commit such powers to an individual at the distance of half the globe." The latter, when his new India Bill was in a fair way to pass, offered the Earl his choice of the offices of Governor-General or Commander-in-Chief; and when he persistently declined then, and again after the Macartney interregnum, to accept either separately, or to take the former office at all, unless with independent power in cases of emergency, the amending Bill of 1786 was introduced, under which he could no longer refuse to act. By this, which became henceforward the rule of Indian government the functions of the Supreme Council were reduced to those of mere advice or remonstrance, whenever the Governor-General chose to decide for himself. The members might in such case collectively or severally recommend or object, but action belonged to the Governor-General, on whom henceforward lay the real responsibility of administration, checked only by the higher authority at home. As the latter could always receive the recorded opinions of the councillors, the Governor-General would naturally take good care not to override them without showing good cause. This system had been devised at the time of the introduction of the Indian Bill in 1784, but

Mr. Pitt had abandoned the proviso which to Cornwallis and others seemed the pith of the whole Act, in
order the more easily to secure its passage. Two years
later, however, it was found necessary to supply the
omission; and in spite of Burke's powerful opposition,
the arguments of Dundas (then President of the Board
of Control) prevailed, and the Governor-General received
the vast powers he has ever since held. One weak
point was left in the measure. It was open, from the
nature of the government, for the Governor-General to
reduce himself from his rank as responsible ruler to the
mere President of a Committee, by ceasing to exercise
his individual authority, and referring each business
to a single member or to the voice of the Council.
This is the temptation natural to any Viceroy who
would avoid excessive responsibility; and if report be
true, it is precisely in this direction that the Supreme
Government has on the whole for some time past
tended.

    To return to Cornwallis. Voyaging to Calcutta
with Shore, afterwards Lord Teignmouth, for his chief
fellow-passenger, he landed on September fourteenth
1786, and began that career of administrative reform
on which his future fame was to rest more surely than
on American campaigns. It is not necessary to peruse
the twenty pages which Sir J. Kaye has devoted to the
earlier history of the Indian Civil Service, in order to
see that Cornwallis had before him an Augean task.
To pay collectors, judges, even councillors, rather less
than the salary of a merchant's junior clerk, and to
leave these high officials to eke out their pittance by
jobbery and corruption, had been the normal practice
of the good old company. Nearly two centuries

before, Sir Thomas Roe had written the golden truth, which it was left for Cornwallis to reduce to practice. "Absolutely prohibit," said the far-seeing ambassador of James I., " the private trade, for your business will be better done. I know this is harsh. Men profess they care not for bare wages. But you will take away this plea if you grant great wages to their content; and then you know what you part from." As has been well added, Roe was in this matter a great man, obviously in advance of his age. So far from profiting by his wisdom, the company adopted the very contrary policy, attempting by the ridiculous device of temporary edicts, framed 16,000 miles off, to keep the daily habits of their servants down to their meagre salaries. As their rule extended from factories to provinces, and from provinces to kingdoms, the childish fetters they had imposed were silently laid aside or openly scoffed at, and the picking of the Pagoda tree became a recognized art, dividing the attention of the civilian with his care of his office. Thus, as soon as Cornwallis had investigated the state of things, we find him writing of one of the company's civil servants in a manner that gives a lively picture of the existing régime :

" Ill as I thought of the late system of Benares, I found it on inquiry much worse than I could have conceived. The Resident, although not regularly vested with any power, enjoyed the almost absolute government of the country without control. His emoluments, besides the thousand rupees per month allowed him by the company, certainly amounted to little less than four lacs a year, exclusive of the complete monopoly of the whole commerce of the country, with the power of granting perwannahs, etc. It has been generally supposed that in return for all these good things, the Residents at Benares have not been ungrateful to the friends of the Governor-General. I have no reason to suppose that Mr. — took more than his predecessors. God knows what he *gave*. But as he was on bad terms with the Rajah and his servants, and as new measures are more likely to succeed with new men, I thought it better to remove him."

In the same letter he adds, in a passage quoted by Sir J. Kaye: "I am sorry to say that I have every reason to believe that at present almost all the collectors are, under the name of some relative or friend, deeply engaged in commerce, and by their influence as collectors and judges of Adaulet they become the most dangerous enemies to the company's interest, and the greatest oppressors of the manufacturers." So much for the state of things: then came the cause, and the remedy which Cornwallis had already, not having been in the country a year, brought into use without waiting for the directors' sanction to his reform. "I hope you will approve of the additional allowances that we have given, for without them it was absolutely impossible that an honest man could acquire the most moderate competence. After this liberality I made no scruple of issuing the revenue regulations against embarking in trade, and will make an example of the first offender."

The remedy in such a case was, in fact, clear as the disease, being no other than that which Sir Thomas Roe had so long since recommended. Yet it needed all the prestige and influence which Cornwallis had brought with him, to enforce his views on the slow hearing of the directors. The earnestness with which he insisted upon what he felt to be the cardinal point of Indian administration is abundantly illustrated by the " Cornwallis Correspondence," which Sir J. Kaye has freely and usefully employed. The sweeping inferences he has drawn from this valuable work seem to us, in one case, hardly justified, for an expression quoted as written *with reference to the company's civil servants*—" I sincerely believe that, excepting Mr. Charles Grant, there is not one person on the list who would escape prosecution "—appears in the original letter to be applied to a special " list " of persons whose cases were submitted to the Court of Directors for lenient consideration, on the score of their having been coerced by their superiors. The word " list " thus specially used by Cornwallis in the sentence immediately preceding could hardly be applied by him in the next, that already quoted, to the whole civil service without qualification. If not a very elegant writer, he was certainly by no means a loose one.

Be this as it may, the measures already taken for the amendment of the service by the Earl were approved at home, where Dundas rendered him due support. In vain was it asserted that however well men were paid in India, at that distance they could not refrain from fee-taking or corruption in some form. The honorable soul of Cornwallis revolted at this theory ; and the objections raised by the Directors to his grants of salaries were thus met by him in a private letter to Dundas of August twenty-sixth, 1787 :

" If the essence of the spirit of economy of the whole Court of Directors could be collected, I am sure it would fall very short of my anxiety on that subject. . . . If it is a maxim that, pay our servants as we please, they will equally cheat, the sooner we leave this country the better. . . . From the spirit of this letter" [of the Directors] " I conclude that the commission given to the collectors, the allowances to the residents, will all be disapproved of. I see the pay of the sub-treasurer is objected to. When I came I found the sub-treasurer playing with the deposits, amounting to three or four lacs. I fancy of the two he had rather I had taken his salary from him. I have saved" [he forcibly concludes] "since I came, upon the salt upon the various contracts, upon remittances, balances, and jobs of different kinds, ten times, I may say fifty times the amount of the salaries that are retrenched. I am doing everything I can to reform the Company's servants, to teach them to be more economical in their mode of living, and to look forward to a moderate competency; and I flatter myself I have not hitherto labored in vain. But if all chance of saving any money and returning to England without acting dishonestly is removed, there will be an end of my reformation."

A better destiny than he hoped awaited his vigorous measures. The promise made to him by Dundas, "You may depend upon my giving the most exact attention to every suggestion you communicate to me," appears to have been literally fulfilled. As the minister observed in the same letter, "We never before had a government of India, both at home and abroad, acting in perfect unison together upon principles of perfect unity and integrity; these ingredients cannot fail to produce their consequent effects." Those effects began to appear sooner than Viceroy or Minister could have hoped; for we find Cornwallis writing but four months after the receipt of this assurance, "The Company has many valuable servants; the temper of the times is changing. Men are beginning to contrast their

present expenses and their future views." His
unwearied war upon sinecures, jobbery, and fraud had
already reduced the expenditure within the estimates,
"which never," he writes, "happened before;" while
the civil service was beginning to feel the advantage
held out to it by the honester system which refused
(to use Cornwallis's words) "to place men in great and
responsible situations, where the prosperity of our
affairs must depend on their exertions as well as integrity, without giving them the means in a certain number of years of acquiring honestly and openly a moderate fortune."

Not that Dundas and Cornwallis had the opposition
of the Directors for their only difficulty. A still more
scandalous one lay in the system of sending out to
Calcutta the needy and improvident hangers-on of
court officials or party leaders, in expectation that the
Governor-General would provide for them. This practice the innate honesty of Cornwallis did more to check,
it is not too much to say, than the spirit of his times
could possibly have taught him. In truth, his conduct
in this matter was before the age; although to say of
him "he could not perpetuate a job to please the
King," is an instance of the misuse of high-flown language which is our author's besetting sin; and it is the
less excusable, as in a note to the next page we find
that he quotes from a letter of Cornwallis, explaining
his rejection of William Burke's suggestions of modes
of serving him: "I have treated him with the greatest
personal attention, and I have done little favors, as
ensigncies in the King's service, etc., to his friends." It
was quite consistent, at that period, with the honorable
character of the man that such gifts should be made to

conciliate the cousin of Edmund Burke, and yet that
Cornwallis should absolutely decline proposals for
alterations in the mode of payment of the troops,
which were intended to put large sums of money into
the pocket of this same Burke, then Paymaster-General
in India. In the same spirit a gentleman coming out
to be provided for with a recommendation from the
Queen, was put off with a clerkship at 250 rupees a
month ; but Cornwallis's own friends fared much worse.
Their claims were met with inexorable refusal, while
that of a mere acquaintance was treated as summarily
as if the pressing it were a crime. " If I was inclined
to serve you," he writes to such a one, " it is wholly
out of my power to do so without a breach of my duty.
I most earnestly advise you to think of returning to
England as soon as possible. After the first of January next I shall be under the necessity of sending you
thither."

Such vigor and wisdom as this portion of the " Correspondence" shows is well worthy the first place in a
work which set out with the design of illustrating the
high qualities of the Indian services. The measures
which Cornwallis adopted for the improvement of the
civil branch won their way to acceptance. His rule of
securing the whole devotion of the official by paying
him so liberally as " to enable him to save honestly and
openly," became the charter of a great body of gentle-
men ; and by their aid the foundations of our growing
empire were laid deep and strong.

The care of Cornwallis for the military force was no
less. Justice indeed has hardly been done by Sir J.
Kaye or any other writer to this portion of the subject ;
for the abuses which had crept into the contingents

raised by native states were hardly less than those in the political offices, while the regular troops of the Company were in a very low condition, the recruiting of respectable Englishmen being practically interdicted by home jealousies. Of the European troops Cornwallis wrote: " They are such miserable wretches I should be ashamed to acknowledge them for countrymen ;" and added, as the only remedy, some words that seem to us well worth quoting for their curious acknowledgment of the early jealousy of the royal troops towards their brethren of the Company, a jealousy afterwards amply repaid by Indian officers, and which lasted until the Company was merged in the Crown : " I know it will be unpopular with my brother officers at home ; but it is my duty to state, that if these dominions are worth preserving, it is absolutely necessary that the East India Company should be permitted to treat publicly for recruits, and to keep them under martial law until the time of their embarkation." In the same spirit he set himself to abolish all the invidious distinctions hitherto made in India between the military services.

Before his arrival, all field officers of the King's were wont to receive special brevet rank, so as to supersede those of the Company who were of the same standing, while the local commissions of the latter were often altogether ignored, as far as it lay in the power of the royal officer, who looked on their holders as irregular rivals of his profession. Representations on this head came with peculiar force from one who was known at home as the favorite general of the royal troops in the field, the leader who had come out of our American disasters with honor unsullied and military

20

reputation raised. In 1788 Cornwallis received the
needful powers for bestowing, in the sovereign's name,
local commissions for India on the company's officers,
while the special higher rank of the King's field officers
was ordered to be absolutely swept away after eighteen
months' notice. From this day forward the officers of
the three local armies already in pay under the company saw the road open to the highest honors of their
profession; at least as regarded service in their adopted country. It needed, however, three-quarters of a
century's habit, and a formal assumption by the Crown
of the imperial authority in India, before British statesmen could learn the simple elementary lessons that the
military strength derived from our Eastern possessions
is but part of the general strength of the state, and
that our Indian Empire is the natural base of all our
warlike operations in the East.

With certain very irregular contingents raised in
the subject native provinces, the existence of which
was a private profit and no public benefit, Lord Cornwallis dealt in the most summary fashion. .How
abused the power of our Residents had been in this
direction may be gathered from the following letter,
addressed by him to a certain captain, whose pretended battalion had been disbanded, and who made a
large claim on his own account against the Vizier of
Oude:

" Near PLASSY, November 22, 1787.

" SIR,—I am sorry to say that on my arrival at Lucknow
I could not meet with any person, either European or native,
that knew anything of your battalion, or had seen any part of
it. Although I could not help placing proper confidence in

your assurances of its being perfectly complete, both in officers and men, yet as there was not a trace of it existing at
the headquarters where it was raised, and had been so lately
disbanded, and you had been so improvident as to keep no
voucher for any of your disbursements, you did not put it in
my power to say to the Vizier or his ministers that part of the
large sum of money which you received was not issued to discharge your personal pay and allowances. Circumstanced,
therefore, as your claim is, I do not think that my interference
would be warranted by the order of the Board relative to the
reduction of your corps. I am, etc.

                                        " CORNWALLIS."

In short, the care of his lordship for the military
departments, as might have been expected from his
previous training, was as great as that which he bestowed on the civil service ; and, fortunately for the
future of the Indian army, he remained long enough
at its head to see his recommendations carried into
practical working. Under this wiser rule the heart-
burnings and discontents of the company's officer van-
ished, and a commission in the Indian army became an
honorable object for the ambitious and energetic of the
youth of England. A class pressed into the service
from this time by which the government has been
doubly strengthened. The Viceroys have found in it
some of the most able administrators that India has
known, having in its vast list the ready means of reinforcing the civil element in their higher departments ;
while the army has furnished sabreurs as bold, artille-
rists and engineers as skilful, staff officers as sagacious,
as any modern military school from the time of Gusta-
vus downwards.

It has been the fashion of late to suppose that Cornwallis, as a reformer, was but an instrument in the hands of better-informed men, experienced in Indian affairs. A late popular history of India takes this view of his viceroyalty, which would regard him almost as simply an able and honest, yet ordinary executive officer. A mere glance at the first part of the "Correspondence" should dissipate for ever this theory, which deserves to stand with that of a worthy officer not many years dead, who published a work in three volumes to prove that Napoleon rose to the crown of France and the sway of Europe by a series of lucky accidents. Sir J. Kaye has done his subject more justice. He has shown, among other points, that the care of Cornwallis reached not only to financial and administrative measures of every kind, but to the moral and social condition of the Anglo-Indian community. To reform this by mere austerity and simplicity of living would have been impossible. Banquets and balls were the more rational mode adopted by Cornwallis, whose genial hospitality kept him in his proper social position as the head of Calcutta society, and enabled him to influence its tone largely for present and future good. With his usual industry our author has adduced extracts from newspapers of the day, and from an interesting work on Indian society, written soon after Cornwallis had left, which sufficiently proves the vast change for the better made by his personal influence and example. It would seem, therefore, that the very habits of our countrymen in the East are indebted to the same far-seeing wisdom and energy which the best informed of them declare to have founded the prosperity and usefulness of the services of the company, and to have left traces of its happy influence on every succeeding generation of officials.

Cornwallis had not too long a space allowed him for his reforms. They were scarcely complete when the troubles in the Presidency of Madras began, which were to keep us constantly engaged in or expecting war until the death of Tippoo Saib many years later. The account of Cornwallis's expeditions in Mysore is well worth study, were it only for the purpose of seeing how he prepared the way for the final triumph of our arms under Harris and Wellesley. But it is more important to follow him back to Calcutta after he had wrested a hard-won peace from Tippoo, and see him devote the remainder of his Indian career to the completion of his administrative reforms, and their complement of legislation. Those who would understand exactly how far Cornwallis deserves the credit of the famous Regulations of 1793, which have formed the basis of our later administration of justice in India, should study the memorandum of Sir George Barlow (which Sir J. Kaye was the first to bring to light), explaining in the most precise terms what he did in this matter. His reform was that which came naturally from a wise ruler in a country hitherto administered by individual officials who acted personally for the government according to their own views and their separate instructions. He reduced these instructions to definite published laws, and enforced by their means uniformity of practice in the courts. That in doing this he was acting rightly, and indeed anticipating what otherwise his successors must perforce have undertaken, is admitted by men of all parties, and stands deservedly to his credit as a statesman.

It is far otherwise with the celebrated Revenue Settlement effected under his rule. Our author seems to avoid offering any opinion of his own on this debated question, to which he devotes but a single page. Yet as he gives room for the reproval of James Mill, who in his History asserts of this measure that "the aristocratical person now at the head of the government avowed his intention of establishing an aristocracy upon the European model," he, in justice, does not omit to show that the arguments of the perpetual Zemindar Settlement were far older than the days of Cornwallis, having been completely exhausted in reports made before his appointment. Mr. Law, then collector of Behar, he terms "the father of the Permanent Settlement;" but the praise or blame should in truth be allotted rather to the whole service of which Mr. Law was but one active member. A large part of the second volume of the "Cornwallis Correspondence" is devoted to papers concerning this vexed question; and it is there abundantly shown that what the Governor-General recommended was enforced by the deliberate opinion of all the chief administrators of revenue in Bengal, and of his own councillors, excepting always Mr. Shore, afterwards Lord Teignmouth. The latter argued earnestly in favor of the settlement being renewable every ten years, instead of being made in perpetuity, and his arguments were fully weighed before the final decision was arrived at by Pitt and Dundas, who (as appears plainly shown from the "Correspondence") were the ultimate judges, assisted only by Charles Grant. It is plain, however, that Shore dissented merely on the question of the length to which the settlement should run. There was no difference of opinion at the time among those who knew the newly-acquired country, as to the wisdom of creating from the Zemindars of Bengal a territorial aristocracy, or rather of confirming them in the tenure they had already acquired by prescription. The only question much discussed was as to the terms on which this should be done. Possibly Mill's attack upon Cornwallis would have been spared had he known the "Correspondence," or had he written after it had become the fashion with recent Indian rulers, warned by Dalhousie experience, to copy in other districts the original prescription under which Lower Bengal has proved the model portion of our dominions for tranquillity and wealth of produce.

Sir J. Kaye follows Cornwallis from India to Ireland, and gives an epitome of the important events which marked his viceroyalty there. These belong, however, in no sense to the story of our Indian empire, and, as with the American portion of the biography, are too briefly treated to do full justice to the subject. Cornwallis's connection with the Union measures might well have a work to itself, and is at any rate too important a matter in national history to be treated merely as an episode of his Indian career. While occupied thus at home, and subsequently in diplomacy on the Continent, he watched the brilliant schemes and daring policy of Lord Wellesley with the natural anxiety of an ex-ruler who sees much of what he judged a sound policy reversed by his successor. Even the great successes which it was given to the new Governor-General to organize in council, and to see achieved by his brother's sword in the field, hardly reconciled Cornwallis to our new and comparatively aggressive position.

What was written by him at this time, embodies exactly the opinions and difficulties of many able and honest men from that day to the present. " The question is, have we not too much? But I hardly know, when the power was in our hands, what part of our acquisitions we could prudently have relinquished." At last came the supersession of Wellesley, and the almost inevitable recourse to Cornwallis as his successor. The story of the quarrel of the Directors with their representative has nothing very new or striking in it, being but the natural collision between a board of commonplace, narrow-minded men and the bold, ambitious Viceroy whom they sought to restrict by drafting instructions for his guidance from the other side of the world. To displace so able and successful a Governor-General as Wellesley was a serious step, and fully accounts for the warm desire of the Directors to secure Cornwallis's return to the post without supposing (as some have done) that his great name was the only help open to the British Government in a dangerous crisis, which, but for him, might have ruined our Eastern Empire. For although Cornwallis accepted the offer and went, he went, as is well known, only to die, and left his former administration of India the single and sufficient groundwork of his reputation in that country.

Before passing from the subject of these two great men and their varying views of Indian policy, it is but just to pause and point out that it was not in the power of either, or of any of their successors, wholly to shape or even to control the limits of our sway in Hindostan. There is a general darkness on this subject of Indian conquest which is hardly creditable to a

nation whose public writers are usually well informed
on questions of merely practical policy. It has not
been either a national or individual lust of empire which
has carried our standards from the Hooghly to the
Indus. The force of circumstances has been too strong
for the most pacific in our list of governors. In fact,
from the day that our factories began to hire troops.
and take independent dealings with the native states,
the result was sure. It must be remembered that when
we first set foot in India, the foundations of the old
Mogul Empire were thoroughly broken up. Wave
after wave of conquest had passed over it, destroying
and altering ancient landmarks, but without raising up
any single central power strong enough to control the
rest, and to restore order to the peninsula. The seeds of
such a one once planted by the company, the process of
growth went on in the same constant form. Insult and
aggression on the new civilization came naturally from
the native states whose robber-chiefs had made invasion of peaceful neighbors the normal practice of their
rule. Defeat of the invader must needs involve punishment for the past and indemnity for the future, and
these could rarely be secured but by the rough expedient of annexation. That this process should be constant until Affghanistan was reached was simple necessity, for a reason too generally overlooked. There
never was any strategic frontier to our dominions until
they touched the mountains which separate Hindostan
from the rest of the world; and an empire like ours,
won by the sword, and mantained at first mainly by
the force of arms, must needs find such to cover it
before it can rest. Only since we were secure from
outward enemies has it been found possible to throw

the energy of our government into the path of peaceful development of its resources. A military empire, such as ours was purely until of late, must conform its policy to military necessities : a truth we have been unconsciously illustrating ever since Clive began the long series of conquests forced on us by those we have conquered.

We have dwelt before on what Cornwallis did for the services which owe to him their efficiency and virtue. The absorbing policy of Wellesley and succeeding Governors-General, willingly or unwillingly pushing our frontiers ever forward, gave to the young Englishman who entered them such a field for energy and ability as the whole world beside could not offer. The constant political changes of the peninsula, and the increasing dominions forced against our will as it were on us, raised up a class of officers in whom the military and administrative elements seem to combine so closely that it is hard to distinguish where the soldier ends and the diplomatist or ruler begins. Of such men in the earlier part of this century, Malcolm, whose life in the work before us follows that of Cornwallis, may be taken as the type, or at least as a very happy example. Sir J. Kaye has so fully written on the same subject in his "Life and Correspondence of Sir John Malcolm," that we proceed to deal with this part of his volume chiefly for the purpose of entering a gentle remonstrance against his treatment of his subject. The whole picture of Malcolm which he gives is one overcharged with colors existing in the biographer's brain rather than in the realities of his hero's life. The Malcolm of Kaye is a man not merely of eminent abilities and buoyant spirits, but of perfect

purity of motives; badly rewarded for his services, yet
unwilling to conceive himself ill-used; exquisitely sen-
sitive to disappointment, yet always hopeful and
cheery; overflowing with kind feelings for his friends,
and seeking promotion and honor solely to glorify a
beloved service. This just man, it is implied, won his
way slowly up to fame and fortune in spite of official
neglect, infirmities of health, and personal unwilling-
ness to remain in ungrateful duties. Of course this
statement is not put into so many words, either in the
" Life and Correspondence" or in the works before us;
but such is the general effect the author would, perhaps unconsciously, impress on his readers. The tra-
ditional view of Malcolm in India is a very different
one, and one which Sir J. Kaye's own materials appear
fully to justify. According to this, his hero was simply
a very hard-headed, pushing, active man, with a fund
of remarkable spirits and energy, who never lost anything for want of asking for it, and had the good luck
to start early in life in as fine an opening as young
" political" ever knew, at the most stirring period in
the whole of our stormy annals. Let us look a little
closely at his early progress and see if the latter opinion be not that which best agrees with the facts as
they come before us.

After a course of boyish dissipation and indebted-
ness we find Malcolm carried with his regiment into
the field at the age of twenty. He sees service, and,
what is more to the purpose, observes the professional
advantage the " politicals," of whom there are several
in camp, possess over the mere soldier. Not until after
this, having been now seven years in Madras, does he
begin seriously to study, and in the next year we find

him applying for an appointment of the coveted civil order. In Sir J. Kaye's characteristic words:

"A subordinate post was vacant: he applied for it, and was just half an hour too late. It had been bestowed on another young officer. His disappointment and vexation were great. He went back to his tent, flung himself down on his couch, and gave way to a flood of tears. But he lived, as many a man before and since has lived, to see in his first crushing miscarriage the crowning mercy of his life. The officer who carried off the prize so coveted by John Malcolm went straight to his death. On his first appearance at the native court at which he was appointed an assistant to the Resident, he was murdered. This made a deep impression at the time on Malcolm's mind, and was afterwards gratefully remembered."

Disappointed of his first hopes, he was willing to put up with an interpretership to a detachment. He left this soon to go home on sick leave; and here was more fortunate, for we find him returning to Madras as aide-de-camp to General Clarke. Clarke went on later to Bengal to command there, but "there were circumstances which prevented him from appointing John Malcolm to the military secretaryship in that Presidency." In plain words, General Clarke had some one whom he cared more to serve by the bestowal of a very valuable situation. However, Malcolm had now become known as an active and useful man, and Harris who succeeded to the command at Madras, kept him on his own staff at first, and from this put him temporarily into the then lucrative post of town-major, of which he wrote, being then apparently more bent on making money than seeking fame, "I cherish hopes of being town-major a few months longer. If I remain one year I shall have a little foundation on which to erect a goodly castle."

Lord Wellesley (then Lord Mornington) now touched at Madras on his way to Calcutta. The town-major took advantage of the opportunity to call on the new Viceroy and submit some reports he had prepared on our relations with the native states, and soon afterwards received his reward in the appointment of assistant to Kirkpatrick, then Resident at Mysore, for which he had made instant application on the vacancy occurring. He was twenty-nine years old when this first step in the desired ladder was gained.

He reached Hyderabad just as the French trained levy in the Nizam's service was mutinying. In the dispersion of this contingent he played a prominent part, being aided partly by his own address and boldness, and partly by his being recognized by some sepoys of a French battalion as an old officer of the regiment they had once served in. He carried the colors of the extinct corps to Calcutta, and received the warm thanks of the Governor-General, whose patronage he had now fairly earned. When the Nizam's contingent soon after joined General Harris's force for the siege of Seringapatam, Malcolm accompanied it officially. On the fall of Tippoo, Lord Wellesley rewarded him for his share by appointing him to a special mission to Persia, and from this time forward his official fortune was made. He wrote hard, worked hard, and did excellent service, though not without some strange blunders here and there, as when he wrote to General Lake of the Mahrattas that "one short campaign" would for ever dissipate their power.

Attached to the force of Arthur Wellesley in the new war at its opening, sickness took him from the camp before Assaye was won, and his absence, in his biographer's hardly appropriate phrase, " was long afterwards a thorn in his flesh."

Regaining his health, he settled into his appointment as Resident of Mysore. He declined to follow Lord Wellesley to England, in order to defend the policy he had carried out for his patron, and prepared instead to assist in carrying out Cornwallis's desire " to wind up the Mahratta war with all possible dispatch." There was much in the pacific policy of the time " that was distasteful to Malcolm," adds the biographer, who takes rather unnecessary credit to the diplomatist for cheerfully carrying out the orders of his superiors, though not in accordance with his personal views.

Malcolm was now thirty-seven years old. He had begun his political life but eight years before, and had ever since enjoyed employment and remuneration as high as the Government of India could give. Yet it appears plainly that he was restless and dissatisfied because he had received no special mark of favor from the Crown. " I have been rewarded, I admit," he writes, " by distinction in the service ; but if a man is wished to go on, further stimulus must be found. . . . I have determined, on the most serious reflection, to retire. . . . If it is conceived that any ability, knowledge, or experience I possess can be usefully directed to the promotion of the public interest, I must be stimulated to exertion by a fair prospect of just and honorable encouragement." Could any man put a higher estimate on his own services than the still young officer who thus wrote to the same Lord Wellesley on whom not ten years before, he had been thrusting his first essays in political writing with a view to a subordinate post ?

Those who know the Malcolms of real life will not be surprised that he did not carry out his " most serious reflection " into earnest, and retire. On the contrary, he stayed and carried on the duties of his Residency with tact and ability until something better came. Sent again to Persia to threaten, and to obtain the material guarantee of an island in the Gulf, his mission was suddenly stopped in favor of a more pacific one dispatched from England. His next employment was an unfortunate one, being to quell the mutinous spirit of the garrison of Masulipatam, where his too lenient management brought on him the disapproval of his immediate superior, the then governor of Madras. From this he was, however, soon relieved by a new and genuine appointment as Ambassador to Persia, and the varied ability he displayed there increased his already high reputation, and gave him the fair claim he enjoys to literary distinction. Another visit to England sent him back to a further course of honorable service in India, where, however, he appears as little satisfied as after the Mahratta war. The government of Bombay was vacant and sought by him, but conferred on Elphinstone. " He regarded such a nomination as a supersession of his rightful claims." Nor was he less disappointed when Sir Thomas Munro was soon after appointed to be governor of Madras, the other post he desired. Some years later, however, he won the dignity he had long sought, and was appointed to the government of Bombay, his last official employment. He soon (1830), in his biographer's words, " was eager for

England and for rest," having in reality the vision of a seat in parliament in his ever active brain. He gained it; but only to lose it in a few months by the borough being disfranchised under the Reform Bill, where his public life may be said to have ended.

Of such an one, to assert with Sir J. Kaye that " he was a man *sui generis*," seems to us a misconception. No doubt it is correctly said that " of all those written of in these volumes he had the most perfect physical organization;" and this, and perhaps the high value he put on his own services, are his distinguishing marks, when we separate the man from the special opportunities of his time. Many others of the same bustling type, quick with the pen, and ready with the sword, have succeeded him, and to their conjoint efforts we owe much of what we are in India. Those who read carefully the " Life of Burnes," as our author gives it, will discern at once the family likeness; the same fondness for writing, the same love for stirring work, the same discontent too if his reward proved anything less than his highest desires. Indeed there are several of whom Sir J. Kaye has written who have shared the energy and talent which carried Malcolm to fame and fortune, and shared his foibles too. But in Sir Henry Lawrence a nobler and higher model is offered; for he was one of those great men whose unselfish heroism rose beyond the thought of his own desert and reward, and who throughout life, as he wrote for his own brief memorial, " tried to do his duty," rather than to win fame. Take indeed our governing classes in India for all in all, no other nation administering wide conquests can boast of servants who, amid all the temptations set before those who rule a subject race, have so steadfastly sought the public good, and even in their very ambition advanced the prosperity and cared for the welfare of those committed to their charge.

Or for mere soldiership, a quality hardly less necessary, take from the records before us the story of Nicholson—name ever to be bound up in history with the turning point of the great Mutiny, the fall of Delhi— one of whom it is impossible for even so eulogistic a writer as Sir J. Kaye to speak in exaggerated terms. Those who are most conversant with the details of that season of trial are most ardent in their praise of the lost hero. While the gallant little band, wasted by sickness and by sword, held with unflinching constancy their post in view of the rebellious fortress, awaiting the reinforcements preparing in the Punjab, it was the arm of Nicholson which first quelled each attempt to spread disorder in that province, and then brought them timely succor. From that day the British forces, no longer struggling for their own existence, became in truth a besieging army instead of a camp beleaguered by the rebels. They went to their hard but glorious work with confidence, for their long line of supply was guarded with a fierce vigilance that mocked the enemy's attempts to break it. When the day arrived on which their hopes were to be crowned, none murmured that the post of honor at the head of the attack was given to one whose name seemed a pledge of victory. And when Nicholson fell, sacrificing his life to give an example to reluctant followers—although the breach was won, the avenging column lodged within the city, the hopes of the mutineers broken for ever—the joy of the victorious army and their sympathizing countrymen was dimmed by the knowledge of the hero's fall. His

21

late chief, Lord Lawrence, but expressed the universal feeling when he wrote, "his loss is a national misfortune." "Few men," adds Sir J. Kaye, in words which we borrow with pleasure, "have done so much at the early age of thirty-five—few men thus passing away from the scene in the flower of their manhood, have ever left behind them a reputation so perfect and complete."

And if the Indian services have been thus honorably distinguished, if purity has gone hand in hand with the valor, zeal, and energy that have gained and consolidated for us the inheritance of the Mogul, it is due far more than to any other personal cause to the far-seeing judgment and wise liberality of the true founder, the great and good Cornwallis. From the time he bequeathed his finished work to others, India has never lacked—our severest critics admit it—such administrators and defenders as subject empire never knew before. And if this be indeed so; if men like Malcolm, Lawrence, and Nicholson be but fair specimens of the growth which Indian responsibilities and Indian work can nourish from the British stock; shall we lament the existence of our Eastern empire, and shrink from the duties its possession devolves upon us? Rather let us take heart for the work, in faith that the same honesty, courage, and sagacity that have won Hindostan for Britain will be found ready at call to maintain the trust, and make the mingling of their races a blessing to far generations.

A CAROLINA LOYALIST IN THE REVOLU-
. TIONARY WAR.

[The following memoir is strictly authentic, and is here published nearly as left by the narrator for the information of his children. A family interest in it would be no proper excuse for the introduction of it here. But it paints the American Revolutionary War in the Southern States, where Cornwallis won his military fame, from a point of view that has been hitherto quite unknown to English readers at any rate. And to mention but one of several curious parallelisms in the two strug- 'gles ; in the account of the chief action the writer shared in, the fight at King's Mountain, military men may discover the birth of that tactical use of mounted infantry with which Sheridan won the battle of Five Forks, and ended at a blow the greater American Civil War of our own day.]

I WAS the eldest son of a large family who emigrated from Ireland at the advice of some relatives who had been settled for several years in South Carolina. In 1773 our family were living on Packolet River, about twelve miles from where it empties itself into Broad River, fifty miles below where the line of the Cherokee Indian reserve then existing crossed that river. The plantation was about 200 miles north-west of Charles- ton. We were established in our new residence, and working hard at the usual farming occupations, increas- ing stock, and clearing additional land, when in 1775 resolutions were presented for signature at the meet- ing-house by the Congress Party, and I opposed them.

When war broke out between England and America, the Congress Party, early in 1775, were sending a quantity of ammunition and clothing as presents to the Indians; on which the loyalists who had not joined them assembled, and went to Fort '96, a post on the Georgian frontier made against the red men, and after besieging the fort for several days took it and the stores. After distributing the ammunition among the loyalists, both parties agreed to a cessation of arms for some weeks, until several of the leading men could receive directions in the business from Lord William Campbell, the governor at Charleston.

Owing to the assistance I early afforded, and my activity in the cause of my king, I was shortly after made a prisoner by the revolutionary party, my house being ransacked, and was kept a prisoner in the camp on Reedy River for about a week. Colonel Richardson released me; but the Congress Party wished that I should be tried at Richardson's Camp, or be forced to join the rebel army; which latter alternative I should have been driven to choose, in order to save my father's family from threatened ruin; for he had been made prisoner already for harboring some loyalists, and his life was in danger. But the first disturbances ended soon after.

I returned to farming in June, 1777, when I purchased a tract of land on Packolet River, where I remained a short time. But at a muster soon afterwards, when the Indians rose, taking advantage of our divisions, I was chosen lieutenant in Captain Bullock's company of militia by my loyal friends. I went with a party to Earlsfort, on the Indian line, at the head of Packolet River, about fifty miles from home, and repaired the fort; continued some months there, and was relieved the May following (1778) by the white inhabitants making peace with the Indians at Duet's Corner.

It was firmly believed in the beginning of this year that Charleston would be reduced by the British, which happened accordingly, on May twelfth following; and Sir Henry Clinton having issued a proclamation commanding all his Majesty's faithful subjects to embody for the defence of his government, I obeyed it. About the middle of June, being embodied with the militia as lieutenant, I commanded in an affair at Bullock's Creek, when the rebel party was defeated in attempting to cross the ford.

I then joined Colonel Balfour, and was in an affair at Wood's house, above the Iron Works on Packolet River. Colonel Balfour then returned to Fort '96, and Major Ferguson, who had raised a corps of loyalists known as Ferguson's Sharp-shooters, succeeded to the command, under the title of Colonel and Inspector-General of Militia. Shortly afterwards he marched to Thickety Creek, encamped, and requested me to carry an express to Captain Moore, then Commandant of Anderson's Fort, on the North Carolina side, with a private message to hold the fort till the last minute. Before I could return the army had moved, about midnight, and retreated towards Tiger River, where I joined them; and we got an account that Colonel McDale had, without opposition, reduced Anderson's Fort and made the garrison all prisoners, Moore having shamefully surrendered it. This disappointed Ferguson's scheme of bringing the Americans to battle while attacking it. Major Gibbs came to me in this situation of affairs, showed me a paper containing instructions to go to McDale's Congress camp at the Cherokee Ford, on Broad River, and learn their commander's name, what carriages they had, how many horses and foot, and whenever they made any movements towards Colonel Ferguson. I was to return and let him know, and he added that there would be a handsome reward. I told Major Gibbs that what services I could do were not with any pecuniary view, and that I would undertake this difficult task for the good of his Majesty's service, since he could not procure a better qualified person to undertake it. I set out immediately (August eighth), and at Packolet got a man to go with me who was acquainted with the North Carolina people. We went to McDale's camp at night, without being noticed, and found who were their leaders, and that 500 horsemen were gone over to attack Michell's Fort. With this news I returned, and found a loyalist in whom I could confide, and sent him off with the particulars by one route to Colonel Ferguson while I went by another, and the colonel got intelligence in time enough to intercept the enemy at the Iron Works and defeat them. In returning I was taken by a party of rebels, who took from me a rifle borrowed of my brother-in-law; but as soon as they set out for the rebel camp I made my escape, joined Colonel Ferguson, and received his thanks and friendship.

On August ninth I was appointed captain and assistant adjutant-general to the different battalions now gathered under Colonel Ferguson. The same day we attacked the enemy at the Iron Works, and defeated them with little trouble to ourselves and a good deal of loss to the Americans, in whose hands I found some of our men prisoners, whom I released. Our next route was down towards the Fishdam Ford, on Broad River, where there was a fight (August twelfth) near the mouth of Brown's Creek, with Neil's militia, where we made many prisoners, among the rest Esau Smith, one of those who had taken me so recently. After this we crossed that river and formed a junction with the troops under the command of Colonel Turnbull and the militia under the command of Colonel Phillips, and having received accounts that Sumter, with a detachment of General Gates's army, had cut off our retreat to Lord Cornwallis's camp at Camden, we had it in contemplation to cross Broad River and retreat to Charleston. At this time the *half-way men* (as those not hearty in the cause were called) left us; we then marched to an estate of the rebel Colonel Winn's and encamped there, waiting for more authentic accounts. On the sixteenth we heard a heavy firing towards Camden, which kept us in the utmost anxiety until the eighteenth, when a letter was received from Captain Ross, aide-de-camp to Lord Cornwallis, informing us that his lordship had attacked and defeated Gates's army, and killed or taken 2,200 men, 18 ammunition wagons and 350 common ones, with provisions and other stores. But the next night we received an express that the rebels had defeated Colonel Ennis at the Enora. This occasioned a rapid march that way. The main body having crossed the Enora, I was left behind in command of the rear-guard, and being attacked in that situation, we maintained our ground until the main body recrossed to our support. The Americans retreated after suffering some loss (August twenty-first).

While at the Iron Works shortly afterwards a party

of loyalists with whom I was, defeated Colonel Banner-
man's party, and dispersed them. I was present also
at a small affair at Fair Forest, the particulars of which
as well as the numerous other skirmishes, have escaped
my memory; scarcely a day, however, passed without
some fighting.

A dissatisfaction prevailed at this time among the
militia, founded on General Clinton's proclamation,
which required every man having but three children,
and every single man, to do four months' duty out of
their own province when required. This appeared like
acting under compulsion, instead of voluntarily, as they
conceived they were doing, and they were in consequence ready to give up the cause; but, owing to the
exertions of their officers (and, indeed, I believe very
greatly through my instrumentality), the tumult was
happily appeased, and the same night we marched with
all the horse and some foot past Gilbertstown against
Colonel Grimes, who was raising a body of rebels to
oppose us. We succeeded in dispersing them and
taking many prisoners, and then joined the force at
Gilbertstown, and encamped there for some time, sending away the old men to their houses, and several officers to raise men to supply their places and strengthen
us. Colonel Ferguson soon after got intelligence that
Colonel McDale was encamped on Cain and Silver
Creeks, on which we marched towards the enemy,
crossed the Winding Creek twenty-three times, and
found the rebel party strongly posted towards the
head of it near the Blue Mountains. We attacked
them instantly, and after a determined resistance defeated them and made many prisoners. The rest fled
towards Turkey Cove, in order to cross the mountains

and get to Holstein.* On this occasion I commanded a division, and took the person prisoner who was keeper of the records of the county.

Our spies ffom beyond the mountains brought intelligence in October that the rebels were embodying rapidly. Other spies brought in word that Colonel Clarke, with a corps of backwoodsmen raised in the mountains towards the Tennessee, had taken Fort Augusta with its stores. This proved to be false, for he had been beaten off by the loyalists there after a stout fight. However, we at that time believed it and marched towards White Oak and Green River to intercept him on his return from Georgia. Colonel Ferguson detached the horse in three divisions, one under my command, with orders to proceed along the Indian line until I could make out Clarke's route and join Captain Taylor at Earl's Fort. I proceeded as far as Tiger River, and there learning that Clarke was gone up the Bushy Fork of Saluda River, I took six of the best mounted men, and got on his track until I overtook the main body, and made one of the enemy prisoner within view of it. I carried him to Colonel Ferguson, who then obtained the required information. Our spies from Holstein, as well as some left at the gap of the mountains, brought us word that the rebel force amounted to full 3,000 men; on which unexpected news we retreated along the north side of Broad River, and sent the wagons along the south side as far as Cherokee Ford. Here they joined us, and we proceeded to King's Mountain with the view of ap-

---

* Now known as the Holston Valley, in which is Knoxville, successfully defended by Burnside against Longstreet at the crisis of the American Civil War in 1863.

proaching Lord Cornwallis's army and receiving support from Charlottetown or from some of the detachments of his regulars. By Colonel Ferguson's order I sent expresses to the militia officers to join us here; but we were attacked (October ninth) before any support arrived by 1,500 picked men from Gilbertstown, on the Blue Mountains side, under the command of Colonels Cleveland, Selby, and Campbell, *all of whom were armed with rifles, and being well mounted could move with the utmost celerity*. So rapid was the attack, that I was in the act of dismounting to report that all was quiet when we heard their firing about half a mile distant. I immediately paraded the men and posted the officers. During this short interval I received a wound, which, however, did not prevent my doing my duty, and on going towards my horse I found he had been killed.

King's mountain,* from its height, would have enabled us to oppose a superior force with advantage, had it not been covered with wood, which sheltered the Americans and enabled them to fight in their favorite manner. In fact, after driving in our pickets, they were enabled to advance in three divisions, under separate leaders, to the crest of the hill in perfect safety, until they took post, and opened an irregular but destructive fire from behind trees and other cover. Colonel Cleveland's was first perceived, and repulsed

---

* It is a far-outlying spur of the Blue Mountains. The defeat and death of Ferguson here crushed the royalist cause on the mountain border of South Carolina entirely and decided Cornwallis to retire from Charlottetown and abandon his inland operations in North Carolina. The reader will notice that the victors owed their surprise of and success over the loyalist militia as much to their acting as mounted riflemen as to superior force.

by a charge made by Colonel Ferguson ; Colonel Selby's next, and met a similar fate, being driven down the hill; lastly, the detachment under Colonel Campbell, and by desire of Colonel Ferguson I presented a new front, which opposed it with success. By this time the other Americans who had been repulsed had regained their former stations, and, sheltered behind trees, poured in an irregular, destructive fire. In this manner the engagement was maintained near an hour, the mountaineers flying when there was danger of being charged by the bayonet, and returning again so soon as the British detachment had faced about to repel another of their parties. Colonel Ferguson was at last recognized by his gallantry, although wearing a hunting-shirt, and fell pierced by seven balls at the moment he had killed the American Colonel Williams with his left hand, the right being useless. I had just relieved the troops a second time by Ferguson's orders, when Captain de Poyster succeeded to the command. He soon after sent out a flag of truce ; but as the Americans renewed their fire afterwards, ours was also renewed under the supposition that they would give no quarter, and a dreadful havoc took place until the flag was sent out a second time; then the work of destruction ceased. The Americans surrounded us with double lines, and we grounded arms with the loss of one-third of our number.

I had been wounded by the first fire, but was so much occupied that I scarcely felt it until the action was over. We passed the night on the spot where we surrendered, amid the dead and groans of the dying, who had neither surgical aid nor water to quench their thirst. Early next morning we marched at a rapid pace towards Gilbertstown, between double lines of mounted Americans. The officers in the rear were obliged to carry two muskets each, which was my case, although wounded and stripped of my shoes (for the silver buckles) in an inclement season, without covering or provisions, until Monday night, when an ear of Indian corn was served to each. At Gilbertstown a mock trial was held and twenty-four sentenced to death ; ten of them suffered before the approach of Tarleton's loyalist cavalry force obliged our captors to move towards the Yadkin, cutting and striking us by road in a savage manner. Colonel Cleveland then offered to enlarge me on condition that I would teach his regiment for one month the exercise practiced by Colonel Ferguson, which I refused, although he swore I should suffer death for it when we got to Moravian Town. Happily, his threat was not put to the test, as I had the good fortune to make my escape one evening when close to that place. In the hurry to get away I took the wrong road, and did not discover my error until I was close to the town. I then retraced my steps until close to the pickets I had left, and taking a fresh departure I crossed the Yadkin River before morning, and proceeded through the woods towards home. John Wedyman, one of my company, had supplied me with a pair of shoes, which were of great use on this occasion ; but as he remained a prisoner, I never had an opportunity of making him a return.

The first night I slept in the woods, and next day I was supported by haws and grapes as I could find them.

The second or third day, in pushing through the woods to get to a ford, I heard a noise of some people (whom I knew to be Americans by white paper in their hats), on which I lay down, and was so close to them that I could have touched one of their horses in passing; fortunately, I was not observed, and soon after crossed the creek after them. I then made for the mountains in order to be guided by the Apalachian range (the higher part of the Blue Mountains), and get over the rivers with greater facility. After crossing Broad River, I met one Heron, who had been with me in King's Mountain, and who had, with some others, taken flight early in the action, putting white paper in their hats, by which disgraceful stratagem they had got through the American lines. I passed a night at Heron's house, and one at another man's on whom I could depend; from both I got some provisions: all the other nights I slept out, amounting to about twelve or fourteen.

I reached my home on the Packolet on October thirty-first, and found the Americans had left me little there. But not knowing where to find any British troops, I continued for some time about the place, during which, as the Americans had possession of the country, I was obliged to conceal myself in a cave dug in the branch of a creek; here, with two of my cousins, we remained, although there was not room to sit upright. My cousin's wife brought us food and intelligence every night. After learning that Colonel Tarleton had defeated the rebels under Sumter at Blackstock's Fort on Tiger River, and so revived the King's cause, I raised with great difficulty a company, and joined a strong party at Colonel Williams's house on Little River, where there was a force under General Cunningham, a loyalist colonel who had just been appointed brigadier of militia by Lord Cornwallis.

Major Plumber having been wounded at King's Mountain, the command of our regiment of militia devolved on Major First, who directed me to assemble my company and follow him to an appointed place on the Enora. On coming to the rendezvous, I found to my surprise and mortification that it was occupied by Major Roebuck, an American officer. His detachment immediately disarmed us and marched us off. Major First, in order to retrieve the blunder, pursued Roebuck, and attacked him when advantageously posted. First was killed, and his party retreated. Roebuck, who was formerly acquainted with me, parolled me to Fort '96, where I was exchanged for a Captain Clarke. I was then directed to assume the command of the fort which I strengthened. Soon after Colonel Tarleton came into the district in quest of General Morgan, who had been sent that way with a brigade by Gates, the Commander-in-Chief of the rebels in this country. Failing to get intelligence of his situation, Tarleton sent me for that purpose, as well as to compel the mills to grind for the army. My knowledge of the country enabled me soon to discover the enemy; but I found that his party had destroyed or carried away everything from my own house.

On January seventeenth, 1781, Colonel Tarleton attacked the enemy near the Cowpens on Thicket Creek. We were totally discomfited. The Americans were posted behind a rivulet, with their riflemen in front and cavalry in the rear. Colonel Tarleton charged at the head of his regiment of cavalry called the British Legion, which had been completed from the prisoners taken at the battle of Camden by Lord Cornwallis. The cavalry were supported by a detachment of the 71st Regiment under Major McArthur. The enemy's riflemen were broken without difficulty, but the late prisoners, seeing their own regiment opposed to them beyond, would not proceed against it, and broke; the remainder charged, but were repulsed; this gave the front line of the enemy time to rally and form in the rear of his cavalry, which charged the 71st (who were then unsupported), making many prisoners. The rout was almost total. I was with Tarleton in the charge, who behaved bravely but imprudently. The force was dispersed in every direction, besides losing the guns and many prisoners.*

My men being dispersed, I desired them to meet me at General Cunningham's, and proceeded towards my home, now despoiled of everything. I had not even a blanket left, or a change of clothes; added to this, I had no money and no pecuniary resources. Being unable to persuade General Cunningham to use any exertions towards embodying his regiment again, I proceeded to Charleston, where unexpectedly I met several British officers who had been taken at King's Mountain. These aided me in getting remuneration for some cattle and provisions I had supplied Colonel Ferguson's detachment with, and superadded the kind-

---

* This action of the Cowpens, fought by Lord Cornwallis's orders to clear his rear of Morgan, before commencing a second contemplated invasion of North Carolina, caused him to abandon his design, and so gave the last blow to the loyal interest in that quarter. Its details have never before been fully explained. In all these petty affairs defeat to the loyalists proved almost annihilation, says a local historian—a strong proof of the unpopularity of their cause. The "rebels," when beaten, soon got together again, as they found shelter and friends in all quarters.

ness of introducing me to Colonel Balfour, Commandant of Charleston, who, hearing from them of my great activity, and that I had lost my all, gave me an order to Mr. Cruden, commissioner of sequestrated estates, to accommodate me in one of them with my family. This produced an order to Colonel Ballingall and Mr. Kinsay at Jacksonsborough, who ordered me a house and provisions, with the use of three negroes to attend my family. Thus was I at once introduced to a new set of loyalists; and I immediately removed to my new residence near Parker's River on Pondpond River.

The rebels however increased much in the neighborhood of Pondpond, and a general rising being expected, I sent an express to Colonel Balfour to acquaint him with it. He detached 100 men to bring off the militia from Pondpond. By his desire I went to communicate confidential intelligence to Captain Kime at Mott's house, near Nelson's ferry, on the Santee River, which journey of 120 miles I performed in twenty-four hours. I then returned to Charleston, and, at the instance of Colonel Balfour, raised a troop of horse, and was stationed at Dorchester, a strong British post, and moved my family thither. We had not been at this place long before I ascertained that Major Snipe, Colonel Haynes, and Marion, the famous rebel cavalry partisan, had returned, crossed Pondpond River, and were embodying troops. I communicated this to Lord Rawdon (afterwards Lord Hastings), who had served in the first Carolina campaign as brigadier under Cornwallis, and took command when the latter general went northwards to Petersburg under orders to make a junction with Clinton in Vir-

ginia. His lordship immediately ordered out a detachment, of which I was one. We crossed Pondpond
River at Parker's ferry; and the boats having been
removed to impede our march, I swam my horse over,
accompanied by some others, and procured feather
beds to transport those across who could not swim.
We then proceeded rapidly and reached Snipe's plantation by daylight, which we soon cleared of him and
his party, driving them out with loss. On this occasion I was wounded in the thigh with a spear by a
man concealed in a ditch while in the act of leaping
my horse over it; but I took him prisoner, and conveyed him with the others made on this occasion to
Dorchester. About this time a detachment was sent,
and succeeded in taking Colonel Haynes, who soon
after deservedly suffered for treason, as it was discovered that he had communicated with the rebels
while acting as a British commissary. At this period
there were daily skirmishes, the Americans constantly
contracting our posts in every direction.

In the beginning of July I joined the army under
Lord Rawdon, then marching towards Fort '96 to
relieve the place. On our approach, the Americans
who were besieging it broke up, crossed Broad River,
and proceeded along the left bank towards Charleston. This was our last movement inland, for the
loyalist party was now either exterminated or forced
to hide its opinions. Lord Rawdon, finding that the
country must be abandoned, detached his light troops
towards Longcanes (a branch of Savannah River), to
bring away the loyalists and their families, taking
himself with the main body the route of Charleston
as far as Conquer. Here the Americans had recrossed

15

the river, and made a fruitless effort to oppose his march by preventing our passage across the creek. This we effected, however, without difficulty, and proceeded to Orangeburgh, where we expected to meet reinforcements from Charleston, and be joined by the light troops and loyalists. But we were disappointed in both, and soon after surrounded by the Americans, who pressed us so closely that we had at length but one pound of wheat in the straw served to each man in every twenty-four hours. The parties going out daily to forage had constant skirmishes with the enemy. On one occasion, Lord Edward Fitzgerald having broken his sword on the back of an American, I supplied him with another to continue the attack, for which he expressed himself greatly obliged.

A day or two afterwards Major Doyle came to me with a message from Lord Rawdon, to know if I could find any one well acquainted with the road to Charleston, and willing to go thither with a message of great importance, for all the expresses sent hitherto had either been killed or taken prisoners. Being perfectly acquainted with the whole of the neighboring country, I immediately went and offered my services to his lordship, which were readily accepted. I was offered any horse in the camp I might think better than my own, but conceiving myself the best mounted officer present, I preferred my own. I found before many minutes, use for every muscle of the good animal that carried me. I set out instantly for Charleston, and had scarcely passed the sentries when I found myself pursued by four or five of the enemy, two of whom kept up with me about twenty miles through the woods. My intention was to come into the Charles-

ton road where it crosses the Cypress Swamp at Cunningham's house, two miles above Dorchester, but I
unintentionally kept too much to the right, and crossed
the swamp by another path a little lower down; and
soon after I saw a picket of the enemy on the Charleston side of the swamp, who in all probability must
have taken or killed me had I not providentially missed
the common path, which they were carefully guarding.
I passed through Dorchester and remained there while
a fresh horse could be saddled and I could give Captain Brereton a message from Lord Rawdon to Colonel
Cootes (at Monk's Corner), of the 19th Regiment,
desiring him to be on the alert, as the Americans had
crossed Broad and Santee rivers in great force. This
was sent express to the colonel, and I continued my
route to Charleston, where I delivered my letter to
Colonel Balfour (the commandant), at four o'clock
P.M., twelve hours after I received it from Lord Rawdon, at Orangeburg—a distance of eighty miles. The
force was immediately turned out and marched to
relieve Lord Rawdon from his uncomfortable situation.
On reaching Dorchester I found to my grief that the
American cavalry had visited that place during my
short absence and taken away my horse, with 300
others. So soon as we joined Lord Rawdon, he found
himself strong enough to force his way through the
enemy, which he did immediately, marching towards
Charleston, and encamped without opposition near
Monk's Corner, where we had some trifling skirmishing, but no important occurrence.

In October the Americans by degrees got possession of all the country except the small part inside the
Quarter House where I was posted, Lord Rawdon

having then moved his force to another part of the country. I then joined a force of three companies raised for the protection of sequestered estates by the Commissioner, Mr. Cruden. In one of our excursions up Cooper's River, with the view of obtaining a supply of rice, the schooner upset and twelve men were drowned. I saved myself by swimming, as did six or seven others; but I lost my watch, sword, and other articles.

Soon after this period (December 1781) the British were obliged to abandon the neighborhood of the Quarter House and confine themselves entirely to Charleston Neck. Considerable quantities of wood being required for fuel, I was appointed to superintend the operation, which was giving employment to a vast number of people. I selected the destitute loyalists who were within the lines, and thus afforded them immediate relief. In consequence, however, of dangerous ill health and affliction, I relinquished the charge to Captain McMahon early in January 1782. My illness continued without much hope of recovery, so taking my passage in the Lady Susan transport, we sailed for Europe on April fifth, under convoy of the Orestes sloop-of-war, commanded by Sir Jacob Wheaton. The fleet consisted of fifty-two sail, and we had a pleasant passage. We made Mizen Head, on the coast of Ireland, May nineteenth, and put into Castle Haven next day, in a hard gale of wind. From thence we proceeded to Cork by land, and purchasing a horse, I proceeded to Dublin, accompanied by Charles Philip Campbell and Solomon Smyth, both like myself from Charleston. From this time forward, I need hardly say, I saw no more of America.

SIR WILLIAM GORDON OF GORDON'S BAT-TERY.

(Originally published by the Institution of Civil Engineers.)

MAJOR-GENERAL SIR J. WILLIAM GORDON, K. C. B., was the eldest son of Colonel T. Gordon, of Harperfield, in Lanarkshire. This estate came to him while he was still young, at his father's death; and through his mother, Miss Nisbet, the heiress of Carfin in the same county, niece of Andrew last Earl of Hynford, he not long after inherited Carfin and Maudslie Castle, formerly part of the Hyndford property. He was therefore born to such good prospects as would have indisposed most young men to steady exertion; but of his own choice he entered a hard-working profession, thenceforward devoting himself wholly to it, and throughout life he literally may be said to have treated his ample means, on principle, as a steward for others rather than an owner. From a private school at Bexley, in Kent, he passed the entrance examination, not very difficult in those days of nomination, into Woolwich Academy. During his cadet life he was remarkable chiefly for his great physical powers, his carelessness of danger, and his steady application to work. To the latter almost entirely—for young Gordon had not been gifted by nature with quickness of parts—he owed the prize he worked for, a commission in the Royal Engineers.

The times were those of the most profound peace modern Europe has known. In no part of our army did mere soldiership promise any special advantage, and perhaps least of all in the Engineers, whose war duties were almost ignored from the day that each officer left the school of instruction established for his corps at Chatham. Gordon passed from his first home station to North America, undistinguished from other subalterns; for his simple habits of life, which were to him as a nature, prevented his being even known generally to be more wealthy than his fellows. He left Halifax after a long term of duty there, much regretted by a few friends who had discovered the sterling worth which was concealed by a reserved exterior, and learnt something of the kind deeds which he had already begun to practice the doing of in secret. But to the many he was known chiefly by his great height and the endurance and activity which he displayed in the moose-hunts for which Nova Scotia was then noted, or for his avowed adherence to earnest and, to those not conversant with Scotch Presbyterianism, what seemed somewhat gloomy religious convictions. Promotion was of course in those days very slow in a seniority corps, and Gordon looked a middle-aged man when, in 1845, he was raised, after sixteen years' service, to the rank of captain, and sent to Chatham to take charge of the first company of Engineers, or Sappers and Miners as they were then called.

A neglected cold at this time brought out a predisposition to chest disease, and to those about him seemed to threaten his life; but his company was

under orders for Bermuda, and the change to that
mild climate soon restored him to his natural vigor
and the out-of-door habits in which he always delighted,
though never allowing them to interfere with the
duties of the desk. During the next five years he
was constantly employed on the large works which
were to create out of the sand-hills that ages have
solidified into Bermuda stone the Gibraltar of the West.
His spare time, of which he allowed himself but little,
was devoted wholly to the manly exercises which he
looked on as due to his profession, to practice, and to
the good works which formed part of his daily life.
Among the latter was a night-school kept by himself
for the instruction of his men, and which he never
allowed any engagement to interfere with. Frugal
and temperate in his own habits, his ready hospitality
was known to all passers-by who visited his station. Sparing in expenditure on himself, his liberality
towards the poor near him, or in cases made known from
any distance, was exhaustless. He not only gave as a
matter of course to those that asked, if they deserved
it, but his delight was to send help to those who
deserved it and had not asked. The venerable bishop
of the diocese, revealed after Gordon's death the fact
that he maintained the private charities which he
began at Bermuda for many years after he had left the
island, and that his name is still familiar there among
those who have heard it blessed by the aged and
infirm whose special wants he had carefully ministered
to. No case of distress or difficulty in his own corps,
however far from him, but received instant attention
when brought to his knowledge.

But it was not so much for his large-hearted chari-

ties that he by degrees became well known at this time
as for his marvellous physical powers and endurance.
The former he made it a principle to conceal, as
though practicing literally the injunction " Let not thy
left hand know what thy right hand doeth;" but his
feats of strength and swiftness, done on water and on
land as regularly as other men took their daily meals,
could not be hid, and the report of them spread far
beyond the little world of his garrison. His theory
was, that a soldier, to do his duty properly to his
country, must keep his body in the highest perfection
of its powers. Acting stringently up to this idea, he
lived constantly, except in his exceeding temperance
of diet, in such a state of regular training as few men
ever reach, even for a special purpose and a brief time.
His work never slackened any where in consequence of
this. It was confessed that no one ever saw so much
labor got out of working parties of soldiers or of con-
victs as Gordon did, and that without a harsh word.
No office detail, however petty, was below his attention. A favorite fancy of his was the preparing of
working drawings, which he might well have left to his
subalterns, but for his passion for labor; and after
returning from a run of twelve miles, done within two
hours, he would go straight to his high desk, without a
moment's intermission, and fall to work with a steady
hand in the standing attitude which he invariably
used.

He returned to England about the time of the
Great Exhibition of 1851, which was designed to usher
in an era of universal peace. His reputation for
strength and fearlessness, for liberality and honesty of
purpose, went before him; but many of his comrades

were ready to laugh at his favorite theory of being ready for the active service which in their time could never come. Two years afterwards the nation was rushing into the Crimean war, and no department which had the choice would have overlooked such a born warrior and practical engineer as the subject of this memoir. Gordon was at once put under orders for the Crimea, being then a captain of some standing, and fifth in seniority of the Royal Engineers selected for service in the east. But when the siege of Sebastopol was a month old, casualties had already made of the captain the Commanding Royal Engineer of the army, and honors and rank were coming thick upon him. Gordon carried on his duties under the superintendence of Sir John Burgoyne, who had come out as adviser to Lord Raglan; and he acted afterwards as second to Sir Harry Jones, when government sent that officer to take Sir John's place. To write, it may truly be said, the story of the duties of Gordon of Gordon's battery, and how they were performed, would be to write the history of the siege. His long-practiced endurance now enabled him to do without difficulty far more than any other man would have attempted in the way of personal supervision of the works as they went on unceasingly; and during one bombardment it is reported of him that he never sat down to take a meal for three days and three nights, and at its close was seen still walking along the trenches, sound asleep though refusing himself rest. His valor was not so much mere courage as a perfect indifference to danger, which became a proverb in the lines. It won for him the special favor of the Naval Brigade, whose soubriquet of "Old Fireworks" expressed their keen sense of his constant readiness to give the example of facing the enemy's fire whenever personal example could be of use. Nor was his influence felt only in leading others on to deeds of daring. He made no secret to those who questioned him on his habits of his never-failing daily study of his Bible. At such a time hearts were easily impressed by a few words coming from one whose heroic character and unsparing devotion to the work in hand had made him conspicuous to the whole army. And the great siege, more than any other part of his career of usefulness, has left abundant witness of the marvellous influence that pure life had on others for good.

A severe wound received in the right hand and arm in the great March sortie, and much neglected afterwards, broke down his health just before the siege closed, and he was absent when the stronghold was surrendered which, more than any other single man, he had contributed to make our prize. In the following year, being still regimentally a captain of engineers, but a colonel by brevet and aide-de-camp to the Queen, he was called suddenly from a holiday in Scotland to be practically the military head of his corps as Deputy Adjutant-General. "It's a splendid appointment," he said, in answer to a friend's congratulations, " but one I would rather not have, for the principal duty lies in refusing different men different things they want." With this somewhat morbid view of what discipline should be, it is not surprising that he was not as popular at the Horse Guards as his friends could have desired to see him ; but his translation to the important charge of the great fortifications of Portsmouth, the largest engineer-command then in the world, which happened not long after, gave his zeal and energy and his natural kindliness better scope. His Sunday evening entertainments, a custom begun by him when first in charge of a small detachment long before, were open to all his command weekly without special invitation, and drew his young officers together once more, as they had another generation of young officers fifteen years before, the survivors of whom warmly own the valuable influence these genial meetings had on them. With the design of the works of the Portsmouth district Sir W. Gordon (who received his knighthood while employed there) was not concerned. His duty was merely executive, and as an executive officer it may be fairly declared that he has never been surpassed. His command was broken by a temporary call to Canada at the time of the Trent affair; but the alarm over he returned once more to the charge of the great works around Spithead, of the execution of which his old opponent, Todleben, after being escorted by him round them, publicly expressed his unalloyed admiration.

As Deputy Adjutant-General of his Corps he had become an Associate of the Institution of Civil Engineers, and his keen sense of duty to his profession made him a constant attendant at its meetings; but with his usual extremely retiring habits he shrank from taking any more active part than listening. Not many weeks before his death, however, he rose to return thanks for the mention made of his corps in the President's address, which pointedly alluded to himself, and made a short speech full of manly feeling and of sensible acknowledgment of what the education of Royal Engineers owes to the civil branch of the profession, " their intercourse with which he desired to express his warm hopes might on all occasions be close and friendly as it had been heretofore." He had then not long been appointed by popular wish, as it were, no less than by royal choice to the revived office of Inspector-General of Fortifications, which his friends thought to see him fill with the same dignity with which he spoke that night. Alas, a secret disease, produced by the irritation of his severe Crimean wounds acting on the nervous system, was even then preying on his brain. The pain in his arm had gradually increased, and latterly never left him. His very efforts to suppress outward signs of suffering served but to increase the mischief that was working within. Traces of aberration of mind had been observed some time before by watchful and anxious friends, and a few weeks later he passed from among us by the saddest end a gallant soldier could know. In strength a giant, in modesty a maiden, in humility a child, so pure and noble a life never came to a more painful close than his, when his mind losing its self-control, he suddenly laid violent hands on his own life.

Left by his parents at the age of twenty-one the care of a younger brother and sister, he had discharged his difficult duties as though he had been the most loving and thoughtful of fathers. Of his practical goodness let this one trait suffice : when defrauded of several thousand pounds by an agent he had implicitly trusted, he insisted on charging his own want of supervision as chiefly in fault by the temptation it had offered, and absolutely refused to prosecute the offender. More than this, when he found the wretched man afterwards starving (who had robbed his employer only to fall into deserved penury), he himself, having long since forgiven him, and having sought him to express his forgiveness, now ministered to the needs of the only living being who had ever done him serious harm. The sudden loss of such a hero may well have cast a gloom over the service which was proud of him, even had the circumstances been less painful. It had seemed his part to bring visibly before their eyes, in a hard and sceptical age that loves its own comfort and doubts of others' goodness, all the pure and knightly qualities of the ideal "chevalier sans peur et sans reproche." To his personal friends their bereavement would have been most bitter in any case, and it was doubly hard where the sad consolation lies chiefly in the words our Laureate has addressed to such sufferers:

> "Friends, this frail bark of ours
> May wreck itself without the pilot's guilt,
> Without the captain's knowledge."

CHINESE GORDON AND THE TAIPING REBELLION.*

"THE Abyssinian campaign," wrote Sir Francis Head soon after the fall of Magdala, " promoted the corps of Royal Engineers from darkness to daylight. For in the London War Office it had in former ages been a time-honored axiom that a practical knowledge of the attack and defence of fortified places, of the application and construction of field-works, bridges, pontoons, roads, water-supply, surveying, sketching, and signalling, rendered an officer of Engineers *incompetent* to command an army in the field—for the very reason expounded by Festus when, with a loud voice, he exclaimed, ' Paul, thou art beside thyself; too much learning hath made thee mad!' But the Abyssinian campaign, conducted throughout all its ramifications by an Engineer, has indisputably established that in that competitive examination which in the council of statesmen must henceforth guide their selection of the fittest officer to command an expedition, or to defend the mother country, the corps of Royal Engineers can no longer be excluded."

If an apology were needed for publishing this brief narrative of one of the most wondrous series of suc-

---

* *The Ever-Victorious Army :* A History of the Chinese Campaign under Lieut.-Col C. G. Gordon, C. B., R. E., and of the Suppression of the Taiping Rebellion. By Andrew Wilson.

cesses that military annals record, it would be found in that reticence of its hero, which combined with other causes to keep his exploits too long unknown to his countrymen ; so unknown indeed, that it is not surprising that Sir Francis Head should have shared in the popular belief, as his words just quoted imply, that the Abyssinian expedition was the first occasion on which a British engineer had held a soldier's most important trust, the command of an army.   Yet before his eulogy of Napier appeared, a work was written which from its title, recited at the head of this essay, would seem intended to make known an earlier campaign, in which an engineer was the sole general : a campaign where the enemy was vastly more numerous, the powers of the commander more limited, the supplies scantier, the support more uncertain, the reward, oh ! how infinitely less, than in the case of Abyssinia.   And the issues ! Who shall compare the punishment of the drunken tyrant of Magdala, and the rescue of a dozen British captives from his grasp; or even the assertion of the greatness of British power, of the reality of our eastern resources, and, best of all, of our moderation ; with the accomplishment of a task which restored tranquillity to an empire whose population outnumbers that of Europe, repaired her desolate cities, and gave her toiling millions of peasantry the longed-for peace, waiting for which in vain, they had ceased to till their paternal lands, lest they should but be offering fresh temptations to the spoiler ?   And in accomplishing this great achievement a greater still was wrought.   The victories of the young Engineer-General of China shook to its fall the foul fabric of a blasphemous religion, which at one time had threatened to take rank in importance with those of Buddha and Brahma, and whose head had aspired to usurp the most ancient of earthly thrones, under the claim of a pretended revelation.

But in truth Mr. Wilson's work has buried a great epic amid heaps of mere book-maker's rubbish. What he intended no doubt to illustrate he has but obscured. That which should have been the main subject is so overladen by details often little relevant, that the reader who desires to know the story of Gordon's campaign may leave the volume at its end with confused impressions of the Chinese system of philosophy, the foreign policy of Pekin, the ability of the arch-impostor and his generals, the superiority, in a sense, of Chinese officialdom to that of Europe, and a dozen other collateral subjects, but without having thoroughly grasped that which he came to seek. As Mr. Wilson most truly remarks in his introduction, the book should have been written in three volumes at the least. We may add that the attempt to cram all the intended matter into one has spoilt the whole as a general work of reference, while it has confused and made tame his narrative of that single episode of recent Chinese history which, in the first page of his introduction, he declares to be "the topic of this book." It is not our business or wish to discuss at any length, what the writer has intended for the philosophic accompaniment of his particular task. He seems to us to have said a great deal too much, or not enough, when he hints that the Chinese empire is founded on principles similar to those shadowed in "Plato's Republic;" or declares that the ordinary Chinaman is universally so educated as to take an intelligent interest in the theory as well as the practice of his government; or states the para-

dox that the infanticide of China " does not arise from
any tendency among the Chinese to destroy infants ;" or
finally winds up his book with the alarming but somewhat vague declaration that, in Great Britain, " there
must be a return to some connection between its
higher intelligence and the wielding of its power, otherwise it will soon share the fate of Carthage and Venice,
of Spain and Holland." A writer who is capable of
putting down on paper such nonsense as this, unconscious that he is merely jumbling historical names in
pairs, instead of drawing historical parallels, is not
likely to be a very safe guide through a survey of the
forty centuries of civilized life in China, or of the philosophy by which its government, in theory at least,
subsists. Not to dwell on these longer, we are content with total dissent from the hints which he, though
" no Mandarin worshipper" by his own account, scat-
ters plentifully through his pages, that modern Europe in general, and England in particular, are vastly
behind the Flowery Land in civilization, decency, and
religion. Europe, it is true, has known evil days under
the hands of fierce conquerors, plundering and destroying in religion's name ; but its annals may be ransacked
in vain, without finding any parallel to the miseries
endured in those provinces of China over which " The
Heavenly King," the Taiping prophet, extended his
fell sway for ten sad years.

Hung Sew-tsuen (better known in China by his
assumed title, Tien Wang) must be a character with
some considerable attractions about him to a biographer, for Mr. Wilson, unintentionally it may be, seems
disposed to make him his hero, forgetting that this
was not the purpose of the book. That he had the

talent of imposing on others a sense of his divine mission is undeniable ; but that he should have done this with such ease and with so little question of proof; should, unlike his prototype, Mahomet, have been able to dispense personally with the fighting part of his mission, and found others ready to do the hard work for him; should never have attempted to create a system that would spread and maintain itself without an army ; and should have been allowed, so soon as he gained his temporary throne at Nankin, to shut himself up in seclusion and devote himself to foul licentiousness, undisturbed, save once, by the remonstrance of one chief follower, who paid the penalty of his rashness with his life ; proves to demonstration the degradation of sense and manners to which the calm Philosophy of Harmony our writer so much admires had reduced the people who had no better guide. As Mr. Wilson so often strains for a comparison between Chinese and European civilization, we will offer him a special one ; that between the most bloody and ruthless government of modern days in the West, and the rule of the Taipings. Bad as the triumvirate of 1794 at Paris and their proscriptions were, their administration was mild and decent—nay, honest and even saintly—when compared to that of the Heavenly King amid his concubines and disciples at Nankin. Such as he was, however, he was a power in the land, and one to be taken much into account in considering the forces acting in Western China in the years 1860–63. For he was aided not only by the blind superstition of his chief followers, but by two powerful extraneous supports which seemed often ready to intervene and save him, even when the reviving energy of the Imperialists, and the detestation in which the subjugated people around held his armies, seemed likely to turn the balance of the war against him.

The first of these was the favor or indifferentism of the European trading communities, who were now strongly established on the coast at various points. To many of these gentry, who had merely come to China to make money and go away again, it was a perfect matter of indifference which party succeeded in the contest so long as trade went on. To them " the Mandarins," the politest name they ever gave a government 4,000 years or so old, and the arch-rebel who had brought ruin on the southern provinces of China, were regarded on equal terms as contending powers. There is abundant evidence of this in the work of Mr. Wilson, who knew the class well; and that the Taipings could obtain supplies from some of these accommodating merchants as freely as the Emperor's government, is a patent fact in the whole history of the war. But for the absolute folly of the rebels, which led them unchallenged to threaten the Treaty Ports when they found themselves in their vicinity, it would have been as hard apparently to get the cosmopolitan society of these marts to declare itself against their pretensions, as to procure a decided intervention on the part of the British Government. This local feeling, nourished too often by personal differences with the Mandarins, in which the foreign traders were in the wrong, influenced our own national policy to some extent: but a more powerful sentiment than even that of gain held Britain back; for the missionary element among her people had taken up the cause of the Tai pings with a perversity such as the whole History of

Human Error, should it ever be written, will find it hard to match.

In condemning that monstrous misuse of a divine principle which made heroes of the Taiping chiefs, we desire to guard ourselves from any charge of depreciating the value of missionary effort. It is a noble boast of Englishmen that, wherever their merchants have penetrated into heathendom, preachers have been found willing, without hope of gain, to stand by their side. But the Founder of Christianity himself taught its first missionaries to combine the wisdom of the serpent with the harmlessness of the dove; and some of their later successors have ignored this part of their instructions altogether. Hence those noble efforts to Christianize other nations which in their spirit adorn the nation and the age, have been mingled with such effusions of folly and bigotry as have tended, with many harsh-judging minds, to throw contempt on the whole cause. New Zealand, Africa, Jamaica, have each their complaint to make on this score; but never was the erratic spirit of modern missionary enterprise so wholly thrown away, and so open to the censure of the prudent, as when a powerful party at home took up the cause of the Taipings, misled by a few local writers, whose ignorance of Chinese language and customs was only equalled by their audacity. Tien Wang had read Christian tracts, had learnt from a Christian missionary; and when he announced publicly three years afterwards that part of his mission was to destroy the temples and images, and showed in the jargon of his pretended visions some traces of his New Testament study, the conclusion was instantly seized by the sanguine minds of a section set upon evangelizing the East,.that their efforts had produced a true prophet, fit for the work. Wedded to this phantasy, they rejected as the inventions of the enemies of missions the tales of Taiping cruelty which soon reached Europe: and long after the details of the impostor's life at Nankin, with its medley of visions, executions, edicts, and harem indulgence, became notorious to the world, prayers were offered for his success by devotees in Great Britain as bigoted to his cause as the bloodiest commander, or " Wang," whom he had raised from the ranks of his followers to carry out his " exterminating decrees." The Taiping cause was lost in China before it was wholly abandoned by these fanatics in England, and their belief in its excellence so powerfully reacted on our policy, that it might have preserved us from active intervention down to the present time, had not certain Imperialist successes elsewhere, the diminishing means of their wasted possessions, and the rashness of their own chiefs, brought the Taiping armies into direct collision with us. And with the occasion there was happily raised up the man whose prowess was to scatter their blood-cemented empire to pieces far more speedily than it had been built up.

South of the lower portion of the course of the Yangtsze is Kiangnan, the district which was the scene of the future operations of Gordon and the " Ever-Victorious Army." It lies chiefly between the river and the deep and narrow bay of Hangchow. The width of the peninsula they form, from that city at the head of the bay across to Nankin on the Yangtsze, is 150 miles; its length from this line to where the ocean bounds it, about 200. The great treaty port of

Shanghai lies near the extreme western point, some twenty-five miles inland, on one of the numerous creeks which are the main features of the country. To picture to ourselves the events which were to follow, we must conceive first the general features of the district, as Mr. Wilson describes it, before being devastated by the bloody partisans of the Heavenly King. Densely peopled, it is generally but a few feet above the level of the ocean, and in some places below that level. Here and there isolated hills rise to the height of a few hundred feet; but for the most there is a dead level, rich with trees, growing various kinds of cereals in great abundance, thickly studded with villages and towns, and intersected in every direction by rivers, creeks, and canals. Look across any portion of this vast plain, and boats, with mat-sails spread, seem to be moving in every direction over the land. In some places, and especially round the great city of Soochow, the waters spread out into lakes of considerable size. Except on a few lines there is no convenient land transit but by raised foot-paths, so narrow that they must usually be traversed in single file : but the net-work of waters affords vast facilities for the movements of boats and small steamers. Upon the peaceful people of this plain the Taipings had descended in a desolating swarm, half robbers, half fanatics.

"We must conceive them," [says Mr. Wilson] " coming down on its rich towns and peaceful villages, moving flags, beating gongs, destroying images and temples, seizing valuables, occupying houses, dealing with all disobedience according to the exterminating decree of heaven, and being a terror unto young women ; but still not at first destroying the crops or.many of the houses, or slaying many of the males. Then we have the Allies driving them back, firing into their masses of men with long-range rifles, and pounding at their stockades with heavy guns and shells. On the retirement of these we have the rebels again advancing to the neighborhood of Shanghai, but this time in an infuriated demoniac state, burning and destroying everything in order that there may be a waste around the starving city, and murdering or driving before them all the villagers. Lastly, the Ever-Victorious Army appears on the scene—not by any means always victorious, but very frequently so—and bringing European drill and officers, with heavy artillery, to bear on a settlement of the question. Let this be embellished (as the scene appeared to me in 1860) with views of rich fertile plains, where the crops are trampled down or consumed, a few narrow bridges of the willow-plate pattern, a dilapidated pagoda or two, broken blackened walls of village houses, the deserted streets of towns, innumerable swollen blackened corpses lying on the slimy banks of the muddy streams, or rotting underneath the graceful bamboos, red flames at night flashing up against the deep dark sky ; let us imagine, also, the Taipings throwing themselves into all sorts of postures impossible to the European, and uttering cries scarcely less painful or hideous than those from the ravished villages, and we may form some conception of the great Chinese tragedy which was enacted in Kiangnan."

Looking at this country in a purely military aspect, it is evident that warfare carried on in it in a systematic way would necessarily have peculiar features of its own. The narrowness of the roads, and the abundance of lateral creeks, would compel all land movements to be conducted on a very reduced front ; while the aid of a flotilla would enable an attacking force not only to turn the opposing enemy undiscovered, but in many cases to fall upon him in flank and cut his columns in two. The walled towns situated on the great roads would become points of vast importance in a strategical view. Furnished with high walls, huge stockades, and large garrisons of fierce but rudely armed Taiping soldiers, they were proof almost to impregnability against the unscientific assaults of the Imperialist generals; but were ready on the other hand to open to the superior powers of a European siege-train, backed by disciplined and properly armed troops. As several of them, Soochow in particular, were situated partly on great sheets of water crossed by causeways, they might be completely blockaded by a force of resolute men smaller in numbers than the enclosed garrison, but holding the vital points of passage out. In this very manner, and for the same reason identically, was Napoleon able to enclose Marshal Wurmser's corps within lake-girt Mantua in 1796 with a mere detachment of his own army, while with the bulk of it he met and beat the relieving force of Alvinzi. Kiangnan is a country of Mantuas, and Soochow the chief of all, as we shall by-and-bye discern. Carrying further the same idea of seizing and occupying points vital to the enemy, it was evident that the capture of a few well chosen towns in succession might at once give a line of supply to the attacking force which held them; a line which could be held for it by inferior troops, and would thus enable it to seize successively such places as would cut the enemy's communications one by one, until his armies should be divided and destroyed in detail, or compelled to fly the province. Of course to do this any commander must have a fighting force morally and mate-

rially superior at the actual points of contact to those
it would encounter. Of course it must further be supplied with locomotion by water far beyond those of its
opponents. And these conditions would be of little
avail, if it had not for its chief a man of genius, instinctively able to see the vital points in the theatre of war,
and of daring to seize them at all risks. Whether
the Ever-Victorous Army and its general were such a
force and such a chief, let our after-story tell, to which
these remarks are but a prelude, indispensable to the
understanding of what follows.

The Taiping rebellion was ten years old, and had
from a rapid series of conquests become a vast but
desultory struggle with the regular governments of
China, before its force came into collision with the new
power from without, the armed civilization of Europe,
represented by the protected settlements on the sea-
board of the empire. The rapid growth of the movement and its chief successes were comprised in the
period between 1850, when Hung Sew-tsuen, the self-
styled Heavenly King, proclaimed his mission, and
1853, when, at the head of large armies, he established
his headquarters at Nankin, the second city of China.
But, as Mr. Wilson's work almost too mildly states it,
" the rebels were essentially destroyers, and possessed
no capability for reconstruction." The very extension
of their conquests limited their means of aggression
by reducing the productive powers of the unhappy provinces which came under their sword. At first, indeed,
they were not everywhere so cruel as to destroy blindly
their own means of subsistence ; but large contributions
of provisions, of rice especially, were exacted as a condition of existence from the country districts; and

when the delivery of these became uncertain, owing to the approach of Imperialist forces, or to any real difficulty of producing the necessary quantity, plunder, devastation, and murder were the mild means employed for bringing the refractory villages to submission. Thus, as the rebellion became checked and localized by Imperial successes, its cruelties grew more detestable, until the provinces that it had held became the howling wilderness of ruin which that of Kiangnan was, as described by Mr. Wilson in the latest stage of the rebellion. The first great check sustained by the Taipings was the destruction of the army sent by the Heavenly King against Pekin soon after his establishment at Nankin. Growing ferocious under disaster, he then began the series of "exterminating decrees" by which his government was, during the rest of his career, mainly carried on. Soon afterwards, in 1856, he put to death, in a fit of jealousy, his chief general, the true author of early Taiping success, known as the Eastern King; and from that time his cause began to languish, and that of the Imperialists, supported by the naturally conservative element of the Chinese people, made head against it even under the walls of Nankin. In 1859–60 the humiliation of the emperor's government by the French and English, which followed upon the reactionary policy of the Pekin government and its useless quarrel with the Allies, once more gave a great impetus to the rebellion; and the Faithful King, one of the Hung Sew-tsuen's best commanders, succeeded in raising for a time the Imperialist blockade of Nankin, driving the investing armies down towards the estuary of the Yangtsze, and opening for the first time to the Taipings the rich province of Kiangnan. Following up this advantage, he advanced to the southwest, defeating and almost destroying the first Imperialist army which encountered him. Another large force which held Soochow was so terrified at the news of this disaster, that its commander committed suicide ; and the wealthy city, the central point of the peninsula before described, containing, according to not extravagant estimates, two millions of inhabitants and the chief silk manufactories of China, fell unresistingly into the spoilers' hands. Hangchow, which is only inferior in importance to Soochow, next was occupied ; the whole district, except a few posts towards the mouth of the Yangtsze and near the city of Shanghai, was in Taiping hands ; and the rebellion had reached so great a height that, in the words of Mr. Wilson (p. 57,) " had it not been for the assistance given by foreigners towards its suppression, it might possibly still be useless by devastating the country."

We have quoted these words the more particularly, before proceeding to speak of the intervention, because they directly contradict sundry hints of the same author's that the liberation of China from the scourge which had for twelve years oppressed it was not due to foreign aid in general, nor to that of Colonel Gordon in particular. There is such a thing as damning with faint praise, and surely it is little better to quote high panegyrics of the commander whose deeds one records in order to follow them with a page of such remarks as :

" There is no doubt that Gordon's force unaided could not have cleared the province. While the brunt of fighting fell upon him, he required Imperialists to hold the places which he took, and their forces fought along with him so as greatly to contribute to his success. . . . It is quite clear, judging by the situation and its results, that the Imperialists allowing the Taipings to advance against the posts was no proof whatever of their being unable to deal with the rebellion effectually in their own slow and systematic way."

To write in this fashion after the proofs his own work furnishes that the campaign of the Ever-Victorious Army found the rebellion active and flourishing, and left it crushed, shows that if Mr. Wilson can tell the story of Gordon's successes, he is wholly incapable of drawing from them the broad and obvious conclusion. In one still more contradictory passage on the campaign, Mr. Wilson states that a right understanding of its military results and political relationship "is absolutely essential to correct the erroneous supposition that the Chinese were in any very great need of an assistance for the suppression of the rebellion." So far from correcting this supposition, we are certain that any one who carefully weighs Mr. Wilson's own narrative will come to the very conclusion which he deprecates. That he himself should have missed it, having had the advantage of perusing the original documents since placed in our hands, adds but another proof that it is useless to look for the historian's judgment in one who has been trained to regard the current events around him with the petty view of a local politician. But it is time to pass entirely away from the criticism of Mr. Wilson's work to the story which he has undertaken to tell.

In January, 1862, despite the warnings previously given by Admiral Hope, the Faithful King, now chief-commander of the Taipings, put his army from Soochow in motion for the second time against Shanghai. According to the theory of Mr. Wilson—which at this point we beg to take leave of—he moved because pressed by the Imperialists that way. But as he had, in fact, attacked the place in 1860, and been beaten off by the French and British garrisons, when he was at the height of his successes, we must decline to believe that this aggressive policy was the result of certain reverses of 1861. Its meaning was announced plainly enough by the invader's proclamation, " We must take Shanghai to complete our dominions," as the manner of warfare by which this was to be accomplished, by the smoke of the burning villages which obscured the city, and hid the surrounding country from the eyes of its terrified inhabitants. The foreign residents formed themselves into volunteer corps ; the allied admirals prepared to act decisively against the invaders. General Staveley resolved, with our Minister's countenance, not merely to save the city, but to maintain a clear radius around it of thirty miles. Finally great importance was suddenly attached to the American adventurer Ward, who with about a thousand half-disciplined Chinese, held Sung Kiang, a place eighteen miles above Shanghai on the Whampoa, which he had taken from the rebels at the time of their advance in 1860, being commissioned by the Chinese governor of the city, and paid for his services from means furnished by some of its leading merchants. His force was officered by such wandering Europeans and Americans as he could pick up; and on the first repulse of the rebels (who had occupied some places to the south of the city, from which Ward, aided by the admirals, drove them) it received from Pekin the title by which it was afterwards officially known, that of The Ever-Victorious Army.

During April and May, 1862, the Allies, notwith-standing the death of Admiral Protet, shot dead at Najou, obtained considerable successes. They recov-ered several walled towns in succession which had been too easily given up to the Taipings, and seemed likely without difficulty to maintain the clear radius resolved on. No better thing could have happened to the rebels, as afterwards appeared: but at this time they obtained a sudden success which proved ulti-mately of most disastrous result to their cause, though favorable to it for the moment. The Faithful King learning that the Imperialists near Shanghai, embold-ened by the reverses of their enemies, had resolved to advance against Taitsan, a considerable place on the direct line between the former place and Soochow, marched to meet them, and on May sixteenth suc-ceeded, by the old ruse of placing among them a body of his own picked men under the guise of deserters, in utterly routing them. A small part only escaped to Kading, the place from which they had advanced. This town was one of those recently recovered by the Allies under Staveley: and that general, growing nat-urally anxious about the advanced positions into which he had thrown his detachments, and their exposure to overwhelming masses of the victorious Taipings, aban-doned these new acquisitions and withdrew to Shang-hai, a step not taken without some remonstrance on the part of his staff.

Staveley's retreat naturally gave an impetus to the Taiping advance. The Faithful King now occupied the towns within the lately protected radius, and laid waste the country up to the city's walls. Beyond them there was nothing free from the marauding parties he sent out, but the ground the fire of the Allies could reach and the two small towns of Singpo and Sung-kiang. The latter place had been the headquarters of Ward's force ever since it was raised in 1860; the other was one of those lately taken by Staveley, and now occupied by a detachment of the Ever-Victorious Army. An attack was made on Sungkiang, but repulsed by Ward, aided by a party from the fleet. Singpo, on the contrary, was soon so closely invested that it was resolved to abandon it, and great loss was suffered in the attempt of the garrison to escape on June eighteenth, in which their commander, Forester, was captured by the Taipings. The Faithful King, now master of all the district but Shanghai and a few miles of the river, was for pressing his successes against "the foreign devils;" the rather so since he doubtless hoped (as he had endeavored two years before) to gain an entrance into the city by treachery. At this point, however, he was recalled by his master, against whose capital at Nankin new Imperial armies had moved from the interior, and so Shanghai was left to breathe freely again. The interest of Chinese affairs concentrated for the rest of the year 1862 on the treaty port of Ningpo, to the south of the bay of Hangchow, which the Taipings had some time since seized. Hither Ward repaired with part of his force to aid the operations of Colonel Roderic Dew, of the navy. This gallant officer (whose achievements are worthy of far more notice than we can give them) had become entangled in the conflict of the Imperialists and Taipings for the possession of the city, and after a vain attempt at armed neutrality, took part so decisively with the former as to recover the place for them, and then, following up his success, cleared the desired radius of thirty miles around it. The barbarities of the defeated Taipings in their attempts to recover this exceeded all description, and made the country people their determined enemies; so that, in spite of the death of Ward in one of many affairs in which he showed great gallantry, the district near Ningpo was fairly freed from the Taipings by the beginning of 1863.

Ward's skill and courage in action caused him to be much lamented; but he had never been able to restrain the marauding propensities of his force, which the Ningpo successes had shown in their worst colors. His successor, Burgevine, a young American of more activity and pretension than genius, was so inflated by his sudden elevation as at once to become almost immediately involved in quarrels with the Chinese governor (or Futai), the Imperialist generals near him, and the bankers who supplied the means of payment to the force. With the moral support of General Staveley to back him, the Futai dismissed Burgevine, and took officially over for his government the Ever-Victorious Army, the command of which was refused by its next senior officer. At the Futai's entreaty, Staveley gave it in temporary charge to Captain Holland, one of his staff, until authority should be obtained from Sir F. Bruce at Pekin to attach a British officer permanently to it as commander. Holland, unwilling to let his force grow rusty, advanced forthwith against Taitsan, a place already noted for Imperial disasters, but only to be repulsed with heavy loss. At this juncture the

reply of Sir F. Bruce was received, and under his sanction the command was conferred on Gordon, a young
captain of Engineers, just breveted major for his services in the previous operations.

Gordon had first seen war in the hard school of
"the black winter" of the Crimean war. In his humble
position as an engineer subaltern he had attracted the
notice of his superiors not merely by his energy and
activity (for these are not, it may be asserted, uncommon characteristics of his class), but by an extraordinary aptitude for war, developing itself amid the trenchwork before Sebastopol in a personal knowledge of the
enemy's movements such as no other officer attained.
"We used always to send him to find out what new
move the Russians were making" was the testimony
given years since to his genius by one of the most distinguished of the officers he served under; and the
reputation he then made he had fully sustained during
the brief services he had lately been engaged on in
China. If General Staveley had made any mistake in
the operations he personally conducted the year before
(and it must be remembered he·was painfully hamper-
ed by the doubt whether active intervention would be
approved), he more than redeemed it by the excellence
of his choice. The Ever-Victorious Army found itself
under a leader whose courage it had constant occasion
to admire, whose justice it honored, whose firmness
availed to suppress the daily quarrels of its officers
and to shield the men from abuse of their power. The
private plundering which disgraced the force when with
Ward disappeared under a general whose eye was as
keen as his soul was free from the love of lucre. Stern
against iniquity as the Baptist himself (for Gordon was

24

of the religious type of soldier which England has learnt to reverence in such characters as Havelock and Hedley Vicars), he from the first taught his force to "do violence to no man, and be content with their wages;" while the milder side of the gospel by which he lived was displayed to the defeated Taipings; and the humane treatment which their prisoners met with at his hands did almost as much, after the first, for the cause which he served as his inborn skill in the art of war. Among the strange medley of adventurers who held commissions under him were Englishmen, Americans, French, Germans, Spaniards. Some were ex-mates of merchant ships, some old soldiers of good character, some refugees of no character at all. Among them were avowed sympathizers with the rebels, and avowed defiers of Chinese law; but all classes soon learnt to respect a general in whose kindness, valor, skill, and justice they found cause unhesitatingly to confide; who never spared himself personal exposure when danger was near; and beneath whose firm touch sank into insignificance the furious quarrels and personal jealousies which had hitherto marred the usefulness of the force. The influence he gained over their rude minds, and the degree of education that qualified them, may be illustrated together by the following pithy note addressed to him by an excited subaltern before the greatest of his conquests, and after some very heavy losses of officers in previous assaults:

"Camp before SOOCHOW: 3rd De 63.

"Sir, i wish to volunteer my Service to be one of the Stormers.

"W. H. ——, Lieut. —— Regt."

The difficulties that beset the commander in enforcing the most necessary discipline before the enemy appear from the characteristic letter following, written by an officer after the execution of a deserter at one of the detachments, during a long series of desperate engagements at the close of Gordon's operations, near Chanchufu. (The colonel complained of for his severity was killed, it should be noted, in a night affair, four days later, when some of Gordon's own troops fired on his party; and it has been shrewdly doubted whether the firing was wholly accidental.)

April 21, 1864.

"Sir, It is with Great Regret, that i ame forced to apply for permission to retire from your force but the transaction of this afternoon so Disgusts me that i can no longer serv in So Corruptible a force i hope you will not forget an officer whom has servd at Chingwan and at those hills at Whosun lately, without the chance of any Loot. Sir i have hardly a farthing i leave it to your generosity for the means of reaching Engeland but i cannot possibly serv in this force after Col.—'s act of this afternoon. Now Sir Some men who Deserted from Soochow and whom you ordered to be Shot, were Sheltered and husbanded by Col.—and eventualy released. a Corpl who deserted from my late gunboat i was told that i had Ill-Treated him, by Col.—, for why, because he was one of his old croneys i could tell you more if I had a private Conference with you. Sir I have servd in the british army for a long time and never heard of a man being Shot, for desertion (and without a court martial) Sir if you cannot give me the means of returning to Engeland i hope you will Give me a recommendation that i may obtain a Situa-

tion and not join your Enemies the Taping rebils Sir it is
with Sincere regret i tender this resignation from 31st.

"I remain your most Humble Servant.   —— —— —

"The late Capt. Artillery."

"Sir as authority for a Character i present you with my
discharge."

"Gen. C. GORDON."

The organization of Gordon's army we have not
space to give in detail, nor is this essential for the
purpose of our story. Its numbers, varying from
3,000 to 5,000 men, under about 150 officers, were
easily maintained, after the first successes, by recruiting among the captured Taipings. The infantry were
armed mostly with the smooth-bore musket, but had
plentiful supplies of ammunition; and some picked
men had rifles. The artillery was very formidable,
comprising a well-arranged siege-train for the attack
of walled towns, and supplied with complete boat carriage for water transport. A flotilla of armed steamers
and gun-boats served, in that water-intersected country, both to cover and flank all movements, and also
by suddenly transferring the force from one point to
another to multiply it to the enemy's imagination.
A light pontoon equipment was ready for the passage
of the numerous creeks to be crossed on every march.
Though formidable in these particulars, the value of
so small and so irregularly formed a force, acting
against masses often tenfold its own numbers, must
needs depend greatly on the nature of the country
and the powers of strategy in the commander. Of the
former we have already spoken: the latter's operations
we have now briefly to recount.

The force now placed under Gordon, and the means he commanded for its rapid transport, might be employed by an active and daring commander in two different ways. The one would be to carry on connected operations, supported by, or at least bearing on, those of the Imperialist commanders in this part of China, and directed, as before pointed out, against the main lines by which the Taiping armies communicated one with another. A more obvious and apparently more brilliant course, but one leading to less decisive results, would be to transfer the Ever-Victorious Army suddenly from one point to another in the province, so as to strike a series of blows at isolated posts of the enemy. It might be said, indeed, by one reasoning from preceding events, that neither of these, but rather a purely defensive attitude near Shanghai, or the gradual recovery bit by bit of the places near that city which had been lately captured, would have been the natural way of employing the force at first. But the new commander's instinctive genius told him at once that a vigorous aggressive was, in a case like this, certain to prove the best defensive; that the Taipings would not attempt to hold the vicinity of Shanghai when they found an active enemy in their rear, threatening the places through which their retreat would lie; and that the moral superiority attaching to such an offensive would not only be good for his own men, but would extend its advantages to the Imperialist armies, which would gain heart from the moment they saw the common enemy reduced from his usual threatening attitude to one of defence. The feebler notion of protecting Shanghai by operations confined to the thirty-mile radius was never therefore entertained by Gordon; yet in resolving to attack beyond it, in order to completely free the district near the city, it is probable that he could not foresee wholly how far success might lead him, and was content to leave the thorough breaking of the Taiping power as a question for future circumstances to decide. But for the immediate present, before his entering on his more regular operations, he resolved to try the second mode indicated, and to strike one sudden blow at a distant point, such as should give heart and cohesion to his followers, and inspire them with confidence in their new chief.

About seventy miles north-west of Shanghai, and on the southern shore of the estuary of the Yangtsze, lies Fushan, a town long infamous as a haunt of pirates, and now held by the Taipings, who had captured it in 1862, for the second time, after it had once deserted their cause. Their garrison not only held this place, but shut off from the river Chanzu, a town ten miles inland, which had returned to its allegiance at the same time, and whose governor, closely pressed by a Taiping force, had now great difficulty in restraining the Imperialist garrison from surrender, by which they hoped to avert the threatened vengeance of the rebel commander. To relieve this suffering garrison as swiftly as possible was the first task to which Gordon applied himself after taking command of the Ever-Victorious Army; and not many days after he was on his way thither, carrying part of his artillery, and as many of the infantry as his two available steamers would transport. Under cover of an Imperialist force, which was intrenched not far from Fushan, Gordon landed without opposition, and disregarding a large body of Taip-

ings which kept the open field to watch his proceed-
ings, went directly to the attack of the town. A
32-pounder planted cleverly in the night near the wall
made an easy breach in the defences next morning
(April 4th), and the garrison, losing heart, fled at the
advance of the assaulting column, and gave up the
place, which thus fell with very trifling loss. A march
to Chanzu relieved the faithful governor there (faithful
probably because, as once having been a Taiping
leader, he dared not risk a surrender), and showed such
traces of the cruelty of the rebels as might well have
hardened any heart against their cause. The dreadful
sight in one place of the putrefying corpses of thirty-
five Imperialist soldiers, burned partly first, and then
crucified, testified that the tenacity of the Chanzu governor had in it something of a wise discretion. Having executed his purpose, Gordon returned as speedily
as he had come to his headquarters Sungkiang. His
success had confirmed him in the good opinion of his
force and of the Chinese authorities, from whom he was
now able without difficulty to procure the necessary
means for that liberal payment of his officers by which
he superseded the loose practice of special rewards for
their captures which had existed under Ward, and which
had supplemented a still more irregular system of private
plunder. Firm in maintaining his own authority as to
discipline, he affected none of the autocratic airs of his
predecessors, but loyally treated the Chinese governor
of the province, Li (the same who had got rid of
Burgevine by Staveley's aid), with the respect due to
the representative of the government he served. In
vain did Burgevine intrigue at Pekin for restoration to
his charge; for even Burlingame, the American minis-

ter, was not in his countryman's favor. His successor
had already, both in the field and in quarters, won
golden opinions from all with whom he had to do ; and
Li, when appealed to from Pekin, wrote of him pithily
and truly: "He wishes to drill our troops and save our
money; he fully comprehends the state of affairs, and
in the expedition he is preparing his men delightfully
obey him and preserve the proper order." For Gordon was now making ready for the campaign which
was to restore Kiangnan to the Imperial arms, and by
breaking the neck of the rebellion, lead to the general
pacification of China.

It must be remembered that the great city of
Soochow forms both a natural capital and central
point to the peninsula which was to be the theatre of
war. About thirty-five miles north-west of Shanghai
lies the walled town of Taitsan, connected, by a main
road running onward through the still larger town of
Quinsan, with Soochow. Quinsan was a place of the
very greatest strategical importance; for the principal
approaches to Soochow on the eastern side met there,
and it served also as the arsenal of the Taipings in
that country, they having established in it a manufac-
tory for shot under some vagabond Englishmen.
Against this town Gordon was making his advance at
the end of April, sure of the after fall of Taitsan, which
in fact depended on it, when he was called aside suddenly to the latter town to avenge one of the acts of
treachery by which a Chinese civil war, beyond that
of any other nation, is apt to be defiled. The Taiping
commander at that place, intimidated apparently by
the fall of Fushan, which left him exposed to an attack
on that side or from Shanghai (Taitsan lies halfway

between the two) had made proposals of surrender to Governor Li. Either these meant nothing, or he changed his mind after the first negotiations, for the affair only ended in the surprise by treachery of the first part of an Imperialist column which was marching in by agreement to occupy the place. Three hundred of the prisoners were slaughtered and beheaded, their heads being sent to Quinsan as a proof of the fidelity of the Taiping general; but the news reaching Gordon, he turned aside at once and moved swiftly to avenge this act of barbarity. Reaching the south side of the town on April thirtieth, he worked round to the east of it, keeping out of gunshot, and capturing some small forts which protected the Quinsan road, cut it off from that place. His heavy guns, protected by mant-lets (for the slow process of trenchwork was seldom needed against the imperfect fire to be met in these sieges), opened on the place next day, and on the second an effective breach was formed. Never did the Taipings fight better than here. They had not yet been discouraged by frequent defeat, and, more-over, had good reason to distrust the mercy of their enemies. They mustered ten thousand strong, and had among them to work their guns several of the reck-less and untameable adventurers whom European merchant-ships cast out in the course of their distant trade, and whose chief aim is to keep beyond the reach of the civilized law, which they have probably too good reason to dread. But all defence was in vain against the perseverance and energy of the new commander. On the first repulse of his attacking column, Gordon, imitating Grahame at San Sebastian, caused a battery of eight-inch howitzers to play over his stormer's heads and clear the breach. On the second essay the defenders gave way and made a general attempt to escape. It is to the credit of the soldiers of the Ever-Victorious Army that they spared the Chinese prisoners (seven hundred of whom were soon after enlisted in their ranks), while the foreign adventurers naturally met with little mercy. Seven of these were killed after the assault, three of whom proved to be deserters. At this early stage of the campaign it is curious to observe that the old immoral sympathy for the Taipings took the form of attacks on Gordon's force, who were accused by anonymous writers in the press of the treaty ports of acts of "the most refined cruelty" towards their prisoners. Such letters would have been of but little importance, had not the Bishop of Victoria been misled by them, and addressed a dispatch to Lord Russell on the subject. These charges were not left to Gordon only to refute, though he did so effectually by showing the confidence with which the Taiping prisoners took service in the ranks of the accused force. They were rebutted by General Brown (who had succeeded Staveley in command of the regular troops about Shanghai) upon the most direct and detailed evidence; and the origin of the fiction was traced to its source in the execution by an ordinary but cruel Chinese official mode, "the ignominious death," of seven of the runaways of the late garrison of Taitsan, who fell into the hands of an independent Imperialist force which lay six miles from the place on the Shanghai side.

Taitsan had offered considerable temptation to plunder, and Gordon was glad, therefore, to withdraw the Ever-Victorious Army from its new conquest. His abolition of the old license to pillage, and other measures taken at this time to secure the necessary regularity and discipline, were not carried out without much resistance, especially from the European element. At one time all the commanding officers of battalions sent in their resignations simultaneously to support an extravagant demand; at another a number of those below them became still more mutinous, and their insubordination threatened to spread to their men. Gordon quieted the seniors, who had most to lose, by a firm but determined refusal, and replaced the obstinate portion of the others by volunteers from General Brown's troops; so that before the end of May, with order restored, a complete and well-organized commissariat, and the moral advantage of recent successes attaching to it, the Ever-Victorious Army was moving onwards to new achievements. There was no question now of remaining on the defensive, or even of confining the operations to the neighborhood of Shanghai. The capture of Taitsan had at once cleared more than the necessary ruins around the city, the Taipings near it naturally retiring as they found the enemy established between themselves and Soochow. The Imperial forces taking advantage of this, followed them up westward to the neighborhood of Quinsan, and then intrenched themselves under their general Ching, waiting till their disciplined ally should arrive to deliver the place into their hands.

The importance of Quinsan in a strategical view has been already noticed generally; but to understand it more accurately it is necessary to point out that it was the key to all further operations against Soochow It lies nearly thirty miles eastward of that city, being connected with it by a single causeway running along a canal, to both the north and south of which the creeks spread out into large lakes, making all other direct land communication from that side impossible. Close to the west of Soochow lies the principal of all the numerous lakes of Kiangnan, Taho, a sheet of water nearly square-shaped, and forty miles long and broad. Hence there are but three main accesses to the city, two running north and south along the eastern side of the lake, and the third through Quinsan, thus forming with them the letter ⊢, Soochow being at the cross, Quinsan at the (proper) foot, and the Taho lake lying along the top or left-hand side. Quinsan once taken would supply a base for separate operations against the necks of land north and south of the city ; and these once occupied and closed, the fall of the place, to a force having command of the water communications, would be but a question of time. A right understanding of these broad features of the case will make clear the nature of the operations that followed.

Gordon's reconnoissances and reports of Quinsan told him that the place was strong. The ditch around it was over 100 feet wide ; the various approaches were furnished with forts inside stockades ; the garrison was estimated at from 12,000 to 15,000 men. But if strong in itself its communication with the rebel headquarters at Soochow was extremely bad, being, as before stated, along a single causeway, narrow in places, with lengthy bridges across the creeks, and easily approached at any point by Gordon's chief armed steamer the " Hyson." This causeway then was the weak point of the defence, and against it Gordon accordingly, seizing hold of the fact with the clear insight of genius, led his attack on

May thirtieth, carrying as many of his land forces as his flotilla would convey, under the protection of the Hyson. This steam-vessel, a small iron river boat, mounting a 32-pounder gun and a 12-pound howitzer, having her crew and gunners protected by timber-proof breastworks, and for her commander a rough but valiant Yankee named Davidson, did extraordinary service on several occasions, but never so much as on this day, a memorable one in the annals of the Taiping war. The point where Gordon's flotilla struck the vicinity of the causeway on its south side was Chunye, one-third of the way from Quinsan to Soochow. The approach was protected by piles in the water, and these again by stockades on the neighboring land, within which was a strong stone fort. Gordon had intended to carry the land defences, if necessary, by assault, and thus cut the enemy's communication at once by road and canal. The Taipings, however, saved him all trouble on this occasion ; for no sooner had the piles been torn up and the steamer appeared making her way through, than a panic seized the defenders, and stockades and forts were alike abandoned, their late garrisons flying both ways, and spreading alarm to the gates of Quinsan and Soochow. While Gordon landed his troops, the Hyson was sent down the canal to follow up the fugitives towards the latter place, and fulfilled her task completely, clearing the causeway the whole way to within sight of the city, and occupying two stone forts which guarded it at different points. Towards dusk she returned to Chunye, and not too soon, for the road from Quinsan was now crowded with a dense column of men, at the head of which Gordon's troops were briskly firing. The Taiping garrison, finding their main outlet closed, while the passages eastward from the town were held by the Imperialist general Ching, had sallied forth at evening, determined apparently by mere numbers to crush Gordon's small force (one battalion of infantry and some guns were all that had been brought up), and make their way out. The fore-gun of the steamer was at once brought to bear, and her 32-pound shells soon decided the engagement, driving the Taipings in a shrieking rout of fugitives back on the beleaguered town. So fearful was their loss from the firing and their own panic crowding (the steamer appearing to them, no doubt, a relentless and invulnerable monster, which could neither be escaped from, nor injured, nor stayed in her pursuit), that no thought of further resistance was left to the disheartened garrison, and the Imperialists, who had been on the watch on the opposite side, entered the town unopposed from the east next morning. Of the Taipings many thousands dispersed over the country; but the villagers here, as after the capture of Taitsan, revenged abundantly on the fugitives the oppression they had long suffered from, and but few of the number reached Soochow, or any other place of safety. Up to this time Gordon's actions may be considered as having cost the rebels not less than 25,000 men. This last extraordinary success, gained, with a list of *seven casualties*, by one decided and well-planted blow, did not occur without being accompanied by some fresh difficulties. General Ching's jealousy of his ally's achieving with a handful of men what his own army had not dared to attempt, broke out in a serious form, and led to some of his gun-boats firing on a party of the Ever-Victorious troops, whose flag they pretended to ignore

Governor Li, however, compelled the apology which Gordon found it necessary to insist on, lest the mistake should be repeated; and this difference was settled for the time. A more serious matter was a mutiny of the artillerymen, who disapproved strongly of Gordon's intended change of headquarters from Sungkiang to Quinsan. The former was associated in their minds with the easy days and loose discipline of Ward's command, and they openly refused to obey orders when they heard of the proposed transfer, adding threats of destroying their officers rather than submitting to it. It was not until Gordon, drawing the revolver which he was never seen but on this single occasion to display, had dragged from the ranks the foremost man of the mutineers, and forced him to embark under threat of instant death, that obedience was restored, and the rest of the company, in the words of an eye-witness, " obeyed their general's formal word of command and embarked without hesitation or demur. It may be said," continues the same narrative, " that any other determined officer might have done likewise, and with the same results. Not so. It was generally allowed by the officers, when the event became known, that the success in this instance was solely due to the awe and respect in which General Gordon was held by the men; and that such was the spirit of the force at the time, that had any other but he attempted what he did, the company would have broken into open mutiny, shot their officers, and committed the wildest excesses." But this act of energy made him master of the situation and he had no occasion to continue or repeat his severity towards his Chinese rank and file. His artillery officers were the next to give him trouble. They objected to a new commander whom he had given them ; and it was not until he actually started on his next expedition without them that they returned to their allegiance and were restored to their posts upon apology. This last difficulty overcome, and his force considerably augmented by largely enlisting from his Taiping prisoners, he moved, towards the end of July, to a still greater achievement than those he had attempted—the conquest of Soochow itself.

The situation of this city has already been described. It should be added that the Grand Canal, which crosses the peninsula from Hangchow in the south to Chinkiang on the Yangtsze, with a wide semicircular bend to the eastward, passes by Soochow on its eastern side. Certain branches or natural openings connect the Grand Canal with the Taho Lake, cutting, at various points, across the necks of land which, as before pointed out, formed the only accesses to the city when Gordon's force held Quinsan to the east, and his steamers commanded the lake to the west. These points became of the highest strategical importance to the series of operations by which he designed to thoroughly invest the place. The town of Wokong stands about fourteen miles to the south of the city, commanding one of these points; and on July twenty-eighth Gordon moved against it so rapidly as to surprise some of the stockades outside which had been left unguarded, and to carry others with little loss. A judicious distribution of the Ever-Victorious troops now enabled their commander to shut in the garrison with ease, and the Taipings, to the number of 4,000, soon afterwards surrendered. Here occurred the first of certain acts of Imperialist treachery which ultimately caused Gordon's retirement; for General Ching, who had taken charge of part of the prisoners, under promise of good treatment, violated his word, and put five of them to death. Indignant at this causeless breach of faith, Gordon resolved to lay down his command, and actually left the force for Shanghai. But he arrived there on August eighth to find that Burgevine (who, though carrying on a friendly correspondence with him, had been long in vain seeking to regain his lost command and replace him) had suddenly left that place with 300 Europeans, to join the Taipings at Soochow, carrying off also a small steamer, and throwing the great port into a new fit of consternation. To abandon the Imperialists was not to be thought of now, for it would have left his own troops to be seduced from their allegiance by their old commander, who had had the art to attempt to make them believe that this dismissal was the result of his insisting on their rights. Gordon started alone for Quinsan, and resuming his command, took immediate steps to counteract the intrigues of the American, sending his siege train temporarily back to Taitsan till he should be surer of his being able to maintain his advanced position. His troops near Wakong remained on the defensive, but successfully resisted the attacks directed against that place from Soochow with a view to recover the southern passage into the city; and presently their general, having received some reinforcements, resumed the offensive, and advancing northward along the strip of it, carried Patachiao, a small place close to the southern defences of the place, and rested there purposely for awhile to carry on negotiations with the foreign part of the defenders. It was his two-fold object to bring these

25

over, in order to weaken the Taipings and to save
European lives; but in entering into the private proposals to treat, which he soon received from them,
Gordon undertook a task no less difficult and dangerous than the most vehement assault upon the place.
Those he desired to win would inevitably try first to
seduce his own men. His ally, General Ching, was
carrying on independent operations against the garrison. Burgevine, disgusted with his new service, where
he found himself kept by the chief Wangs in an inferior position, had new plans in his restless brain, and had
the audacity to communicate to Gordon one of them,
which involved their both betraying their employers,
and seizing Soochow as the seat of a new Eastern Empire for themselves. Over all these and other difficulties
Gordon's coolness and skill, as conspicuous in diplomacy as in war, carried him triumphantly, and brought
him to his end without bloodshed. Before the end of
October the chief part of the foreign allies deserted the
garrison, under pretence of the sally: and soon afterwards Burgevine, by dint partly of Gordon's personal
entreaty to Moh Wang, the Taiping commander, was
allowed to follow them; so that the great obstacle to
the fall of the city and the breaking up of the rebellion
was quietly removed.

Freed from this, Gordon resumed his operations
against the place, and soon worked his way almost up
to the city walls on the south side. Abandoning his
posts there to be tenanted by his Chinese allies, he
transferred his force round the west side, by the lake,
to the northern, the only remaining outlet, and on
November first carried by assault Leeku, a place not
many miles from the city, and which almost shut it in

On the tenth and nineteenth of November further points were captured and occupied which completed the investment. In vain did the 30,000 Taipings enclosed seek for a way out. In vain was another army planted at Wusieh, twenty-five miles off on the Grand Canal, in rear of Gordon's posts, while the Faithful King (still the chief general of the arch-impostor) arriving from Nankin with another force of equal amount, intended for the relief of Soochow, took up a position in the open country between the city and Wusieh in the vain hope of making Gordon relax his grasp. Of the peculiar strategy of this campaign, which neutralized numbers by the skilful distribution of the better provided army, no higher instance can be found than that by Gordon's arrangements. 14,000 *men all told, including the contingent which aided him under Ching,* sufficed for the immediate work in hand of hemming in a force of more than double their numbers, and keeping off others nearly threefold in strength. Judging the Taipings to be already dispirited by their situation, Gordon, impatient for the surrender of the place, resolved on a night attack on a portion of the walls. It was made on November twenty-seventh, and despite the daring self-exposure which seemed both natural to the man and necessary as an example to this motley army, but which in the commander of a more regular force would have been a vice, Gordon found himself repulsed with a loss of 200 of his force. This success did not however alter the condition of the garrison, who were now losing heart; and two days later an assault undertaken by daylight, after a heavy fire, was made with success on the stockades and detached works outside the east gate. Once more Gordon exposed himself in front of his own storming column, armed as was his wont on such occasions, with no visible weapon more formidable than his favorite cane: and his men, nerved by his example, carried the points of attack, so that on the thirtieth he was enabled to issue a general order, congratulating the troops on their success, which, it was pointed out, " had made the city untenable by the rebels." Gordon was not too sanguine ; for a day or two later dissensions broke out among the rebel generals within ; Moh Wang was murdered by his subordinates at the council-table ; and on December fifth the city was surrendered to the Imperialists. Then took place the saddest incident which the British officer, acting with semi-civilized allies, can have to endure. Gordon had not been able to guarantee the safety of the Taiping chiefs ; but hearing from Ching that the highest authority, the governor (who had lately arrived on the scene), had promised them mercy, he removed his own force, with a promise of two months' pay, from the approaching scene of plunder, and went into the city to have an interview with the Wangs. They expressed themselves confident in Li's word, and after a second interview left the city to give themselves up, Gordon (whose force was already on the march to Quinsan) remaining himself with the intention of protecting those inside from the Imperialist soldiers who were entering.

It was at this time, on December sixth, when the deliverer of the provinces was surrounded by armed Taipings, his troops removed from him, and the great city, which had so long been the object of the campaign, incapable of further resistance, that Li, under pretence or on account of a difficulty in arranging terms with the

Wangs, caused them suddenly to be seized and executed, and ordered the city to be given up to plunder.

Those who are curious in Chinese sentiment, and
wish to know exactly how far it justified Li's actions,
may consult the work of Mr. Wilson, which is very full
on this point. Unfortunately Gordon had not been
brought up in those broad principles of the Doctrine
of Harmony on which, we are assured, the Chinese
fabric rests, but in the narrower philosophy of Christen-
dom. It is not surprising therefore that his grief and
indignation burst forth at the sight of the headless
bodies of the Wangs; that he, in his first impulse,
sought Li to exact personal satisfaction from him ; and
that, failing to find the wily governor (who with good
reason kept out of his way), he departed after his force
to Quinsan. Here he remained in inaction with the
Ever-Victorious Army for the next two months, pending the inquiry which had been instituted at Pekin on
his demand into the governor's conduct, and refusing
curtly to receive the reward of a decoration and a present of 3,500*l.* transmitted by the Imperial Government
for himself on the first news of the capture of Soochow.

The Ever-Victorious Army thus withdrawn, the
rebellion soon appeared likely to revive. Foreigners
once more began to join the Taipings. The province
was infested by lawless Chinese and still more lawless
foreigners ; and the Imperialist forces, despite the aid
of some of Gordon's disciplined artillery, appeared
unable to do more than hold their own against the
enemy. Mr. Hart, who had lately taken charge of the
Imperial Customs, now strongly urged Gordon's resuming the field, since his inaction was the strongest

encouragement to the disaffected, and pointed out with great clearness that, as he had nothing more to do to add to his reputation (since Soochow had fallen) and constant personal risk to undergo, this action could only be ascribed to his laying aside private feeling for the welfare of the province he had delivered. Urged by this and the like opinions, and with the special sanction of Sir F. Bruce, who wrote that he had obtained at Pekin "a positive promise in writing from this government that, in cases of capitulations, where you are present, nothing is to be done without your consent," Gordon retook the field towards the end of February, 1864.

To understand his remaining operations, it is necessary to remember that Soochow is at the central point of the Kiangnan peninsula, and Nankin at its north-west corner, 100 miles off; that the Taipings were now confined chiefly to the western side of the district, and that, if this were cut through by a line carried across from Soochow to the Imperialist intrenchments near Nankin, their armies would be reduced to acting within two separate strips of no great size, and would probably be unable any longer to exist. Gordon's plan, therefore, was to take and occupy the towns of Yesing, Liyang, and Kintang, upon this line, and thus connecting the Imperialists at Soochow with those before Nankin, to divide their enemies completely. Yesing, being on the Taho Lake, was captured without much difficulty on March first, and Gordon advancing rapidly on Liyang, and offering its garrison easy terms, it was surrendered without resistance on the fourth. The district around was found to be fearfully wasted by the Taipings, who had held it undisturbed for three years, and exercised a rule so exacting as fully to account for that animosity of the country people which has been already noticed. Gordon proceeded next against Kintang, but here he was forced to leave his steamers behind him, and some part of his land forces had naturally remained to guard his late captures. He had therefore with him but three of his infantry regiments and his guns, when, after some days' delay, caused partly by bad weather, but more by the necessities of the people of Liyang (who had been plundered of their last stock of provisions to fill the Taiping stores on his approach), he arrived before the place. The garrison here proved obdurate to his offers, and the heavy guns being brought up, a breach was formed. Before this had been done a pressing dispatch arrived from Governor Li for aid to the Imperialist forces. The latter had advanced on their own account against Chanchufu, a place about forty miles to the east of Kintang, and had been repulsed with much loss, the Taipings threatening in consequence to retake the offensive. A second dispatch told him that they had detached a force down the Yangtsze, turning the Imperialists by the north and threatening Fushan, his own first conquest. This was on March twenty-first, but Gordon's guns were now brought up, and he, judging it too late to retire from Kintang, resolved to assault. Once more he exposed himself in the manner that for a year past had given him among his men the reputation of being a magician, bearing a charmed life—but not again to escape, a severe wound through the leg compelling him to be carried off, after he had remained giving orders and concealing it until he fainted from loss of blood. The

attack then failed, and next day the wounded commander withdrew his force to Liyang, which was reached
on March twenty-fourth. The weather had been bad,
and the men required rest hardly less than their
wounded general: but when news was received on
arrival at Liyang that the Taipings had taken various
places on the way southwards towards Quinsan, and
had scattered on a long semi-circular line towards that
place the large force lately held about Chanchufu, he
thought the opportunity of striking at their flank too
good, and the object of checking their advance too
important, to be neglected. On the twenty-fifth he
was far on his way north-east to look for them, taking
with him, however, only two regiments, one of them
composed of Taiping recruits just enlisted at Liyang.

Never, surely, did commander show more confidence
in his own resources than this wounded man, pushing
forward along the creeks in his flotilla (for he was
unable to walk or ride) with a few hundred troops, part
of whom had been in arms against him a few days
before, into the heart of the district occupied by
unknown thousands of the Taipings. On the twenty-
sixth parties of their foragers were driven off from their
plunder, and a proclamation found which announced
to the villagers that their general was on his way to
Shanghai, and would take Soochow on his way. By
the thirtieth it was ascertained that the central point
of the Taiping line was at Waissoo, where they had a
strongly intrenched position, and that a creek conducted to it, up which the artillery and commander
might be carried by boat. His infantry—about 1,000
strong—were to march by a separate route, and the
combined attack was fixed for next day.

At dawn on March thirty-first both parties moved ; but the flotilla reached the neighborhood of Waissoo only to find themselves wholly unsupported, and to escape with some difficulty (for the banks were high and their guns useless) from a somewhat perilous posi- tion. Gordon's wound and his adventurous spirit had here combined to cost his force rather dear ; for the infantry arriving near Waissoo, had been surprised, in the absence of the watchful eye of their commander, by an attack in flank, and had been routed with a loss of over one-third of their number, including seven officers. All of these had perished, of course ; for the Taipings, who had remorselessly murdered the vil- lagers by hundreds, in the country about, were not likely to spare such of their enemies as fell alive into their hands. On learning these particulars, Gordon, who, though the very boldest of generals, was not an imprudent one, fell back some distance from the neigh- borhood of Waissoo, and remained on the defensive until he had brought up some fresher troops of his force from Liyang to augment the demoralized regi- ments which had suffered, and had partly recovered from his own wound.

When next he advanced, on April eleventh, to attack Waissoo, he did so (to quote the words of his own journal) "with the greatest caution, for the men had not yet got over their fears." Threatening the position by a feint from the south, on which side the enemy was fully prepared for an attack, he quietly moved round undiscovered with a regiment and two guns to the north of the place, and surprised without loss a stockade which laid bare to him the interior of the position. The result of this successful stratagem was the speedy abandonment of their lines by the Taipings. They were vigorously followed up by 6,000 Imperialists brought up by the governor himself (who had waited, as usual in these operations, ready to profit by the expected victory of their ally), and were driven across the country they had lately harried without mercy. "Armed with every sort of weapon," continues the journal, "the peasantry fell upon the rebels, who suffered fearfully among the creeks that abound there. They were cut up in every direction." The last advance of the rebellion was finally checked. Three days later the Taipings were either dispersed hopelessly through the country, or shut up in Chanchufu, whence they originally had started.

Hither Gordon and the governor had followed them. Once having enclosed the rebels, the former called up the rest of his force, borrowed 1,000 of the Imperialist soldiers for his trenchwork, and carried on the siege in due form; for the place had in it 20,000 Taipings, was stoutly defended, and repulsed his first attack. It fell on May eleventh to a combined assault, Gordon with his storming column effecting their entrance just in time to prevent any ill consequences from a panic which had seized the Imperialists after they obtained a lodgment in the place. And well it was this crowning mercy of the war had been thus swiftly won, for on May thirteenth the Ever-Victorious Army was on its way back to Quinsan to be paid off. The British Government, which had never given more than a half-hearted and, as it were, tentative support to that of China, had become intimidated at the outcry the massacre of the Soochow Wangs raised among the party sympathizing with the Taipings, and had withdrawn the permission under which Gordon served. Had he been less energetic and decisive in his last operations, the rebels would have taken heart at his withdrawal, and the struggle might have been prolonged for years. As it was, their cause was shattered beyond all revival. The southern district around Hangchow, cut off from that near Nankin strategically as before explained, by Gordon's advance in march on Liyang, had succumbed to the army under Ching. Notwithstanding the death of that general during these operations, his successor, aided by a small Franco-Chinese contingent, had captured Hangchow, and driven the remnant of the Taiping force into a desolate mountain district beyond its borders. In the north Nankin itself was all that now remained to the Heavenly King and his adherents. The Imperialists shut him in more and more closely. Starvation did its slow and dreadful work on the bodies of the invested garrison, and the city fell finally on July nineteenth, the impostor having shortly before ended his vile life by the most fitting death, the hand of the despairing suicide.

The disbandment of so peculiar a force as the Ever-Victorious Army, under a weak administration like that of China, was obviously no easy task. Its chief handled this, his last duty in China, with the same firm yet delicate touch which had brought him through so many difficulties before, and let us add, with an admirable disinterestedness which commanded respect alike from the force, his countrymen, and the Chinese officials, and greatly smoothed his immediate difficulties. Refusing absolutely the munificent pecuniary reward pressed upon himself, this young general, who had lived in the field an example of plainness and economy, and spent his surplus pay in supplying the needs of his force, now insisted on and obtained fair gratuities for his officers and men, but especially for those that had been wounded, before he laid his commission aside.

So parted the Ever-Victorious Army from its general, and its brief but useful existence came to an end. During sixteen months' campaigning under his guidance, it had taken four cities and a dozen minor strong places, fought innumerable combats, put *hors de combat* numbers of the enemy moderately estimated at fifteen times its own, and finding the rebellion vigorous, aggressive, and almost threatening the unity of the Chinese Empire, had left it at its last gasp, confined to the ruined capital of the usurper. Leaving his late command well satisfied, Gordon himself sailed for England, taking with him no more substantial treasure than the highest military title of China (Titu, equivalent to commander-in-chief of an army), the rare Imperial decoration of the Yellow Jacket, and the good-will and respect of all with whom he had to do. "Not only," wrote the Prince of Kung, the Chinese Prime Minister, to Sir F. Bruce, "has he shown himself throughout brave and energetic, but his thorough appreciation of that important question, a friendly understanding between China and foreign nations, is worthy of all praise."

Much has been said, and fairly said, in eulogy of the moderation and patriotism of those volunteer generals of the victorious armies of the Union who, at the close of the American Civil War, laid down their important charges to return cheerfully to the counting-house, the factory, or even to the humblest appointment in the regular service on the frontier. Englishmen who bestowed admiration on this conduct of their trans-Atlantic kinsfolk, should certainly yield no less to that of their own countryman; since he, his task once accomplished, sought for no irregular employment in China, asked for no prolongation in any form of his high command, but laid it down to return straightway to the ordinary life of a captain of Engineers on home duty, his highest ambition the furtherance of some local good work, his daily business for years to come the building obscure forts from the designs of others on an Essex swamp. The very papers in which the record of his services was inscribed lay thrust out of sight, their existence forgotten save in Mr. Wilson's mention of them. They might have mouldered for him away unread, but for the appeal, made almost as a demand, of certain of his brother officers, awakening to the knowledge that out of their own corps there were few who were aware of the extent and bearing of Gordon's services, and the importance of the Chinese campaigns of 1863–4.

The writer is far from being one of those who would have the world racked with war in order that we may learn what generals lie hid among us; but he cannot be insensible to the fact that England's interests are so vast, so numerous, so complicated, that it is impossible to predict that the day shall ever come when the hero's arm and the captain's brain shall be unnecessary to her greatness or her safety. Ever and anon, too, there comes across the ocean the cry of some one of her scattered offspring, abandoned perhaps by a vacillating policy and false humanitarianism (akin to those

which misguided us in our Chinese dealings) to a disastrous war. Fitly, therefore, may we close this brief
record of great deeds done from no mere love of glory
or of gain, with words suggested long since by one
who, himself a soldier whose name has become a
household word in England, had been among the first
to note the warlike genius of young Gordon when
together they bore the fire of Sebastopol:—" Another
Colonial war, and no help to be given! If we can't
spare an army, if we can't spare a staff, let us at least
send them one captain of Engineers. If there is a
man in the world who can conduct such a war with
honor, thoroughness, and humanity, and bring it to a
satisfactory close without needless delay or expense,
England has that man in Chinese Gordon."

THE END.

Printed in the United Kingdom
by Lightning Source UK Ltd.
119650UK00001B/16